D1095621

RITUALS & SABBATS

SACRED RITES AND SEASONAL CELEBRATIONS

RITUALS & SABBATS

LADY PASSION, HIGH PRIESTESS,
& *DIUVEI,
HIGH PRIEST, COVEN OLDENWILDE

STERLING ETHOS
New York

An Imprint of Sterling Publishing Co., Inc.
1166 Avenue of the Americas
New York, NY 10036

ISBN 978-1-4549-2677-1

Distributed in Canada by Sterling Publishing Co., Inc.
c/o Canadian Manda Group, 664 Annette Street
Toronto, Ontario, Canada M6S 2C8
Distributed in the United Kingdom by GMC Distribution Services
Castle Place, 166 High Street, Lewes, East Sussex, England BN7 1XU
Distributed in Australia by NewSouth Books
45 Beach Street, Coogee, NSW 2034, Australia

For information about custom editions, special sales, and premium and corporate purchases,
please contact Sterling Special Sales at 800-805-5489 or specialsales@sterlingpublishing.com.

Manufactured in the United States of America

2 4 6 8 10 9 7 5 3 1

sterlingpublishing.com

Image Credits:
Britt Sabo: 117; Shutterstock.com (throughout): allraspberry: sunbursts;
LanKS: paper texture; serazetdinov: hand, hourglass, key; Trikona: sun;
Valeriya_Dor: dirt texture; Naci Yuvuz: sun

TO OUR ELDERS, WHO KEPT THE WHEEL
TURNING AND TAUGHT US ITS RITES.

CONTENTS

INTRODUCTION

"Audentis Fortuna iuvat."
(Fortune favors the daring).

—PUBLIUS VERGILIUS MARO (VIRGIL)

WITCHES ARE PEOPLE OF POWER, BUT WE'RE NOT CONTENT WITH
ONLY OUR OWN: WE ADD THAT OF GOD/DESSES AND *DAIMONS,*[1]
AND USE THE MAGNIFYING POWER OF THE CIRCLE WE CAST, OUR
EMOTIONAL INTENSITY, THE AMOUNT OF PHYSICAL ENERGY WE
RAISE—SAY, BY DANCING A FRENETIC CONE OF POWER—AND ALL
OTHER DETAILS OF THE SPELLS WE WORK, TO TARGET, SHAPE, AND
AMPLIFY SUCCESSIVE LAYERS OF MAGICAL POWER UNTIL THE WORLD-
BENDING FORCE WE'RE RAISING REACHES A FEVER PITCH. THEN,
LIKE A BOW BENT TAUT FINALLY RELEASING ITS ARROW, WE LOOSE
FORTH OUR WILL IN THE WORLD.

Witchcraft isn't wish-craft—shallow talking and fantasizing about how things ought to be. Of all the wonders of Witchcraft, ritual best reveals how ours is a "cunning art," acting on a deep understanding of the hidden workings of reality. Whether done by a Solitary Witch or a Coven, a powerfully performed ritual runs like a spy thriller in which the lone protagonist or the team don disguises, meet in a secret lair, exchange cryptic passwords, write in code, and perform the crucial procedure required to prevent oblivion—all following a carefully thought-out,

---

1. We use "daimon" in the olde, non-judgmental sense of a lesser spirit, like the daimon that accompanied Socrates. See *The Goodly Spellbook*, "To Conjure a Personal Helper Spirit."

well-rehearsed plan. Like the thriller's surprise plot twists, along the way there's always an element of the unexpected: one or more unanticipated, even daunting challenges that would distract and defeat untrained dabblers, but that well-taught Witches know to take in stride and spontaneously take advantage of to enhance their working.

Just as transcendent lovemaking begins with a kiss, powerful rites[2] start small, with the idea of a spell or the feeling of a need, and gradually build until they peak with a roar. Witches who experience such rituals soon grow attuned to sensing exactly when to discharge their power to achieve maximum effect—typically, the split second before the energy teeters like a toy top whose spin begins to wobble.

The tradition-based magic ritual techniques that you'll learn here commence in a primal void of darkness penetrated only by the spark of a flickering candle, a cloaking nebula of scented smoke, and a murmuring rhythm of invocation. Light gradually dawns as more candles are lit—space taking form from East to South to West to North, tracing out the track of the Moon and the Sun. The murmur crescendos into a rousing chant as a gleaming blade or a numinous wand, staff, or hand slices thrice round a compassing circle to erect the boundary of this momentary universe. The powers of the Four Elements are summoned and mingled, their Guardians called forth, Gods and Goddesses named and evoked—and now, to cast the spell, the humans gathered here clasp hands and whirl, around and around like a spinning galaxy, till by spirits, minds, and bodies in concert, they generate the energy that brings what they will into being.

Ultimately, the Cone of Power dance spends their force like sexual climax. Eyes glassy-gleaming, everyone grins devilishly at each other, in emotional thrall to the wicked-cool secret they share.

Words have been rendered superfluous; the Mystery impossible to define. A

---

2. The terms rite and ritual are practically interchangeable. Insofar as there is a distinction, ritual connotes a structured ceremonial process, and rite either a specific practice, or ceremonies in a more generic sense. For example, dancing around a Maypole is one of the classic "rites of Beltane," whereas consecrating the pole itself beforehand and carrying it to the dancing site with a virgin sitting astride it incorporates that rite into a "Beltane ritual" (though for the virgin, riding the pole may in turn be a "rite of passage").

self-imposed taboo descends—silence, again, for fear that sound could shatter the afterglow they cherish. Hearts swell with a fierce desire to cling forever to the circle bliss. At last, everyone slowly absorbs the rite's magnitude as the Cakes and Wine ceremony ensues. . . .

Witch ritual sets up the type of spiritual atmosphere that encourages magic to happen. In a full ritual, things are said and done in circle much as they were in antiquity: participants are anointed, candles and incense burned, a space marked out as sacred, and, in time-honored ways, all readied for spellworking. Yet a valid ritual can *also* be as basic as simply casting a circle, calling the Quarters, working a spell, then closing the circle by dismissing the Quarters, or doing it all in your thoughts.

Even if you practice magic as a Solitary, either by choice or of necessity, you are never *really* alone because somewhere in the world Witches are casting spells—often for the very thing you desire yourself—and if you faithfully observe the Sabbats, Esbats, and other Craft customs and traditions, you are one with all Pagans who have spelled since time began.

Witches do ritual because no successful spell is an isolated act—it's the product of many interwoven factors. Some of these are internal, such as the amount of prior preparation, knowledge, experience, skill, reverence, Divine inspiration, will, and intention that you bring to the spell. Other factors are external, from the timing and location of the spellcasting, to the particular chains of cause-and-effect, karma, luck, and natural/magical/universal law that have led up to the circumstances that necessitated the spellcasting. The internal factors are usually under your personal control; the external factors, however, are rarely so.

A ritual is like a magic loom that weaves these tangled, intricate, interconnected threads together into an archetypally ordered pattern, allowing the internal factors to affect the external ones so as to alter the fabric of reality.

All rituals—from the simplest and most spontaneous to the most formal and ceremonial—accomplish this task of transformation by using words, actions, symbols, and tools that are structured according to magical sounds, numbers, shapes, colors, correspondences, etc., as explained and illustrated in *The Goodly Spellbook*. Ritual applies the powerful magical principle of rhythmic repetition, which can entrain our brain, body, and life rhythms—synchronizing them with the chanting of our spells or the cycling of Earth's seasons.

This art of re-ordering reality is primordially ancient, as old as the human mind. Indeed, the prehistoric Indo-European root of the words "rite" and "ritual," *ar-*, meaning "to fit together," is also the root of words such as "art" (as in the Art Magical), "harmony," "rhyme," "reason," "arithmetic," and—you guessed it—"order."

We have well over two decades' experience circling with Witches throughout the United States and abroad; in conducting elaborate, popular, public Sabbat rituals in the Blue Ridge Mountains; in writing, lecturing, and giving interviews about Witch ritual; and in teaching traditional ritual magic to innumerable students from age seven to seventy.

It's been our privilege to participate in rites so powerful that they defy description, and our challenge to stoically endure rites so lackluster that they should never have been attempted. Simply put, we know what works and why, and what doesn't work and why not.

While we provided some ritual basics in *The Goodly Spellbook: Olde Spells for Modern Problems*, this book teaches how to perform a full ritual in detail, whether you're a Solitary creating a secret rite, or part of a Coven creating a private or public ritual to appeal to adepts or curious masses of folk, from rambunctious kids to the elderly or infirm.

Herein we give our moving Gardnerian-derived Oldenwilde Ritual Script, which will protect you as you grow in magic might and amplify your spell efforts; ritual customs from sources worldwide; creative rite options; monthly Esbat meeting Cakes and Wine serving suggestions; all about seasonal Sabbats, including feasts and food magic; and many more pleasurable surprises.

We present these magical techniques neither as entertainment nor solely for educational purposes. Magic is an authentic spiritual practice, best used in tandem with medical, legal, and other reasonable measures.

Relish mastering delightful spiritual drama to achieve your dreams, please the Gods, and aid others!

*Lady Passion & *Diuvei*
Coven Oldenwilde

ALL AROUND, RITES ABOUND

"Sacred ritual is a private or community action which has a sacred purpose or meaning. That is, through this action, contact is set up between the ordinary world and the spiritual world."

—JOHN MCGRATH AND TERENCE LOVAT, *NEW STUDIES IN RELIGION*

ANYONE WHO'S ATTENDED ONE OF COVEN OLDENWILDE'S SABBATS OR OTHER CIRCLES KNOWS THAT WE BELIEVE RITES SHOULD NEVER FEEL ROTE. A RITUAL IS NOT A ROUTINE: YOU SHOULD ALWAYS FEEL AN ANTICIPATORY SHIVER OF EXPECTANT EXCITEMENT JUST BEFORE YOU STEP INTO THE PRESENCE OF THE GODS, AND SAVOR AN AFTERGLOW OF ECSTATIC EXHILARATION LONG AFTER YOU LEAVE IT. A GOODLY WITCH RITE CAN CHANGE YOUR WORLD-VIEW, INURE YOU TO LIFE'S TRIFLING TROUBLES, WARM YOUR SOUL FOR DAYS.

Sadly, many people have soured on the very notion of ritual, thanks to centuries of stultifying monotheist rituals replete with seemingly arbitrary speeches and actions performed "by the book" even though their true purposes have been forgotten—and their Pagan origins long denied.

One well-known example of such a monotheist ritual spell is the Eucharist—the "transubstantiation" during the Mass of bread and wine into what Catholic and Orthodox Christians teach is the literal body and blood of Christ. This seemingly cannibalistic rite has been so beset by its lengthy history of theological dogma and sectarian controversy that it gave English the magic-deriding word "hocus-pocus"—originally a sarcastic mispronunciation of *Hoc est corpus meum* (Latin, "This is my body"), the spell formula the priest pronounces to transform the bread. Lost in the noisy debate between fundamentalism and skepticism are the rite's ancient roots in the spiritual as well as physical incorporation into ourselves of the yeast-risen life forces of grain and grape, and the universal practice of making food and drink offerings to the Gods—as survives (*sans* implications of anthropophagy) in the Cakes and Wine ceremony that is a traditional part of Wiccan rites.

Outside of church, synagogue, or mosque, people participate in many secular rituals filled with spells and symbolism, but—absent a Witchy lens to view them through—they rarely recognize the magic beneath the bland veneer of "custom." If you've ever blown out candles on a cake to make a wish and sung a special song at a birthday party; donned ceremonial cap and gown to receive a seal-embossed piece of parchment and a valedictory farewell speech at a graduation; jumped to catch a bouquet and tossed rice or seeds at a wedding; or placed a wreath of greenery and tossed a handful of dirt atop a lowered casket at a funeral—then you've already helped cast a spell at a ritual.

It's easy to casually dismiss such practices as merely sentimental superstition. Perhaps that's for the best, because if their underlying magical purposes were to become widely known, religious fundamentalists and scientific skeptics would likely set aside their usual enmity and tag-team to stamp out the surviving magical principles that give these secular rituals their affecting spiritual power.

Birthdays, graduations, weddings, and funerals belong to a specific kind of ritual called "rites of passage"—ceremonies that mark a person's developmental transition from one stage of life to another. The special spell customs associated with these acknowledgments of growth are intended to bless the person or persons who are the focus of the rite, to accord them benefits in the stage of life they're entering—in the above examples, goodly fortune, honor, fertility, and rebirth, respectively.

The rituals that surround these spells give meaning and potency that the spells would lack if performed at random, outside of their ritual context. For instance, you might be arrested for assault if you waited till months after a wedding to walk up to the married couple and pitch a fistful of rice at them!

Craft Rites of Passage extend from the cradle to the grave:

* *Wiccaning (blessing a newborn)*

* *Moontime (honoring a female's first menstruation)*

* *Green Man (honoring a teen's transition into manhood)*

* *Handfasting (temporary Witch marriage)*

* *Croning (honoring a post-menopausal woman)*

* *Rite for the Departed Soul (Witch wake)*

Witches' annual eight seasonal Sabbats are rites of passage on a macrocosmic level because they mark and honor changes that occur throughout the Wheel of the Year. Ritually celebrating these Sabbats immerses us in the rhythm and significance of cyclical time.

Initiatory and Elevation rituals can also be considered rites of passage since they mark a Seeker's entrance into successively deeper levels of magical knowledge and skill. They differ in form and number from one magical tradition to another, but many Wiccan Covens (including Coven Oldenwilde) use or adapt the three-fold Gardnerian sequence of First-Degree Initiation, Second-Degree Elevation, and Third-Degree Elevation—the Witchy equivalent of a medieval craft-guild initiate's passage from Apprentice to Journeyman to Master.

Rites of Passage underline the fact that the art of ritual is itself an art of time. To understand this, consider its analogies to another temporal art: music.

Both ritual and musical arts are built on rhythm and repetition; on themes; on introduction, climax, and close. And learning to perform and compose rituals, whether as a Solitary or with a Coven, is just like learning to perform and compose music as a soloist or as a member of a band or orchestra:

* *Initially, you practice the parts of the ritual script or musical score you are learning by carefully reading and repeating them.*

* *You gradually become familiar enough with them to grow confident that you can perform many or all of the parts from memory.*

* Then you move beyond mere technical proficiency to performing with feeling, power, and flair—finally achieving that mystical state where the ritual or your composition comes to life and seems to perform itself, as though you're channeling the magic or music as much as creating it.

* As you experiment with writing rites or songs, you will eventually become such a skilled adept that you are able to improvise a ritual or composition instantly, without needing a script or score at all.

Drama and ritual parallel one another in the same ways as music and ritual. Indeed, the connection is in some ways even closer, since the earliest stage plays in Western history were religious rituals (the mystery plays of ancient Greece and medieval Europe), and plays in many indigenous cultures still are dramatic enactments at religious festivals of the mythic doings of Gods and Goddesses. Most historians of drama trace its origins in Western culture to the public rituals of the God Dionysus, Whose cult—one of the direct antecedents of modern-day Witchcraft—encouraged participants to explore the perilous boundary between "reason" and "passion" that is still the locus of every great actor's and dramatist's art, just as the best ritualists merge learned method and spontaneous instinct into a cohesive whole.

Dance is also universally associated with ritual. In structured dances, such as folk dancing and the traditional Pagan dances we illustrate in *The Goodly Spellbook* chapter titled "Magical Movement and Gestures," the geometric patterns the dancers' feet trace out on the ground are visible from a "God's-eye view," like a Tibetan colored-sand mandala or a crop circle. Trance dancing at a nightclub or a concert gives many people their first spiritual experience of the kind that a magical ritual induces. Indeed, many of the most influential and popular rock musicians from the 1960s on have consciously incorporated ritual and spellcraft into their performances in order to create a divinely transcendent experience for their listeners and themselves.[3]

....

3. Bebergal, Peter, *Season of the Witch: How the Occult Saved Rock and Roll*, Peter Tarcher/ Penguin, 2014.

OUR TEN FAVORITE SABBAT RITUALS

WE'VE PERSONALLY SEEN AND FELT THINGS DURING RITUAL THAT CONVINCED US OF MAGIC'S MIGHTY MERIT. INDEED, IT'S *BECAUSE* OF OUR EXPERIENCES IN RITUAL THAT TOUCHED US DEEPLY THAT WE'VE DEVOTED OUR LIVES TO WITCHCRAFT. SO FOR US, TRYING TO SELECT OUR ALL-TIME FAVORITE PAGAN SABBAT RITES FROM OUR COMBINED LIFETIMES' WORTH OF POSSIBLE CHOICES IS LIKE EXPECTING DOTING PARENTS TO DECLARE THEIR FAVORITE CHILD.

Ruling out traditionally secret Gardnerian rites, the ten rituals we picked to highlight here we'll always cherish. They stand out in our memory because they were colorful and moving, and they taught us crucial Mysteries of ritual. We tell their tales here to serve as an exhortation for you to circle often and with boldness and joy. Included among them are some of the twenty Public Samhain Witch Rituals we led every October in and around Asheville, North Carolina, from 1995 through 2014.

See photos, videos, interviews, commentaries, and magazine articles detailing our two decades of conducting public Sabbats—their magical themes, challenges, thrills, décor, music, and results—at: http://oldenwilde.org.

Favorite Rite #1: Litha at Pendle Witch Camp
(Pendle Hill, Lancashire, England, 2006)

OUR *THE GOODLY SPELLBOOK* BEING A NEW SMASH HIT AT THE TIME, TRADITIONAL BRITISH WITCH AND SHAMANIC FANS OF IT HAD ASKED US TO CROSS THE POND AND TEACH MATERIAL FROM IT AT PENDLE

WITCH CAMP, THEIR WEEKEND-LONG SUMMER SOLSTICE GATHERING IN NORTHERN ENGLAND. WE WERE DEEPLY HONORED BY THEIR INVITE BECAUSE OUR GARDNERIAN WITCH LINEAGE ORIGINATED IN ENGLAND: IF ANYTHING, WE BELIEVED THAT WE HAD MUCH TO LEARN FROM *THEM*. BUT WE HOPED THEY'D LIKE OUR *GOODLY SPELLBOOK*-BASED WORKSHOPS ON WITCHES' SECRET LANGUAGE, MAGICAL MUSIC, AND TRADITIONAL PAGAN DANCE STEPS.

We sailed across the Atlantic on the regal *Queen Mary 2* and had a splendid time working our way through England doing book signings and radio call-in shows. At last the time for the event arrived. Organizer Adrian Lord picked us up in London and drove us hell-for-leather to the site in the shadow of Pendle Hill on narrow, twisting, stone-wall-enclosed roads through rolling sheep pastureland—the infamous Lancashire home of the rival Witch Crones Chattox and Demdike, whose feud led to the decimation of themselves and their families in one of the most notorious Witch trials of the early 1600s.

The organizers generously provided us a tent and all camping trappings, right down to "wellies" (rubber boots) for navigating the freshly vacated sheep meadow the gathering was held on. Elaborate pavilions of exquisitely embroidered tapestries, gossamer curtains, futons, carpets, and lush pillow pallets pampered participants as they dined on typical hippie sticks-and-twigs fare. Other tents differed little from those of any queen's opulent royal travels, bedecked floor to ceiling with carved antique shelves chock-full of glittering bottles filled with Witch potions and psychedelic tinctures.

Two huge circus-like canvas tents had been erected to commemorate Chattox and Demdike's historical battle of wits and to serve as the venue for the classes, but nothing was ever said as to who "won" or lost, nor any attempt made to foment factional discord among participants or admirers of one matriarch or the other.

Participants enthusiastically received our workshops. We were delighted when they confirmed that some obscure words in Witches' secret language continued to be in use, such as *natterjack*. Musicians among them were fascinated by the olde modes, particularly eery Locrian. In the dance workshop, they glided in intricate hand-in-hand patterns while 'Diuvei played a wooden flute, and stomped till the fields wept mud and all gasped enraptured.

Just before sundown on Solstice proper, kids took to the plain and began silently summoning everyone to the main rite by spinning lights dangling from their wrists by cords. The effect was enchanting, and folk reverently assembled en masse, wielding blazing torches and enormous papiér maché heads on saplings. At the center of the circle was an upright four-spoked Sun wheel woven of straw and withies. Everyone instantly inhabited a time before sermons, beyond words.

We looked around, admiring all their costumes. Their faces radiated content-ment—we suspected in part because we'd watched them settle spats in minutes, whereas our American counterparts nurse grudges for years. Steeped in a magical culture far older than the colonies', they'd developed the reasoned approach of apologizing, hugging, and then wiping the *faux pas* out of mind: Pagan bygones. Their bliss was infectious.

The priest for the main rite, Runic John, rightly avoided dispiriting attend-ees by assigning someone to drone dogma or recite bad poetry at us, in favor of manifesting the feeling of the Sabbat through deeds. Florid speech was unneeded because the fire-dancers embodied the courage associated with high summer, proving the value of practicing for years to perfect an Elemental skill and justly honoring the Sun at His zenith by their passionate delivery.

We sat down on soft grass in front of the wide wooden stage. Everyone around cut us gentle, furtive glances, as if they knew a secret and couldn't wait to see our reactions. Exotic music surrounded us, its source impossible to identify. The notes wafted low and slow down the valley and steadily built in intensity, synchronizing our heartbeats and evoking expectancy.

As the Sun crossed the horizon into the underworld, the Sun wheel was set ablaze. Troupes of skyclad athletes in glorious body paint and exotic feathers took the stage by storm and proceeded to work the most wicked solar magic that we had ever seen. They breathed fire; fondled flames between moth-white fin-gers; risked immolation to spin signal flares atop teased hair; swallowed flam-ing swords; and whipped fireballs around their necks like nunchucks, and fiery hula-hoops around windmill arms and gyrating bellies—tossing the fire high enough to kiss the clouds and resemble a burning phoenix. We whooped, hollered, played drums, and begged them never to stop. The ritual lasted until the blush of sunrise.

We embarked on the voyage back to America impressed with English Witches' friendliness, sincerity, uncontrived approach to magic, and use of ritual characters such as the 'Obby 'Oss—so much so that Lady Passion would be inspired to make a traditional "Mast Beast"[4] version of the 'Oss that she named Ol' Charmer for our Samhain rites, using an articulated replica of a prehistoric horse's skull, complete with wool-yarn mane, Witch-themed horse brasses on leather martingales, and moving glass eyes.

On the return trip home, we were treated to a further demonstration of magic's power to transcend borders when the British luxury liner's Filipino crew found out we were Witches: for the rest of the voyage, scarcely an hour went by without a knock on our cabin door and an earnest request for a divination about a family member back home, a health problem, a love interest, etc.—all of which Lady Passion answered with a Tarot-card reading in exchange for huge bouquets of flowers that nearly overflowed our stateroom by the time we reached New York Harbor.

Ol' Charmer became a beloved feature in our public Samhain Sabbats every Halloween. Children were attracted to his spirit-blue glow (a snapped glow-stick secreted inside his skull) and made a beeline to pet him. And over the years many a volunteer enjoyed animating him by wielding a wooden pole beneath his dun-colored coat and snapping his jaw to nip butts and bestow luck and bounty.

Favorite Rite #2: Beltane at May Moon Madness (Sevier County, Tennessee, USA, 1997)

WE CIRCLED AT THIS WEEKEND-LONG GATHERING IN THE HEART OF MOONSHINE COUNTRY WHERE SOME MEN CONTINUED

---

4. Known in Wales as a *Mari Lwyd*. The 'Obby 'Oss is known in America as a hobby horse, a small rocking horse that children straddle to mimic a horse and rider. In ritual, the 'Oss or Mast Beast is a larger ritual character animated by a human cloaked behind its snapping mouth. It teases and entertains participants, blessing them with fertility.

TO MUTTER IMPRECATIONS AGAINST THE DREAD "REVENUERS."
WE'D CARAVANNED WITH OUR COVEN CREW ABOUT
FORTY-FIVE MINUTES FROM OUR COVENSTEAD IN WEST ASHEVILLE,
NORTH CAROLINA, AND SPENT THE FIRST FEW HOURS
RECONNECTING WITH FRIENDS WHO HAD TRAVELED TO
ATTEND FROM NEARBY SOUTHEASTERN STATES.

Meanwhile, our students and Covenmates erected all our tents, hung a huge parachute above them, made a stone-lined fire pit, erected several altars about, fumigated the circle compound area with incense, and surrounded the lot with bamboo tiki-torches. They did this on their own initiative—very impressive!

Once the compound was complete, we all excised the memory of the mundane world by sunning ourselves skyclad in the balefire field, then returned to camp to don minimal gathering wear: silver and jewels, long sheer skirts, leather-slung drinking horns, blue woad or red madder body paint, feathers and twigs in hair— the usual, according to each of our unique Craft styles. As always, the preparation itself was a fun, creative exercise in opening ourselves up to the delicious pos- sibilities the gathering promised, elevating our excitement and constituting an outward expression of our intent to get the most out of our magical experiences.

We eased into things as well as Pagans who loved to revel could. The annual gathering's site was sprawling, secluded, and owned by Pagans who had created the evolving magical village in the Smoky Mountain woods over many years' time. We checked on the condition of the stone roundhouse, left offerings on stone- slab altars, and made the rounds of groups tucked in pockets throughout the winding acres of streams, woods, and clearings—meeting, swapping tokes and sips of spirits, and seeking the gathering's general tone: Sweet, wild, intense, what? We slept to comforting cricket song, frog croak, cicadas, and unceasing drum rhythm.

The next day, we attended enlightening workshops such as shape-shifter yoga (animal mimicry) and how to smelt a Damascus athamé (a magical knife tool made super-strong by repeated tempering and folding molten metal on itself in successive layers).

We bartered for magical objects at vendor booths and won some prizes in the

Adult Pagan Olympics—a series of Witchy antics such as a naked circle race (in which women deftly led their mates around by their phalli), and the noisy-tent contest (in which a couple zipped themselves inside a tent and outside listeners judged the quality and seeming sincerity of the sexual sounds they made). We won two matching chalices for creativity (Lady Passion had entertained the judges by doing body shadows on the tent wall for added effect, and *Diuvei pretended to clamber in exhaustion halfway out of the tent only to be dragged back in by his ankles), and two of our Initiates were also awarded a prize for having tickled each other into emitting suggestive shrieks of delight.

Conch horns blew, and a hush fell. Men resembling the satyr-God Pan solemnly carried a garland-crowned virgin girl atop a mammoth Maypole, a circlet of fresh flowers capping its front end. We followed down the path to the forest woodhenge, feeling as one with all Pagans who had danced around this symbol of the World Tree for centuries.

The tall, branchless tree trunk was erected in the center with effort akin to setting a stone monolith. Dozens of long, jewel-colored ribbons tied to the circlet floated down to the ground. Kids, teens, and adults each grasped a strip and faced each other according to whichever gender they identified themselves with, alternating male—female style.

Nearby, a line of musicians launched into a merry tune, playing flutes, drums, and harps. The pole dancers began moving in the directions they faced, each one alternately holding their ribbon aloft to let the opposite person dancing toward them pass under it, then holding it downward so that they in turn could pass under the next person's ribbon. Gradually the ribbons wove themselves onto the tree from top to bottom. Laughter reigned as the ribbons' free lengths shrank ever shorter, bringing everyone into closer and tighter body contact and compelling everyone to contort themselves creatively in order to continue dancing. The colorful end result resembled a gigantic Chinese finger-prison. The weave would adorn the tree until weather began beating it to shreds months hence, at which time it would be pulled off to join its predecessors in the rafters of the open-air wood longhouse that served as a banquet hall.

Afterward, we skipped and ran to that longhouse and enjoyed a communal feast of pit-roasted whole boar, innumerable springtime side dishes, ale, and custom lattés. At sunset, everyone assembled on the balefire field for the main rite, each packing their proclivity: a bota bag of wine here, a pouch of finger cymbals there, a *djembe* drum slung across a torso, etc. Encircling torchlight cast comforting, obscuring shadows: since all were masked, painted, or costumed, none could swear with certainty who anyone else really was, giving us liberating anonymity to express ourselves to the hilt—or plausible deniability should we embarrass ourselves.

Circle cast and Quarters called, the owner of the venue began eloquently extolling Beltane's virtues. An experienced Priest of the Order of the Golden Dawn, he held us spellbound with his sonorous voice. His High Priestess seamlessly took turns with him, both of them sizing each other up and flirting, enacting the annual mating of the God and Goddess. Like decisive animals, their courtship dance was brief, participants fairly chomping at the bit to get in on the action themselves.

Men descended on the piled-high pyre and ignited it as the Priest slowed his cadence and deepened his timbre. He intoned about spring's release from winter confinement, its liberation from constraint, its irrepressible wanderlust. . . .

"What do we *do*?" he challenged. "Reject domination," he reminded. "What do we *want*?" he grinned in a way only a Witch would understand. "Freedom!!!" he howled till the air rang reverberant.

His single chant-word broke us out of trance to unbridled exuberance. Everyone danced ecstatically and started circling and leaping the balefire while screaming the primordial yaup.

Musicians struck up beats that goaded us on. We lost ourselves in the moment, then danced past exhaustion, and then past all sense of self. We belted "Freedom!" from the top of our lungs and from deep within our being—appealing to innumerable deities to avenge our collective trauma for every inhumane injustice dealt us, each insane inanity and cruel impediment imposed to part us from our potential simply because we were Pagan.

Women twirled, the balefire backlighting their barely-there skirts and revealing the shape of their lithe bodies underneath. The bota-bag bearers soothed them in the heat, flitting to each and squirting Dragonsblood wine (a local specialty of fermented grape juice) into parched throats. A tall, thin man in top hat and tails vied for their attention opposite a hoofed-and-horned teen with the same desire. A whirling dervish spun nonstop all night. The motley crew was all Cheshire grins from the wicked wonder of it all, and wide smiles as if they'd slept with a coat hanger in their mouths. Shrieks of bliss sliced the air along with the flame-licks.

Come the wee hours, some peeled off to go greenwooding (make love adoors). Others sought an occasional brief break to fuel their stamina. We sat atop split-log benches as close to the fray as possible without risking being crushed by bliss-blind dancers who'd lost all comprehension of boundaries.

We good-naturedly topped each other's magical exploits and drank "burns-blue" moonshine (the traditional test for purity) labeled with humorous disclaimers like "Not responsible for lost virginity, black-out marriages, crashing into a police car," etc. We counseled folk in grief, apologized for slights, and traded hugs of fealty. Soon an astonishing profusion of glow-worms phosphoresced on the dark ground all around us, billions of stars mirroring them in the black sky above until it was impossible to differentiate land from sky. It was all sparkle, and we soaked up the experience in awe.

We had always taught our students that when a rite was truly affecting, they might have a bittersweet price to pay for the experience—an urge to share the inexpressible, and difficulty retaining its rapture when they returned to the mundane world. So before we crashed out in our tents, we tried to forfend the phenomenon by gathering ephemeral flotsam-and-jetsam ritual detritus and balefire ashes to use as future spell components. We left languidly the next day, rejuvenated by our magical catharsis.

We still occasionally visit the Pagan place and imbibe mint juleps on Derby Day.

Favorite Rite #3: Samhain III, "The Light Fight" ("Dark of the Moon Dance" at Memorial Stadium, Asheville, North Carolina, 1997)

By 1997, we'd held two free public Samhains on successive Halloweens in the center of downtown Asheville, on the plaza in front of our county courthouse and city hall. Occasionally we'd quip tongue-in-cheek that they were intended to show our gratitude for residents letting us wild Witches live for another year—but in actuality, they were opportunities to encourage closeted Pagans to be proudly public, and for curious townsfolk to have fun circling with real Witches. Each ritual had garnered wide coverage, such as by National Public Radio and the television series *Extra!*

Hundreds of families had reveled at these night rites despite Christian fundamentalists' attempts to impede them: we'd quickly learned to set signs on-site posting the North Carolina law forbidding anyone from disrupting a religious ceremony, with our resolve to prosecute violators. We then turned our backs on any ragers, and drowned out their hate-speech with Witchy music or djembe drumming. Lady Passion led attendees hand-in-hand behind her and parted the bigots like the Red Sea, because they didn't want to risk Yahweh's wrath by inadvertently touching a happy heathen, or accidentally getting encircled and, God forbid, participating in the spiral dance.

Our popularity likely explains why, for the third Samhain, nervous bureaucrats tried to shut down our application to circle in a public stadium. Seeking a site less exposed to bright lights, loud sirens, and disruptive protests, we had inquired about holding our event in any of the city's larger neighborhood parks but been flatly turned down by the Parks and Recreation Dept. So we reserved the small, somewhat neglected Memorial Stadium tucked in the hills behind much more famous McCormick Field, which is featured in seminal scenes in the Oscar-winning movie *Bull Durham*.

The Sabbat was to happen during a New Moon, so the ritual's theme was

"Dark of the Moon Dance." We got permission to light the site primarily with tiki torches and glow sticks, although it was already bathed in enough ambient urban light to read a book by.

But as soon as our plans reached the desks of the higher-level officials who, at that time, still ran our small Southern city like a private fiefdom, they rescinded our lighting permission and insisted on shining all the stadium's floodlights on our ritual. They deemed our rites, in the words of a city attorney, "as dangerous as street luging," and compared our event to a recent Ku Klux Klan march through downtown that had drawn furious protests.

After we made our case in a City Council meeting and the media picked up the story, officials agreed to let us turn out the lights—but only if we posted a $3 million insurance bond. With difficulty, we finally found an insurance company that would provide such an expensive policy with only three days to spare before the ritual. In return, however, we were compelled to put our home—our Covenstead—up for collateral. Confident that our rites were safe, we did so.

What we didn't realize at the time was that this insurance company was also the city's insurer, holding a profitable near-monopoly on insuring city-owned properties, agencies, and governmental buildings. As soon as we submitted our proof of insurance to the city's risk manager, he placed a call to his contact in the company, just to make sure they knew this event was being sponsored by Witches—and the next day, two days before the ritual, the company abruptly canceled our policy, falsely claiming they'd thought this multimillion-dollar bond for a stadium rental was to cover a neighborhood Halloween party.

We cried foul in the press about the abuse of power by these petty despots—appointed, unelected officials with no accountability to citizens or even City Council—and our prejudicial treatment by the insurance company. We detailed the outrages in near-daily newspaper and television news interviews. An immediate and sustained hue and cry arose in our favor because we paid taxes to maintain, and routinely paid fees to reserve, public parkland on which to hold an appealing religious rite.

Though rightly embarrassed by the public backlash, officials nonetheless doubled down and vowed to keep the stadium lights blazing. Undaunted, we waged what the press dubbed "the light fight" while also focusing on prepping to conduct an enchanting ritual. Asked by a reporter how she felt about the situation, Lady Passion calmly warned, "Go ahead—made six hundred Witches very angry!"

Near rite night, a wannabe shock-jock new to the town's TV news channel ostensibly interviewed Lady Passion about the issues on our Covenstead's front porch. His actual intention, which he wasted no time revealing, was to provoke her to make incendiary sound bites. The High Priestess refused to take his bait and be his ratings fodder, maintaining a confident but non-confrontational tone. Finally, the man lost all semblance of professionalism and threw a chair at her head, in full view of elementary-school kids across the street in the process of boarding buses for home. He missed.

People came to the Sabbat in droves. They marched defiantly across the now-infamous field, caped and black-clad—first entering yards and yards of black tent fabric with hundreds of spiders painted glow-in-the-dark dangling above their heads by invisible threads. They encountered many a spooky thrill within, only to emerge into blinding stadium lights and be met by nine cop cars parked on the stadium grounds, each with two glaring police officers standing in front, arms purposefully crossed in intimidating stance. They had been sent there to make absolutely sure that the Witches did not turn out the lights.

Lady Passion bade all to ignore their provocation and turn their backs on them to face the enormous black cauldron-shaped piñata that was the ritual's focus. She'd made the cauldron and its secret contents—hundreds of pieces of jewelry of sinew, bone, stone, gems, leather, and metal. The High Priestess gently tapped its top with a multicolored ear of corn and then passed the ear to the next person. Sensing that there was a designee for the honor, everyone mirrored her restraint to avoid breaking the papiér maché.

The Lady turned toward the authoritarian threat, fuming internally at the cops' temerity at intruding into sacred space as she walked the line of participants that circled the length of the football field. At last she neared the end of the line, and had arrived at what she thought might be the end of her. She looked the paid oppressors up and down: they reflected back shock at the impressive number of Witches behind her.

The High Priestess turned her back on the cops again, disgusted that they nervously fondled their guns. Wearing a wireless microphone, she exhorted attendees: "*I'm* not afraid! Are *you* afraid?" "*No!*" the crowd thundered back. She repeated the refrain, a challenging mantra, as she traversed the line again.

She hadn't reached two thirds of the way up before she had to do an about-face: she'd whipped up the crowd's fervor to bloodthirsty. They had turned and were menacing the cops with withering glares, their eyes launching elf-darts of contempt. The cops flinched indecisively, trigger-itchy. It was a showdown of wills—one group wielding weapons, the other more powerful without them.

Lady Passion pounded the ground with the base of her 117-faceted smoky-quartz-topped staff to signal all to return to ritual focus. "We got 'em and they know we got 'em," she said. Snap, snap, hundreds of fingers snapped, rattling the po'-po.' The message was clear: they were ridiculously outnumbered, and we could make them quake with a snap of our digits—indeed, snap them like twigs if we chose. The cops realized we couldn't be cowed, so they dropped their bravado for the remainder of the rite. We, in turn, ignored them from that point on.

The designated Initiate cracked the cauldron with his tall oak staff, and it sprang upward on a flexible pole sporting a huge silver wooden crescent moon as it emptied its gifts onto the field. Participants swooped on the spillage like an insect attack, picking the grass pristine with dizzying speed. Suddenly abashed at their greed, they recovered their decorum and gracefully adorned themselves and admired each other's diadems, earrings, pendants, armbands, belly-chains, anklets, and rings.

Next, everyone mounted the stadium's high stone seats to select and crown a Samhain King and Queen. The two best costumed earned the honor. Then we descended to the field again, behind the escorted pair of former strangers, who proceeded to dance together for quite some time. We reveled to lovely Pagan music blaring out across the field from the stadium's press booth. Many readers foretold people's fortunes for the New Year, their plethora of card decks and divination tools atop tables surrounding the arena. And afterward as always, we adjourned to host a raucous after-party in our Covenstead to thank our volunteer helpers.

Within weeks, it seemed, the city's director of Parks and Recreation tried to sell the historic stadium site to a developer, as if our rite had contaminated it. Veterans already upset about the dilapidated condition of the war memorial prevented him and forced the city to repair the stadium instead. Nine years later, the director was forced out of his post, dogged by a city audit that found that his department had mismanaged funds for years.

The city risk manager who'd tried to sabotage the rite eventually retired and ran for City Council on a loudly conservative platform. He was soundly defeated in the primary election. The Chief of Police who had ordered his minions to breach our reserved site soon embroiled himself in scandal and chose to "retire early."

The wannabe shock-jock was promptly fired by the station and founded a chain of shops catering to golfers. The stores were repeatedly robbed, and he's not been heard of since.

We helped win the right for all city nonprofits to pay Parks & Rec only half the normal venue reservation fees; and today, many online-accessible insurance companies cover religious events such as ours for a minimal fee and no concern about our denomination. In 2009, we circled in a local neighborhood park.

To this day, people who were there at Samhain III swear that the lights went out.

Favorite Rite #4: Samhain IV, "The River Styx" (Old Fanning Bridge Road, Mills River, North Carolina, 1998)

OUTRAGED BY CITY OFFICIALS' TREATMENT OF US IN THE PREVIOUS YEAR'S "LIGHT FIGHT," THE CONGREGATION OF A NEARBY UNITY CHURCH INVITED US TO HOLD OUR FOURTH PUBLIC SAMHAIN ON THEIR BEAUTIFULLY WOODED LAND. SIX THOUSAND PEOPLE SHOWED UP, THEIR CARS OVERFLOWING THE LARGE PARKING LOT AND LINING THE ROAD FOR MILES.

To enter the ritual, they walked across a wooden bridge lined on one side with trees, then turned to enter and circle deosil within a hillside yurt decorated top-to-bottom as an Ancestor shrine. Many were moved to leave memorial offerings to their loved ones that Coven Oldenwilde continues to prize.

Then, they descended in a steady stream down a long flight of wooden steps to the valley floor decorated in the spirit of the river Styx, lined with burning tiki-torches and hanging cauldrons wafting dry-ice vapors into the night air across high hill and down dale. Their path from start to finish was illuminated with hanging lanterns Lady Passion had crafted by making colored drawings on two back-to-back sheets of paper that were laminated, attached at the short ends, spread apart, and hung with a snap-stick between them so that the drawings glowed like stained glass.

At the bottom of the stairs, folk waited for Chiron, the underworld ferryman of souls. He came silently and encircled a group with a long cotton rope. People grasped its sides at waist height. He led them by towline to the entrance to the underworld, a large open-air pavilion draped floor-to-ceiling with bolts of black fabric, then released them and returned to the River Styx to retrieve the next "boatload."

His charges had to find their way individually through the labyrinth using their wit, humility, or bravery. At every turn, they encountered a different challenging costumed character such as the Minotaur, and Ma'at, the Egyptian Goddess of Justice, Who weighed their goodly deeds in the form of a feather on one cup of Her balance scales, and their guilt on the other side. Everyone met Her approval and emerged from the underworld to seek reincarnation.

Each next encountered a Wraith dancing in place at the head of a long wooden bridge above a rushing river. Shrouded as she was head-to-toe in sheer blue shreds, none recognized the High Priestess, who mutely barred their way until asked for leave. Past the crossing, they walked a convoluted maze of waist-high ropes on stakes atop a massive wood stage. Lost in introspection, each remembered their beloved dead and reflected on the state of their spirituality.

The maze successfully navigated, a woman clad in a chain-mail bikini welcomed them to a hilltop fire circle and led them in intoning Pagan chants. They sat and warmed themselves, then continued to another beckoning hill.

Once they attained it, their journey was complete, and they took their place in an enormous torch-lit circle, entertained by musicians until the start of the main ritual. When all were assembled, the Wraith quickly untied her costume and left it on her spot as if she'd melted or evaporated, and entered the circle in full High Priestess regalia.

We led a lament for our beloved dead, everyone keening out names of their lost loved ones or famous folk they would miss who had died during the past year. Participants were reborn as Lady Passion led them in a long, hand-to-hand snake dance that culminated in a breathless spiral, thousands wrapped tightly around her.

The night before the rite, Coven members guarding the site saw a footless Goddess float ghostly down the hills and bless the valley in which the rite would be held. That night the High Priestess dreamed that mighty, mighty Hecate, in the form of a gigantic python baring round silver teeth, was trapped in a wooden cage atop the bleachers opposite the stage maze. Lady Passion released Her, and in gratitude of being freed, the Goddess imparted deep Witch secrets to her.

The rite inspired other area groups to begin conducting rites for the other annual Sabbats, many of which continue to this day.

Favorite Rite #5: Samhain XVIII, "Love is the Law" (Pack Square Park, Downtown Asheville, N.C., 2012)

WE HELD THIS RITUAL IN FRONT OF THE BUNCOMBE COUNTY COURTHOUSE TO PROTEST NORTH CAROLINA'S "AMENDMENT ONE," WHICH LIMITED MARRIAGE TO GENDER OPPOSITES—A *DE FACTO* BAN ON GAY MARRIAGE—AND THE COUNTY GOVERNMENT'S REFUSAL TO PROTECT ITS LGBTQ EMPLOYEES FROM DISCRIMINATION. THE CORE OF THE RITUAL WAS A MASS HANDFASTING/MARRIAGE VOW RENEWAL WE CONDUCTED FOR ANY AND ALL COUPLES, TRIPLES, ETC. OF ANY AND ALL GENDER COMBINATIONS, PRECEDED BY A PAGAN SPEED-DATING TABLE WE CALLED "MERRYMEET MINGLE."

While preparing for the rite, we directly encountered the religious bigotry that fueled this law's passage. When we sought a price estimate from the sound-system supplier whom, we were told, most local festival organizers used, he sent back an e-mail turning us down with an all-caps quote by a pop Christian preacher about refusing to use one's talent to "defeat the purpose of God in your life." For him, as for most fundamentalists, it was clear: piety was negatively defined, being not about what you do, but about what—and whom—you deny. We moved on to another—and, as it proved, better—supplier, but made sure to post the first one's name and e-mail on our website as a warning to other potential victims.

In front of the courthouse on Samhain night, we legally married one heterosexual couple and handfasted others of all persuasions, tying their wrists with silver-and-blue commemorative ribbons we'd had printed bearing the theme and date of the rite to mark the occasion and give participants a keepsake they could cherish. Afterward, every couple jumped the broom—an olde Pagan rite of commitment to sharing a household.

Our ritual was the lead story on the local news that night, and, as we note on our website: "[The story's] positive coverage made Witchcraft look fun, ancient, and powerful. For example, a mother of a bride was quoted as feeling that her daughter's Witch wedding was preferable to her own, when she was dressed in boots and blue jeans." Later, we heard from a couple met at the MerryMeet Mingle and fallen head-over-heels in love.

See videos of the ritual at: http://www.oldenwilde.org/oldenwilde/samhain/rite2012/samhain-2012-handfasting-marriage-equality.html.

You don't have to have a horse in the race to practice spiritual activism. We're not gay, but have circled with folk of all conceivable orientations over the years. Repressive legislation breeds a domino effect, encouraging nearby states to pass similar laws. We felt that this one was egregious and required a pro-freedom response, simultaneously symbolic and magical.

Almost two years later to the day, a federal judge ruled the law unconstitutional and made same-sex marriage legal statewide. The following year, the U.S. Supreme Court legalized it nationally. Clearly this ritual was a success!

Favorite Rite #6: Samhain XI, "Bones & Roses (Huesos y Rosas)" (French Broad River Park, Asheville, N.C., 2005)

THE LADY LED PARTICIPANTS ON A WINDING TORCH-LIT PATH THROUGH FOUR RIVERSIDE ACRES OF OAK WOODS DECORATED WITH

INTERACTIVE DAY OF THE DEAD STATIONS, SUCH AS ANCESTOR ALTARS WHERE THEY COULD LEAVE OFFERINGS, AND A CEMETERY OF SLAB ROCK TOMBSTONES, EACH BEARING A SPANISH EPITAPH: *QUERIDA* (BELOVED), *DORMIDO* (ASLEEP), *MURIÓ* (DIED), *LIBRE* (FREE), *HUESOS* (BONES), *PAZ* (PEACE), *RECUERDE* (REMEMBER). PASSING BEFORE A FLOWER-DECORATED SKELETON IN A COFFIN UPON A BIER, THE PROCESSION ENTERED THE CIRCLING GROUND, WHERE WE KEENED THE NAMES OF THE BELOVED AND NEWLY DEAD BEFORE WINDING THROUGH THE SPIRAL DANCE THAT ALWAYS CULMINATED OUR PUBLIC SAMHAIN RITUALS. THE DANCE MUSIC LASTED OVER SIX MINUTES, BEGINNING SLOW AND PLAINTIVELY AND INCREASING IN SPEED AND PITCH UNTIL A CLIMAX THAT LEFT HUNDREDS WRITHING AND PUFFING, PHYSICALLY SPENT BUT SPIRITUALLY RENEWED.

Each of our Samhain rites was unique. We used themes, music, and décor from diverse cultures to show the commonality of Pagan beliefs and practices worldwide. Our inclusive approach promoted tolerance and educated kids and adults alike in the merits of disparate Pagan paths and traditions without having to resort to boring, moralistic preaching.

Favorite Rite #7: Samhain "Kids' Carnival" (Unity Center, Mills River, & West Asheville Park, Asheville, N.C.)

WE INCORPORATED DIVINATION AND ENTERTAINMENT FOR PAGANI KIDS INTO SEVERAL PUBLIC RITES WHENEVER WE HAD ACCESS TO A LARGE OPEN-AIR PAVILION WHERE ATTENDEES' CHILDREN COULD GATHER UNDER SUPERVISION. ("PAGANI" IS OUR SHORTHAND FOR "PAGAN/PAGAN-LIKE/PAGAN-FRIENDLY.") HELD PRIOR TO THE MAIN RITE, THIS SAMHAIN INCLUSION FEATURED DOZENS OF WITCHY GAMES SUCH AS "PRIZE FISHING" (FROM THE COVEN'S IMMENSE CAST-IRON CAULDRON SUSPENDED ABOVE GROUND BY ITS HEAVY LINKS, THE KIDDOS USING BAMBOO AND UNBLEACHED STRING "FISHING POLES" WITH WEE MAGNETS TIED TO THEIR STRINGS, AND COLORFUL CARDBOARD PIECES IN ALL MANNER OF FISH SHAPES CUT OUT FROM THE ADVERTISING ARTWORK PRINTED ON GROCERY STORE PIZZA BOXES AND ALE CARTONS, A MAGNET-ATTRACTING PAPERCLIP ON EACH); HEAD TOSS (A PRIZE AWARDED FOR THROWING A SQUISHY RUBBER SKULL THROUGH A SCARF-DRAPED, SPINNING HULA-HOOP); FORTUNE-TELLING (BY THEIR

SELECTING A NUMBERED, DRIED PUMPKIN SEED FROM A PEWTER
PLATTER); BALANCE RACES (WITH A STONE EGG ON A CARVED,
CROOKED-HANDLED WOODEN SPOON—PLUS A SOFT RUNNING SURFACE
FOR THE EGG TO FALL ON!); BOBBING FOR APPLES; AND MANY MORE.

Big Witches come from little ones, so we held a family-friendly Halloween rite for decades. In time, many children who enjoyed them brought their own kids to revel with us. There's no reason to talk down to kids at such rituals — they love dancing with their family members, adore listening to haunting music, and really appreciate the cool prizes they earn versus being handed ordinary Halloween candy.

Favorite Rite #8: Samhain IX, "Wiccan Woods" (French Broad River Park, Asheville, N.C., 2003)

LADY PASSION LED PARTICIPANTS THROUGH A FOREST DECORATED
WITH TORCH-LIT *TABLEAUX VIVANTS* SUCH AS A DUMB SUPPER—A
COMMUNAL MEAL CONSUMED IN RESPECTFUL SILENCE, AN EMPTY
CHAIR AND PLACE-SETTING OF FOOD AND DRINK RESERVED FOR AN
ANCESTOR, DEAD LOVED ONE, OR HUNGRY GHOST. (HALLOWEEN CANDY
TO TAKE AND EAT SILENTLY SERVED HERE AS THE SHARED MEAL.)
A FAIRY REALM ALLUDED TO AUTUMNAL UNDERWORLD SPIRITS WITH
GLOWING MUSHROOMS[5] ON WHICH BARBIE™ DOLLS SAT OR STOOD, EACH
CLAD IN SUCH NATURAL GARB AS A BARK BIKINI WITH TWIG WINGS;
LEATHER MIDRIFF WITH RAWHIDE WINGS; PHEASANT FEATHERS WITH
PEACOCK WINGS; IVY LEAVES WITH VINE WINGS; LINEN SHEATH WITH
CAPIZ-SHELL WINGS, SPIDER-WEB WITH WIRE WINGS; ETC. . . . .

This beautiful riverside park was free of artificial lighting, and we safely held many more public Samhain rites there, lit only by tiki torches and glow-sticks—and without any multimillion-dollar insurance bonds!

....

5. Translucent plastic bowls mounted upside-down atop bamboo stakes, with glow sticks set inside the bowls.

Favorite Rite #9: Lammas Preceding Magnolia Summer
(In front of City Hall, downtown Asheville, N.C., 2007)

SOME RITUALS TAKE MONTHS, EVEN YEARS TO COME TO A
PINNACLE OF FRUITION THAT'S SO SWEET, SO JUST, SO FULL-CIRCLE
THAT ITS EFFECT IS BREATHTAKING IN ITS ELEGANCE: WE CALL
THIS "A LONG SPELL." ITS FULFILLMENT MAY SEEM INTERMINABLE
IN COMING, BUT PERSISTENCE AND CREATIVITY CAN ENGENDER
SUPPORT FROM UNEXPECTED SOURCES AND GIVE YOU RESULTS THAT
EXCEED YOUR HIGHEST HOPES.

In the summer of 2007, we learned that a millionaire developer, Stewart Coleman, planned to ax an iconic pair of magnolia trees and demolish a historic building beside them in front of Asheville's landmark City Hall, in order to erect a fourteen-story luxury condominium building that would partly block the city hall's world-famous façade, and whose wealthy tenants would lord it over the hoi polloi in Pack Square Park below.

The magnolias at stake were especially Pagani: an embracing couple whose interpenetrating trunks looked as though they were having sex. Thus, they'd long served as a popular photo backdrop for newlyweds married in the adjacent county courthouse—a natural fertility spell. They had grown to great size for nearly a century atop a haunted stone jail built into the slope below them. Gilded Age philanthropist George W. Pack had deeded the land on which they stood as public parkland in perpetuity—only to have county commissioners secretly sell it a century later. Adding insult to injury, the developer named his project Parkside.

Shortly after the news broke about what this unholy cabal had done, we held a public "protest ritual" during the Lammas Sabbat, circling the trees and chanting the barbarous Bagahi Rune in *The Goodly Spellbook*[6] to protect them from peril and raise awareness of the issues: corruption versus ethics; secrecy versus the public trust; private profit versus the people's park; a modern building versus old living trees. The event was the first of its kind; it enchanted the public and local media alike, and succeeded in drawing needed attention to the trees' plight.

6. See *The Goodly Spellbook*, "From Abracadabra to Zomelak: Barbarous Words of Power."

Afterward, we worked relentlessly for many, many months within the city's development-review process to try to thwart the project. A seemingly endless succession of appointed functionaries and pro-development lobbyists all insisted that the condos were a *fait accompli*. But townsfolk consistently rallied to our cause, and we repeatedly won support from reluctant gatekeepers for not moving the plan forward. Local activist-author Clare Hanrahan sat under the trees almost every afternoon.

But on July 7, 2008, the final review committee met in City Hall and narrowly approved the Parkside project. The deciding vote to raze the tree pair was cast by a committeewoman who ran a nonprofit with the mission of saving treasured trees, but who had admitted in newsprint that she'd recently accepted a $10,000 donation from Coleman.

Lady Passion was outraged, and stalked straight out of the meeting to the magnolias a few feet away from City Hall. She sat down beneath the Southern trees that had mysteriously thrived outside their hardiness growth zone and had endured many a wicked North Carolina winter. The Lady pondered the perverse irony of it all—how people who achieved the status of centenarian were praised for their longevity, but it was apparently perfectly acceptable for government and corporate ilk to kill their bark-skinned equivalents. She felt compelled not to abandon the vulnerable trees and risk Coleman's workers' cutting them down during the wee hours when no one was watching.

To be continued. . . .

Favorite Rite #10: Lammas During Magnolia Summer
(In front of City Hall, downtown Asheville, N.C., 2008)

LADY PASSION DID NOT LEAVE THE MAGNOLIA TREES' SIDE FOR THE NEXT TWO AND A HALF MONTHS. SHE LIVED OUT IN THE OPEN BENEATH THE STATELY SHADE OF THEIR LOW-HANGING LIMBS. CLARE AND MANY OTHERS BEGAN PROVIDING COMPANY EVERY DAY, AND AFTER TWO WEEKS, *DIUVEI RECOGNIZED HER RESOLVE AND JOINED THE TREE-SIT FULL-TIME HIMSELF.

We endured drought, harassment, Hurricane Fay, and more during what came to be called "Magnolia Summer." Just a few yards to our right were the front entrances of City Hall and the County Courthouse; across a side street on our left, the headquarters of the fire and police departments. Behind us was the site of the last legal hanging in North Carolina. In front of us, a massive, controversial remodeling of Pack Square Park, the city's central plaza and frequent Samhain site for us, raised clouds of caustic dust to sandblast our faces and choke our breathing every day—but the curtained-off construction zone forced every visitor, employee, defendant, politician, lobbyist, lawyer, or judge who had business in the county courthouse or city hall to walk directly in front of us and the trees, and most stopped to talk to us or read our signs and literature. (The number-one question people asked us: "Where *do* you answer the call of nature when the public buildings are closed in the evening and weekends?" Answer: women's bushes are next to the courthouse, men's in front of city hall, and gender-neutral porta-potties at a nearby construction site.)

We slept on bare ground atop the tree roots, the hoods of our black wool Witch capes a perfect foil against the dazzling downtown nighttime streetlights. In front of the trees, Lady Passion and Clare arranged an inviting outdoor parlor of comfy chairs and info kiosks and tables in a crescent that folk flocked to by the thousands. There people shouted their outrage at the powers-that-be in the governmental buildings above, shaking their fists in outrage at the bureaucrats blinking nervously down at them. They left offerings at an impromptu altar in front of the tree trunks, and decorated the limbs with beautiful handmade wind chimes that adorn our Covenstead to this day. They signed petitions, bought "Save the Magnolias" T-shirts, and got free postcards of a picture of one of the magnolia blossoms with the message "Don't kill our trees" emblazoned on it to mail to Stewart Coleman's wife.

Aperture Focus photographers Edwin Shelton and Chuck Cassidy snapped pictures of the event for posterity. Knitting clubs, clown troupes, Native Americans, and poets met under the trees and entertained. Masseuses brought their tables and gave free massages, and teachers brought their students to hug the trees and learn about preservation in action. Several supporters documented daily events on websites, and Asheville's premier free alternative weekly newspaper, the *Mountain Xpress*, erected a camera trained on the trees to enable citizens concerned about their ongoing welfare to go online and reassure themselves of their safe status moment-to-moment. After we endured several overt, in-our-face threats by chainsaw brandishing yokels, an anti-police-brutality Cop Watch activist and a pair of roving gypsy men helped to guard our backs each night.

Public opinion against Coleman heated to the boiling point and drove him to desperate acts. Unbeknownst to us at the time, he cast a spell against us from a kit that we suspect one of his country-club buddies had given him. It did not work. Toward the end, he and an assistant tried to spray neon-orange paint on the grass in a line where he threatened to erect a fence. Lady Passion made them drop their spray-cans on the spot.

One blazing hot day, she was encouraging new participants when a man wielding a box-cutter ran up and tried to slice her spine like the belly of a fresh-caught carp. She sensed his silent rush, cut her sentence off, and whipped around. She instinctively stood, struck a crane pose, and pinned him stock-still with one open, accusatory eye and a raised, pointed forefinger on the same side while hurling Barbarous Words of Power in a tongue so ancient it gave even *her* chills. He ran away.[7]

We held two more rituals around the trees. On Lammas, we renewed the protective circle we'd initially cast, this time using the "Enos Lases Iuvate" chant from *The Goodly Spellbook*'s protection spell "To Protect Forest, Field, and Stream." The other ritual occurred spontaneously, when New Zealand tourists asked their party-bus driver to take them "to the Witch tied to a tree." Lady Passion was not *literally* tied, but they'd heard about the brouhaha even on their far island.

Political officials and candidates visited us to express their support. We subsisted on the kindness of strangers and friends who brought us coffee, food, supplies, and buckets of water to help the drought-starved magnolias. To wash down our dusty throats, the local Wedge Brewing Company donated a dozen growl-

---

7. We incorporated this spell into the 2014 anniversary edition of *The Goodly Spellbook*'s repulsion spell "To Avert Imminent, Life-Threatening Peril."

ers of ale—which, paradoxically, we and our supporters could enjoy on-site only because the land we wanted returned to the public was now considered privately owned in the eyes of the law. Thus magically singled out by its "between-the-worlds" merit, this gift from Wedge revealed a bridge that would eventually help us to end the standoff between the developer and the people.

Our many years of experience conducting annual public Samhain rituals proved invaluable during Magnolia Summer. Thanks to these, we were able to strike a delicate balance between leadership and autonomy, and to keep our eyes on our spell goal through a continually changing, organically unpredictable situation.

The magnolias provided a central point for everyone to rally around, and they always helped us maintain focus in the midst of many demanding people who had ideas about what to do and who should do it. More than a few were dead set against Witches being the public face of saving the trees; to this we replied: "Do what you will, but where are *you* at four in the morning?" We endorsed and participated only in suggestions that we deemed goodly for the magnolias—not our egos or anyone else's—and for safety's sake worked with local peace activists on how to passively resist cops who might start pepper-spraying us at any time on Coleman's orders, and with Earth First! to be able at a moment's notice to secure our arms through thick iron tubes around the magnolias' trunks should Coleman's crew attack with chainsaws.

After awakening at five a.m. every day, we would be shaken from our torpor by loud, gratuitous pruning of everything green around us by a group of Parks & Rec employees, or their in-our-face watering of hopelessly drought-beleaguered impatiens hanging high in plastic pots, while overtly refusing to turn their nozzles toward the august trees more needful of a spray. Frequent dangerous thunderstorms sent us scurrying into the open shelter of the Art Deco Italian-tiled foyer of City Hall. On one of the first nights, someone sneaked so close to us while we slept that they scattered torn-up Bible page bits all over the foyer's floor, apparently hoping to frame the Witches for anti-Christian vandalism; we discovered and cleaned them up before anyone found them, and promptly took steps to tighten our security.

Every night before our relief guard contingent arrived, *Diuvei patrolled the area, pondering the best solution to the impasse into which we'd forced the developer. The plaza's four entrances were oriented to the cardinal directions, so as he circumambulated he cast a protection spell appropriate to each corresponding Element. As he did so, the dilapidated 1800s-era Hayes-Hopson Building beside the trees, which Coleman also planned to demolish, enamored him with its antique ironwork and architectural detail buried beneath thick layers of ugly paint.

Finally, it struck *Diuvei: saving the building was a key to saving the trees. Stewart had admitted to *Diuvei that his only real interest was in making money—so if the Hayes-Hopson building could be preserved and repurposed into a profitable venture, the trees and building could be saved, and everyone could win. The next day, *Diuvei contacted a historic-preservation expert and arranged for him to meet Coleman and tour the building.

We successfully protected the trees until a court ruled in a suit brought against the county by George Pack's heirs that the sale of his donated parkland had indeed been illegal. At about the same time, Mountain Xpress readers voted Stewart Coleman the city's Worst Villain in their annual "Best of Asheville" issue.

Convinced by the preservation expert that the Hayes-Hopson was structurally sound and ideally located for drawing downtown business, Coleman soon abandoned his condo plans and took Lady Passion's suggestion (inspired by our experience with the growlers) of turning the old building into a speakeasy-themed "people's pub"—even naming it Pack's Tavern. The timing was perfect: the Great Recession would have bankrupted his luxury condos, but Asheville's burgeoning local breweries were about to turn the increasingly popular tourist town into the "Beer City, USA" it's become as of this writing.

Hate-breeding leaders of an extremist group had tried to smear an environmentalist candidate for City Council membership as being "a Pegan . . . dancing with Wickens" [sic] for her participation in the initial tree rite. They swiftly became public laughingstocks when they proceeded to sabotage every cause in which they tried to insert themselves.

The woman who had accepted the developer's donation and then voted to kill the trees tried to distance herself from her bad decision by changing the name of her nonprofit. Conversely, Russ Bowen, a popular local TV news reporter and anchor at the time, won a regional Emmy for his coverage of the tree-sit.

Progressive City Council candidates Cecil Bothwell and Gordon Smith helped save the trees—Bothwell broke the story about the illegal sale of public parkland, and Smith's blog "Scrutiny Hooligans" helped keep the public educated about the injustice throughout the many months of people trying to rectify it. They won the 2009 Council election and flipped the balance of power from previous conservative domination to a more liberal bent.

The tree-sit photographers enlarged and framed many of their pictures for us. We exhibited them for a month on the walls of a popular vegan restaurant, Rosetta's Kitchen, along with other beautiful, multi-medium works of art about the magnolias that locals had been inspired to make and contribute. The photos now adorn our Covenstead walls.

In saving the trees, we also saved the haunted stone jail beneath. Soon, local paranormal investigator Joshua P. Warren leased the space as a museum featuring stories about renowned Blue Ridge Mountain haunted places. We blessed its grand opening at his request—during which he showed us an exhibit of the spell ingredients that Stewart had been given to use magically against us during the tree-sit. Although Coleman had vociferously claimed to Warren that he'd never actually used them, the potion bottle the wooden box housed was empty, an accompanying scroll of instructions was tell-tale crinkled, and the black candle had been burned to a nub.

Our final Magnolia Summer photograph shows Stewart Coleman raising a toast with us at the grand opening of Pack's Tavern. Coleman died soon after, but his true legacy lives on: the remodel of the Hayes-Hopson he commissioned from a local architect won a coveted award for historic preservation. Today, Pack's Tavern helps locals steel themselves for court nearby, celebrate when they win, and console themselves when they lose. The pub feeds tourists as well as locals, attorneys, and courthouse and City Hall staff. Opposite its main entrance, a glass doorway prominently frames the magnolias featured in the Tavern's outdoor dining area. At seasonal times, employees often wrap their trunks in colored LED lights.

The magnolias thrive to this day, nurtured by underground water drip-lines that Stewart installed, and protected by night-vision cameras.

A painted mural in downtown Asheville commemorates the tree-sit on a concrete overpass pillar that intersects Merrimon Avenue and Interstate 26.

For details, commentaries, news coverage, and photographs of Magnolia Summer, see The Magnolia Chronicles at: http://www.oldenwilde.org/oldenwilde/activism/magnolia_intro.html.

YOUR BIRTHRIGHT TO PAGAN RITES

"Everyone has the right to freedom of thought, conscience, and religion; this right includes free-dom to change his religion or belief, and freedom, either alone or in community with others and in public or private, to manifest his religion or belief in teaching, practice, worship, and observance."

—ARTICLE 18, INTERNATIONAL BILL OF HUMAN RIGHTS

GIVEN THE PERVASIVENESS OF RITUAL IN EVERYONE'S LIFE, WITCHES FIND IT BEWILDERING THAT OUR RITES ARE OFTEN DENIGRATED, SINGLED OUT FOR PREJUDICE AND PERSECUTION. CENTURIES AFTER THE BURNING TIMES ENDED, PEOPLE WHO PERCEIVE THE CRAFT THROUGH THE LENS OF A HORROR-MOVIE STEREOTYPE OR AS FILTERED TO THEM BY MONOTHEIST PROPAGANDA STILL SOMETIMES TRY TO PROJECT ONTO WITCH RITUALS THEIR OWN PERVERSE FEARS OR FANTASIES ABOUT HUMAN SACRIFICES AND PORNOGRAPHIC ORGIES.

It may be our preference for night over day that unnerves such folks, since the Manichean dualism underpinning monotheism trains believers to associate darkness with their Devil and light with their God. Or it may be Witches' auton-omy—the freedom Covens and Solitary practitioners have always enjoyed in con-trast to the centralized, top-down hierarchical repression that is characteristic of monotheist religions.

Whatever such people's motivations may be, Witches and Pagans should be prepared to counter the ignorance and misconceptions about our rituals and hol-idays that we may confront.

Employers, for instance, often don't have policies that promote religious diversity. They are often monotheist-biased—familiar with employees taking time off from work for Christmas or Yom Kippur, but shocked to learn that Pagan employees have their own sacred ceremonies that they should to be let off work to attend. Considering the traditionally flexible timing of our holidays—within three days before, the day of, or three days after the nominal date of a Sabbat—it should be easy, even advantageous, for an employer or institution to accommodate a Wiccan religious calendar. A full week within which to schedule this should be a blessing to them.

Landlords or neighbors may not appreciate the wild-sounding noise of the bliss we get up to at Sabbat rites. These folk often assume the worst of our doings because there's an assumption that pious people should be penitently reserved, not exuberant.

Non-Pagan family members may resent your absence during Esbat, gathering, or Sabbat observances, monotheist meetings being quick in comparison to ours. They often don't appreciate why you'd *want* to go to a Sabbat gathering for a three-day weekend and dance naked around a bonfire worshiping Pagan Gods. Too bad for them: if they only worship one male God, they've got a lot of catching up to do!

While you're en route to that Sabbat, a policeman who may stop you for speeding could label your athamé[8] a concealed weapon. Guns, they get: sacred knives, not so much. This goes triply for Transportation Security Administration or other security officials whose gauntlet you'll probably have to navigate in order to travel to Sabbats from afar. (Just pack your magical knife in your checked luggage.)

If you conduct Sabbats in a city park or on public land, bigoted local officials may try to impede your plans or even threaten you with arrest if you plan to do things like divination—which remains illegal in many states. Police may descend in a show of force to harass or film participants, in hope of scaring you off your sacred fun.

And Goddess forbid you're arrested for say, using a sacred substance, and find

---

8. A black-handled ritual knife used to draw magic symbols in the air.

yourself sentenced. You might naïvely assume that a prison chaplain would welcome your pursuit of a wise, ethical spiritual path that can enable you to avoid recidivism. In fact, far too many of them and other prison officials are religious evangelicals who are certain that Witches are deluded devil-worshipers, and think themselves obligated by their faith to ignore and punitively violate constitutional religious protections in order to persecute you.

But when such difficulties discourage you, remember: for two thousand years, Witches have successfully resisted suppressive pogroms, inquisitions, arrests, confiscations, and torture to revel when the leaves fall, rivers freeze, orchards fruit, and grains glisten. Your spiritual freedom is your birthright—not granted by any God or man, but inherent in the very nature of your soul, whose self-awareness gives you the power to choose for yourself.

To all of these and other challenges, Coven Oldenwilde exhorts followers of the Olde Religion to stand strong on firm grounds of conscience and justice. We believe that it is everyone's right to be supported in observing both lunar Esbats *and* seasonal/solar Sabbats without impediment. Just as Esbats unite Witches worldwide because we can all see and are all awed by the Moon, so Sabbats anchor us as one in the human impulse to revere *inviolate things*: seasons that wax and wane, roar and murmur in turns—that surprise us with their intensity and comfort us with the cozy sweetness of summer breeze, autumn crispness, winter stillness, spring scent. We maintain that such wisdom not only is worth preserving, it also merits defending.

In the United States, a lengthy history of court decisions ensures that the First Amendment's guarantee of freedom of religion trumps all unreasonable governmental and corporate attempts to restrict it. The Religious Land Use and Institutionalized Persons Act (RLUIPA) ensures the same rights for prison inmates, and protects Covens and other Pagan groups from discriminatory zoning laws that some prejudiced officials try to use to prevent their meeting in their homes. And worldwide, your freedom to exercise the religion of your choice is guaranteed by Article 18 of the International Bill of Human Rights, which most nations have signed in agreement.[9]

Our experience aiding innumerable persecuted Wiccans and Pagans has shown us that there are three keys to winning your religious rights:[10]

1. *Identify your type of persecution: Different types necessitate specific remedies.*

For example, if your landlord evicted you because you held a Wiccan ritual in your living room, he subjected you to "housing discrimination"; whereas if your boss sacked you because you requested time off to attend a Wiccan ritual, you're the victim of "wrongful firing." Such precise legal labels can determine who may give you aid and how, just as getting the right medical diagnosis makes all the difference in determining the type of medical help you may receive.

2. *Know your religious and legal rights regarding your specific situation.*

For example, your employer should have an anti-discrimination policy that you can cite in your favor, and a grievance procedure that you can follow if they refuse your reasonable request. Similar rights exist in employee manuals—if not, form a local union diversity committee to campaign for change. But if they drag their heels and you know there's a six-month statute of limitations on filing a federal anti-discrimination lawsuit (which is true in the U.S. at the time of this writing), you should remind the appropriate corporate representative that you'll have no choice but to take the company to court if they don't act immediately. Then go straight to your local EEOC (Equal Employment Opportunity Commission) and file a formal complaint before contacting a lawyer.

---

9. Article 18 is part of the International Covenant on Civil and Political Rights, which is a subset of the International Bill of Human Rights. You can read the full text of the Covenant on the website of the Office of the United Nations High Commissioner for Human Rights, at: http://www.ohchr.org/EN/ProfessionalInterest/Pages/CCPR.aspx. For more information, including whether your country is a signatory or party to the Covenant, see: https://en.wikipedia.org/wiki/International_Covenant_on_Civil_and_Political_Rights.

10. As cited at: http://wiccans.org/oldenwilde/gen_info/blk_rib/winfreedom.html.

If your religious rights are being violated because of a federal law, local ordinance, or state statute, such as one forbidding fortune-telling, file a complaint with your state chapter of the American Civil Liberties Union. The ACLU may take your case for free if its merits could provide an opportunity to change a bad or antiquated law; if they can't or won't, appeal to appropriate officials or governing bodies such as federal, state, or local legislators or law-review committees until you find one that will assist you.

If a government-funded institution such as a prison or school is systematically violating Pagans' constitutional religious rights, you should be able to get help from the U.S. Department of Justice or your local school board.

Cast your net wide: even agencies that can't help you directly can point you to ones that can.

> 3. *Document your persecution experience in detail, then get your needs met by availing yourself of every magical, legal, and media recourse.*

Documenting what occurs in diverse forms can serve as supportive evidence—legal basis of proof of your claims—and can be considered just cause for filing a grievance, lawsuit, appeal, etc. *You* know what you're experiencing, so copy down names of offenders, their job titles, and the dates and times that rights violations occur. Quote what they said, slanders they made against you or your faith, and threats they may have made. If possible and legal in your state or country, record, photograph, film, or live-stream them in the act. Often, you can also effectively hang those who would inhibit you from exercising your faith to its fullest with their own bigoted words by using social media, online complaint processes, magical means, or exposure of their intolerance or illegality in the press.

For example, when we held our 8th Annual Samhain Public Witch Ritual in 2002, a busload of Bible-waving men calling themselves "Reverends" showed up outside the building where we were celebrating the rite. They spewed Old Testament curses and screeched threats such as "If my daughter was in there, I'd burn this place to the *ground!*" As it happened, we were playing drums so loudly and circling so energetically that we were unaware till after the rite that these fundamentalist thugs were frightening attendees, including children, who arrived late or departed early.

A Christian youth minister who'd come to learn about Wicca was so appalled by his co-religionists' behavior that he filmed their taunts and threats and turned his footage in to our local TV news station, which aired it and interviewed us. We followed up by publishing "Christians Need to Rein in Their Extremists," a commentary in the local newspaper and uploaded onto our website detailing our experience and the larger issue it illustrated of run-amok religious hate-mongering.[11]

The T.V. news coverage, along with our commentary, evoked widespread outrage over the incident, and support for our position—quite a bit of it from moderate Christians disgusted by what they saw as the Bible-brandishing bullies' abuse of tenets of their *own* religion. In such a way can you spin dross into gold—using bigots' documented excesses as opportunities to educate your larger community about the Witches in their midst, and to demonstrate to the intolerant few the futility of trying to suppress or convert you.

In short, to defend your religious freedom, you don't need a stockpile of guns or a fat bank account—only Witchy backbone, facts, reason, and tradition. Regardless of your circumstances, you have rights and options, although you may not be aware of them until a crisis forces you to seek them out. Underlying them all is the basic human ethical principle of fairness, which is the linchpin of justice.

For example, both Esbats and Sabbats are magical in their own way, so resist any facility's or folks' effort to insist that you should only observe one or the other, or a few of each. This would be the equivalent of demanding that Jews observe only Rosh Hashanah, not Yom Kippur; Christians only Christmas, not Easter; Muslims only Hajj, not Ramadan—or of restricting monotheists to either observing their annual holidays or attending their weekly synagogue/church/mosque meetings, but not allowing them to do both.

If you're an American inmate, we recommend that you petition your state's Department of Corrections Religious Rights Review Committee to allow you

---

11. See http://oldenwilde.org/srasmus/oldentext/samhain/rite02/commentary.html.

and fellow Pagans to celebrate all eight annual Sabbats—not just Samhain and Beltane, or four out of the eight, as many facilities like to insist. If you're institutionalized, find and cite your facility's typical written policy of enabling a person's "whole recovery" or words to that effect: insist on your right to *spiritual healing* by observing your chosen religion's holy times, be they Esbats, Sabbats, or both.

If you're a parent, educate any social worker who tries to castigate your Pagan parenting style, or an antagonistic mate or family member, a well-meaning but clueless advocate attorney, or an insensitive judge as the need arises.

If pressed for Craft religious authority to back up your rights requests or requests for work leave to attend rites, etc., quote our book's rationales, and copy and submit its calendars and diagrams, and so forth. For detailed, experienced information on, and advice about, how to creatively conquer prejudice, see our website: http://wiccans.org, particularly Lady Passion's article "The Bliss of Besting Bigots."

RATIONALE FOR RITUAL ORDER

"The modern habit of doing ceremonial things unceremoniously is no proof of humility; rather it proves the offender's inability to forget himself in the rite, and his readiness to spoil for every one else the proper pleasure of ritual."

—C. S. LEWIS, *A PREFACE TO PARADISE LOST*

SOME WHO ARE NEW TO THE CRAFT DENY THE BENEFITS OF RITUAL, SEEING A CIRCLE SCRIPT AS A NEEDLESS RESTRICTION. THEY FEEL THAT WITCH REVELS SHOULD BE—WELL, WILD, EXTEMPORANEOUS, UNENCUMBERED BY ORDER . . . TYPICALLY IN OPPOSITIONAL REACTION TO THE BUTTONED-DOWN, SNORE-INDUCING WORSHIP SERVICES THAT THEY CHAFED AND FIDGETED THROUGH AS CHILDREN OR MONOTHEIST CONGREGANTS.

Practiced Witches, on the other hand, don't feel inhibited by a circle script, but make use of it as a cohesive structure to wrap their spells around. The truth is that even olde traditional Witch rites had an implicit order: meet and greet, spellwork, Cone of Power dancing, feasting, camaraderie, and raucous merriment.

Just as no experienced musician expects to succeed by arbitrarily playing notes devoid of any form, trying to work spells while ignoring the rules that govern them is innately at odds with the magical principle of "As above, so below." As the universe has order, so should Witches' circles, which work because they are a microcosm of the macrocosmic order of the universe. Nature abhors a vacuum, so it will rush to fill a void of order with chaos[12] that, in turn, will yield disappointing, if not dangerous,

---

12. Meaning not the creative openness or higher-level order that students of "chaos magic" and "chaos theory" explore, but an egotistical muddle of the participants' projected moods, desires, and fears—which some entities are adept at manipulating.

spell results. The tale of the inexperienced "sorcerer's apprentice" who casts a powerful spell that spins swiftly out of control isn't just a Disney fantasy.

When it comes to ritual, it *matters* which way the parts fit together: just as you wouldn't put a cart before a horse, you should follow the traditional order of ritual actions, because there is a reason—a function—for each one and for its place in the sequence. Traditionally based Witch rites such as those Coven Oldenwilde conducts are carefully crafted to open the hidden doors to the Mysteries that give spellcrafters access to the inner workings of the universe. Similarly, the rituals prescribed in olde grimoires and spellbooks such as the *Sworn Book of Honorius* and the *Greek Magical Papyri* are not arbitrary or designed to mystify the gullible, as uncomprehending skeptics sometimes claim, but are constructed according to the universal magical principles of microcosm/macrocosm, correspondence, sympathy/antipathy, and so forth.

Beginners often perceive doing a magical ritual properly as a complicated, even daunting task. However, learning, performing, and adapting a traditionally based ritual script such as the one we provide here is much easier when you understand its overall structure. Once you grasp the function of each part of this basic, general-purpose ritual, you can not only successfully tailor and adapt it to your own needs and circumstances, but also confidently begin to experiment with more advanced and specialized ritual arts. For instance, you'll recognize which parts of a grimoire's spirit-summoning ritual can be freely altered from the original (such as substituting Pagan prayers and deities for Christian ones) and which should not (such as the spirit's name or seal).

Understanding the reasons and purposes for each part of a ritual will prevent you from veering to free-form anarchy's opposite extreme: by-the-book fundamentalism. For example, we know of some Gardnerian Covens that insist that every Sabbat ritual in the *Gardnerian Book of Shadows* must be performed exactly as it is written—without varying a single word or action, without expanding on what often seems clearly intended as a bare outline, without even correcting the grammatical errors that have crept in over generations of hand-copying. These oft wrongly insist that the version of the BoS handed down to them in their lineage is the only "right, true one."

Ritual is meant to serve as a means to an end, not as an end in itself. If you execute every gesture and invocation or every genuflection and hymn flawlessly, only to exit a rite with your soul no more affected than if you were handing in some math homework, then the ritual has failed. Similarly, if you are so inflexible in your religious practice that you're incapable of improvising a rite wherever you find yourself—be it locked in a prison cell with only an iron door and three cinderblock walls to serve as the Four Quarters, or lost in the middle of the wilderness with only sticks and stones to use as tools and altars—then your ritual skills are as useless as a traffic light in a power outage.

In ritual, as in all religion and spirituality, knowing "why" a practice is traditional is the best antidote to both runaway anarchy and rigid fundamentalism. For any particular ritual speech, action, or sequence, you might see a different rationale than we do. What matters is that you are thoughtfully pondering its magical intention rather than reflexively rejecting or compulsively clinging to it—as most people unschooled in magic do, for reasons that have all to do with their own unexamined prejudices or comfort levels, and naught with the practice's intrinsic merits or flaws.

The ritual structure you'll learn here consists of three basic segments: a beginning, middle, and end—or, more precisely, an opening section, a working section, and a concluding section.

* *The opening section involves admitting participants; consecrating the Elements; casting the circle; and calling the Quarters. Its purpose is to transport you out of mundane reality and into a protected, powerful microcosmic sphere where you can affect spacetime and, thus, influence the macrocosm.*

* *Mid-ritual is devoted to the magical working that you've chosen as your reason to conduct the ritual in the first place, be it a spell, a rite-of-passage ceremony, an Initiation ordeal or Elevating a student in rank, a celebratory Sabbat rite, a remote healing, a consecration of a magical tool, a divination, a trance induction, a spirit evocation, a Deity possession, etc.*

* *The concluding section bonds participants during the Cakes and Wine ceremony in the delicious magic they've mutually experienced, reverses the opening section's circle-creation steps, and safely returns all to mundane time and space.*

In short, you're opening a rift in the everyday world, creating magic within it, and then closing it back up. Scholars assert that this beginning–middle–end structure is a universal characteristic of sacred ritual.[13]

You achieve each of these three stages by performing specific actions: the Oldenwilde Ritual Script contains thirteen. You can use the following outline as a cheat-sheet while learning the Script that applies to your situation, be it as a group member or a Solitary practitioner:

Thirteen Parts of Traditional Wiccan Ritual

OPENING SECTION:

1. *Prepare* for the rite by cleaning or making ready your ritual space, assembling your spell components/décor, and bathing your body/focusing your mind.

2. *Admit* yourself or others to the Circle space using "watchwords."[14]

3. *Summon* each of the Powers of the Elements by name (the "Eko Ekos") while lighting candles in each Quarter sunwise.[15]

4. *Cast* the Circle thrice around the participants, intoning or singing the name(s) of your primary deity or deities and

---

13. See, for example, Morrissey, Janet, et al., *Living Religion*, South Melbourne, Vic. Cengage Learning Australia, 2016. In "A Structured Movement Pattern" (1995), Terence Lovat refines this further to a "five-stage structured movement pattern": ENTRY, leaving the mundane world and entering the ritual (as when we admit participants); PREPARATION, engaging in a preparatory rite (as when we consecrate the Elements, cast circle, and call the Quarters); CLIMAX, the central, high point of the ritual (as when we perform the magical working); CELEBRATION (as when we celebrate Cakes and Wine); and RETURN, re-entering the mundane world (as when we dismiss the Quarters and snuff the candles).

14. Or passwords.

15. As in *The Goodly Spellbook*, we use "hemisphere-neutral" Witch words to describe ritual movement in circle. Sunwise, "in the direction of the Sun," is the same as deosil (clockwise) in the Northern Hemisphere, but widdershins (counterclockwise) in the Southern Hemisphere. Ayenwards, "against-wards," is widdershins in the Northern Hemisphere, but deosil in the Southern Hemisphere.

wielding a sword, athamé, wand, staff, or magical gesture.[16]

5. *Consecrate* the Elements on your main altar, using your athamé— water (Water) and salt (Earth), then incense (Air) and candle flame or charcoal (Fire).

6. *Spurge and cense* the circle and participants, with sprinkled salt water and billowing incense smoke.

7. *Call* each Quarter's "Guardians of the Watchtowers."

WORKING SECTION:

8. *Do spellwork,* using such means as ingredients, tools, Witch techniques, magical experimentation, etc. This usually includes building energy or inducing trances by such methods as playing musical instruments, chanting, singing, intoning, or dancing a Cone of Power,[17] etc.

CONCLUDING SECTION:

9. *Bless* Cakes and Wine,[18] with participants gathered and seated before the main altar, and give some of each to the Gods as an offering.

10. *Imbibe and partake* of the Wine and Cakes, sharing them around the circle while speaking freely about magical matters or playing traditional Witch games, etc.

11. *End* the rite by standing and declaring the ritual complete, and verbally charging yourself or others to keep what transpired

....

16. Casting before consecrating is Coven Oldenwilde's practice. Some Covens consecrate before casting. See "Options and Variations: Circle-casting" below.

17. A whirling energy vortex raised by a circle dance that steadily increases in speed and intensity until the energy peaks and is released toward its spell goal. Often accompanied by music, chanting, etc. See *The Goodly Spellbook,* Skills section, "Mystical Dance."

18. Or ale, spirituous liquors, etc.

secret (because no one who wasn't there would be likely to comprehend what transpired and, worse, could easily misconstrue events).

12. *Thank and dismiss* the Quarter Guardians in the order initially summoned.

13. *Snuff* out all candles except the middle "Maiden" or Dryghtyn candle on the main altar, and then form a circle hug and raise a triumphant cheer (or howl, rebel yell, ululation, etc.).

This time-honed structure creates a time-transcending "world between the worlds," as exemplified in these steps:

* ADMITTING *(during which you or others utter a password phrase) puts all consciously and subconsciously on notice that they are stepping into an experience that diverges from the everyday—as when you enter a theater and the attendant stops you, checks your ticket, and then ushers you past the velvet rope.*

* SUMMONING *(in which you begin in darkness and then ignite, one by one, the candles that illuminate the rite) reveals the outlines of this magical world—as when you clamber into a cave, shine your flashlight around, and perceive the vast size and age of the chamber you've entered.*

* CASTING *(when you magically delineate the ritual circle-sphere's circumference) erects a protective boundary around your magical world to prevent interference from without—as when you safely thrive in a blizzard because you had the foresight to don a warm wool cape.*

* CONSECRATING AND SPURGING & CENSING *(in which you transmute four substances into the Four Elements, mingle them, and immerse the circle and participants in them) cleanses and purifies that world—as when you walk adoors and relish the air after a spring rain has freshened it of noxious fumes, dust, and allergens.*

* CALLING *(during which you invoke the Guardians of the Four Quarter directions) animates your magical ritual space with protective, empowering supernatural Beings—as when you can confidently mingle in a crowd because a friend has your back.*

Now, immersed in this magical world through sight, sound, scent, movement, words, song, intent, and trust, you can cast your *Spell* into it like a seed into fertile soil. During the working, a primal sensation may well up in you of being one with all Witches who have ever been, or a devotee appreciated by the God/desses[19] to Whom you're appealing for aid. You may even perceive or do things considered impossible in the ordinary world, such as levitate in ecstasy. Revel in the feeling of unbridled freedom and personal power. Note omens that occur—any out-of-the-ordinary shift in temperature, flickering of shadows, flaring or guttering of a candle, word or name spoken by a distant voice, etc.

Work your spell to the point where you feel the magic peak—naught more is needed, for doing more would be gilding the lily. *At this instant,* discharge your spell intent in the direction you want it to go, be it into a cauldron or talisman or out past the bounds of circle, emphasizing your will with gesture and word (for example, raising your hand and forcefully proclaiming "So mote it be!").

If breathless with effort, you may elect to "ground out" excess energy by putting the fingertips of both hands atop the ground or floor, or flattening them similarly, and silently breathing until calm, letting your goodly intent nourish and thank Mother Earth for aiding your endeavor.

After your spell has been cast, you must minimize psychic disorientation by gradually making your way back to the ordinary world, just as a deep-sea diver gradually floats back to the surface to avoid getting "the bends." Coming down from the high of circle bliss takes getting used to, and you may be especially amazed at how capriciously time seems to expand or contract during spellwork. Hours spent in circle can fly by like seconds, or a rite that you thought took just a few minutes can turn out to have lasted most of the night.[20]

The ritual steps of the important Concluding Section gently take down the temporary temple you've erected:

> *Blessing the Cakes and Wine (or Ale or Spirits) is like a small play within a play—a sweet rite of its own within the larger ritual. You silently calm yourself and relax from the exuberance that you felt during spellwork, or from the intense*

---

19. We use the term "God/dess" as an abbreviation for "God or Goddess," and therefore, "God/desses" for the plural "Gods and/or Goddesses."

20. That is why Witches never wear a watch in circle—and why it's bad for the watch if forgotten and worn, because it typically stops during spellwork and never runs again.

concentration that you exercised, and (in our Covenstead, at least) sit in a semi-circle on carpeting or cushions on the ritual-room floor facing the main altar while the High Priestess and High Priest bless the Wine with chalice and blade, pour a thankful offering splash to the Gods in a special libation bowl, bless the Cakes with paten, plate, and wand or athamé, and offer a portion to the Gods in the same bowl.

* *Imbibing* uses shared food and drink to counter the "sugar shock" feeling you may have after expending a great deal of psychic and physical energy doing spellwork, and conversational camaraderie to ground you back into the world of conventional space-time.

* *Declaring the rite's end* comes when the HPS[21] senses that folks have wound down to the point that they are on the verge of getting cold or tired, or are ready to move on to a planned post-ritual feast or head back home. In our Covenstead, Lady Passion rises from her fabric pallet and raises her athamé aloft. All present follow suit, and she recites the "Witches all . . ." declaration. This does not end a circle abruptly, but rather serves as a cue to let attendees stow cushions and prepare to conclude.

* *Thanking and dismissing* the Quarter Guardians, you release Them from having to help you further, as well as banish any lingering spirits that could cause problems if not returned to their accustomed realms.

* *Snuffing* out the candles that you lit in the Summoning step returns the circle to the original close darkness in which the ritual began—closing the doorway for now on the infinite world and returning you to the finite one.

At this point, Lady Passion leads all in a final hand-to-hand circle. She lets her arms fall and bends downward, all following suit toward the center of the round as she whispers Witchy words. She straightens, arms raised high overhead, and all copy—fingers clasped tightly as everyone shouts *"Harrahya!"* loud enough to raise the hair on the back of neighbors' necks.

---

21. HPS is a conventional abbreviation for High Priestess, and HP for High Priest.

WITCH RITUAL CONVENTIONS

"With the spreading news of Witchcraft—what it is; its relevance in the world today—comes 'The Seeker.' If there is this alternative to the conventional religions, this modern, forward-looking approach to life known as 'Witchcraft,' then how does one become a part of it? There, for many, is the snag. General information on the Old Religion—valid information, from the Witches themselves—is available, but entry into the order is not [so easily obtained]. The vast majority of covens (groups of Witches) are still wary enough that they do not throw open their doors and welcome all and sundry. They are happy to straighten the misconceptions, but they do not proselytize. This leads many would-be Witches, out of sheer frustration, to simply declare themselves 'Witches' and start their own practices. In doing so they draw on any, and ofttimes all, available sources. The danger here is that they do not know what is valid and relevant and what is not. Unfortunately there are now many such covens, operating with large chunks of Ceremonial Magick happily mixed-in with smatterings of Satanism and odds and ends of Voodoo together with Amerindian lore. Witchcraft is a very 'loose' religion, in terms of ritual practices, but it does have certain basic tenets and there are established ritual patterns to be adhered to."

RAYMOND BUCKLAND, *BUCKLAND'S COMPLETE BOOK OF WITCHCRAFT*

WICCAN RITES TRADITIONALLY INCLUDE KEY CUSTOMS SUCH AS SUMMONING, SUPPLICATING, AND THANKING DEITIES, AND USING FOUR ELEMENTAL WITCH POWERS. MASTERING THESE POWERS IN SACRED SPACE CAN HELP US IN TURN PRIZE FOUR ANCIENT CARDINAL VIRTUES THAT SHOULD GUIDE OUR ACTIONS IN DAILY LIFE.

Exercising circle etiquette instills habits of ritual practice that display reverence for the sacred as well as consideration toward other participants. Honoring superstitions and traditional taboos is equally important—such as never walking blithely out of circle but, rather, learning how to "cut out" of it properly. Finally, conjuring the Elements by drawing certain pentagrams in the air is a ritual action in which every attendee at a Witch rite is encouraged to participate—but there are different methods for tracing out these four five-pointed stars, some of which are more magically targeted than others.

GODS, POWERS, AND VIRTUES

A Witch ritual isn't just some metaphysical mechanism for getting what you want: it is a meeting-ground between your world and a realm inhabited by spirits, entities, and Gods and Goddesses—and your soul can't help but be transformed by this awe-inspiring interaction, the more so, the more you experience it.

Witches work with that realm fearlessly; but to ensure that we can also do so safely and effectively, we begin a ritual by calling on certain Deities and Elemental Powers to bless the circle and aid the rite. You can substitute your own preferred entities in these invocations, but before you do, you should understand the nature and purpose of the Beings named in the opening of the Oldenwilde Ritual Script.

Dryghtyn (pronounced DRY-tun, DREE-tin, or DRIKH-tin, and spelled in a wide variety of ways) appears in the blessing "Dryghtyn Prayer" that many Wiccans recite at the beginning or end of a rite. It is the Wiccan name for the mystical One that pervades and unites all things, the eternally present consciousness in which every being participates. The "Dryghtyn candle" (also known as the Maiden candle) is the large candle in the middle of the main altar that is the first lit and is the last extinguished.

Oft mistranslated as "Lord," Dryghtyn was originally an ancient Germanic term for the chosen leader of a sworn band of warriors, and connotes a "first among equals" rather than an autocratic overlord. Both in its etymological word-origin and in its metaphysical meaning, "the Dryghtyn," as Wiccans often call It, is closely related to the words *dharma, firmament, truth,* and *tree* (as in "World Tree").

Like a tree, the One forms many branches. Wiccans are polytheists: we believe that multiple Gods and Goddesses co-exist as aspects of the All, much as a single beam of sunlight is made of a spectrum of many colors.

Unlike monotheists—believers in "the one true God of the Torah/Bible/Koran"—we polytheists don't have to tie ourselves in intellectual knots trying to force-fit the universal, all-transcending Providence and the tribal warrior deity of Abraham into a single, one-size-fits-all God-box. We don't have to contend with the scriptural contradictions of a loving-yet-wrathful, single-yet-jealous God Who's strangely obsessed with foreskins and giving women what-for. We don't feel required to turn to a messiah, prophet, guru, preacher, pope, or other human founder or leader of some particular sect to intercede across the bleak existential chasm that monotheism imposes between our world and a remote Supreme Being. Nor can we be driven into violent fundamentalist extremism by the sociopathic paradox that's at the core of monotheism, to wit: If I'm a true believer in Only One God, then the only true interpretation of Him necessarily has to be the one that I believe in.

Instead, Witches may invoke the Dryghtyn's blessing, but we wisely leave It to Its Mystery and proceed to call on any and all Goddesses and Gods Whose beneficence we seek at the time, and with Whom we have more personal experience. We appreciate that Divine Beings are as infinite as stars in the sky, and that Deities go by many names, display unique traits, and manifest Themselves in diverse guises.

Hecate and *Herne* are the names that we in Coven Oldenwilde invoke while casting circle: They're our Coven's primary Goddess and God—Deities with Whom we've long cultivated a close relationship. They represent the most ancient and widely worshipped pairing of Goddess and God since prehistoric times: the Great Mother and the Horned God, Who go by many different names in many different cultures and timelines, but Who are always identifiably the same Deities. As many polytheists have done throughout history, Witches also often refer to this Divine Couple as "the Goddess and the God" or "the Lady and the Lord" (or, as in the Dryghtyn Prayer, "The Lady of the Moon and The Lord of Death and Rebirth").

During the circle-casting part of our ritual format, substitute the names of the two "opposite sex" Deities you prefer. They don't have to come from the same historical timeline or cultural pantheon, nor do they have to be viewed as heterosexual mates (consider the pansexual Greek pair Aphrodite and Dionysus, for example), but they should somehow support each other in Their types of magical abilities, or things They're associated with in Their mythoi. Don't confine your worship to a single God or Goddess from even a Pagan pantheon—or a single undifferentiated "Great Spirit," "Creator," "Universe," etc.—because that would simply perpetuate the imbalance, inequality, and inescapable self-projection that characterize monotheism. Consider it a polytheist minimum to invoke at least one Goddess and God, or more than one of each, per rite.

God/desses are spiritual Beings of a higher order than humans, much as your brain or heart is in relation to the individual cells that compose it. We propitiate many Deities Who want us to flourish and Who aid us when we appeal to Them justly. But Their motivation isn't to reward us in exchange for praise and offerings—contrary to Their misportrayal in man-written myths, God/desses aren't swayed by flattery and bribes. What the Gods want from humans is our participation in a higher purpose, which manifests itself through that which is noble, heartfelt, healing, ecstatic, holistic, just.

Witches embrace entities, Deities, and spirits, and we don't abuse Their good nature by deluging Them with frivolous demands such as praying that our favorite sports team win or that our exes become impotent so we can exact revenge. We conjure Them responsibly and actively because we *love* Them—Their influence in our daily lives delights us and inspires us to strive to embody ethics and attain spiritual depth.

Azarak, Zomelak, Gananas, and *Arada* are the sacred names associated with the Four Quarters/directions invoked before a magic circle is cast. Azarak and Zomelak are entities, Gananas and Arada are Deities, and beginning at the East/Air Quarter direction and processing sunwise, the Witch powers that They accord are To Know, To Will, To Dare, and To Be Silent, respectively.

Wiccans know these as the Four Powers of the Witch; others, as the Powers of the Magus or of the Sphinx. Witches acquire these advantages by walking the difficult path of wisdom, action, boldness, and discretion rather than taking the easy road of being stupid, apathetic, complacent, and glib.

The famous nineteenth-century occultist Eliphas Lévi described these Four Powers in his final book, *The Great Secret*:

> The great secret of magic, the unique and incommunicable Arcana, has for its purpose the placing of supernatural power at the service of the human will in some way. To attain such an achievement it is necessary to KNOW what has to be done, to WILL what is required, to DARE what must be attempted and to KEEP SILENT with discernment.

The Witch Powers are a moral compass that mirrors the ancient Pagan Four Cardinal Virtues, which remain enshrined in three of an original four Tarot Major Arcana trumps: Justice, Strength, and Temperance.[22] The Four Virtues follow a traditional sequence that corresponds directly to that of the Four Powers:[23]

---

22. The preponderance of historical evidence at the time of this writing indicates that Prudence was one of the forty trumps included in the Tarot when it was invented in the early 1400s, but was part of a sequence of trumps that was stripped out when the twenty-two-trump Tarot was developed somewhat later. Prudence still survives in the Florentine Minchiate Tarot, which is closely related to the original Tarot.

23. The Four Cardinal Virtues are a moral meme that dates back to the Pythagorean origins of Western ethical philosophy. They play an important role in the dialogues of Plato such as *The Republic* and, individually, in Aristotle's *Ethics*. They survived the fall of Rome and persisted during the High Middle Ages in Cicero's perpetually popular book *De officiis* ("On Moral Duties"); Aquinas enshrined them at the center of Catholic ethics in his *Summa theologica*.

The Four Witch Powers were first made popular by Eliphas Lévi in the nineteenth century as the "Powers of the Sphinx." Aleister Crowley followed suit in the twentieth, calling them the "Powers of the Magus." Lévi also wrote about a connection he saw between the Virtues and four animals he associated with the Sphinx: Man (prudence), Eagle (justice), Lion (fortitude), and Bull (temperance). He thus indirectly linked the Powers and the Virtues through a shared symbol, the Sphinx—although these two sets don't completely line up in his writings, since he connects the Power to Will with the Bull and the Power to Keep Silent with the Eagle.

Our correlation of the Power to Will with the Virtue of Justice is the only one of the four we make that might not seem immediately obvious. But the philosophers explain the connection: Justice is a Virtue only when willed—that is, when we voluntarily choose to treat one another fairly. It's not a virtue when you're forced to be just *against* your will by threat of law or fear of punishment.

* *Prudence* — *making practical, wise decisions*
* *Justice* — *treating everyone fairly and eliciting fair treatment for yourself*
* *Fortitude* — *persisting through adversity*
* *Temperance* — *avoiding extreme behavior, acting balanced*

Witch Powers are abilities that you can cultivate in order to master daily behavior-ethics, the ancient Four Cardinal Virtues. By the same token, cultivating the Cardinal Virtues magnifies your mastery of the four magical Witch Powers. The more you sacrifice your ignorance, passivity, fear, and self-indulgence,[24] the more you attain both these sets of skills.

In our own practice, both of magic and in living (which, for Witches, are one and the same), we find the Witch Powers and Cardinal Virtues to be infallibly useful, all-purpose guides for navigating capricious reality. They help us achieve a state of true, enlightened well-being for ourselves, our community, and our planet.

Ancient Greeks termed this way of being *eudaimonia*, meaning the result of all wise, fair, brave, and moderate choices, habits, and actions—literally, "as if cared for by a goodly spirit." Eudaimonia is sometimes translated as "flourishing" or "weal" (well-being), but its most famous translation is Thomas Jefferson's "pursuit of happiness."[25] Just like Jefferson's self-government, leading "the charmed life" isn't effortless: It becomes charmed because you aim for what Socrates summarized as "good and beauty" in all you do—every decision you make, every action you take.

Practice enacting the Powers and Virtues for your and others' benefit. Filter all choices through both their sieves to help you identify your and others' feelings and motivations, and filter all problems through them as well, to help you

---

24. We thank Amber Fayefox, a Wiccan inmate at the time of this writing, for sharing his insight on this subject with us.

25. Jefferson, who described himself as a follower of the eudaimonist philosopher Epicurus, adapted this translation of eudaimonia in the Declaration of Independence from John Locke's Essay "Concerning Human Understanding." Locke had in turn derived it from Aristotle. But the idea is by no means unique to classical Paganism: for example, Estonian practitioners of the native Pagan religion Maausk call this ideal "monus," a balanced, harmonious life.

find solutions. Such filtering is a worthy, life-long exercise whose challenges may change as you mature, as varying hardships arise, and as you spiritually deepen.

Make it a daily ritual to wake and meditate on a Power or Virtue, or perhaps pray the Gods grant you a specific one to help you handle the kind of day you face. Then review your actions at night: Were you thoughtful, honest, courageous, and sensitive, or argumentative, self-centered, aggressive, and inconsiderate? Focus on the skill that you consistently find most difficult to master. Make these sieves second nature and you will both avoid, and rectify, many problems—and begin to live an increasingly "eudaimonious" life.

For detailed information on myriad other spiritual Beings, read *The Goodly Spellbook* and the section "Elementals, Entities, and Deities" in Lady Passion's *Candle Magic: Working with Wax, Wick, and Flame*.

CIRCLE ETIQUETTE

How to behave with basic common respect toward the Gods and courtesy toward your fellow Witches ought to be obvious, but this apparently isn't so to everyone. For starters, no one should arrive for a rite roaring drunk or brandishing a firearm. If they do, calm them down as best you can but firmly turn them away, no matter how noisily they protest. The same goes for anyone who sexually harasses other participants. Harmony and helpfulness should prevail.

Prior to circle, all should turn their communication devices off and doff their shoes. After the ritual ends, no one should critique it aloud until twenty-four hours have passed. The "24-hour Rule" ensures that the rite has time to work without being undercut by doubt and negativity—a principle similar to not looking back as you walk away after leaving a spell offering to Hecate adoors at midnight.[26] This custom is polite, politic, and patient: sometimes a spell's effect sneaks up on you in wondrous ways. Leave room in your heart for the possibility that the rite was more powerful than you thought or felt. Let time tell.

---

26. See, for example, the offering to Hecate in the spell "To Resolve a Dilemma" in *The Goodly Spellbook*.

Here are some other insider circle-etiquette secrets:

* *When in doubt, ask.*

Few Craft teachers appreciate the common sentiment "It's better to seek forgiveness than to ask for permission." On the contrary, it's better to *ask* than *assume*.

During ritual, do as the High Priest/ess[27] directs you, as the script directs, or as others are doing. But if you are still unsure about what to do, or whether something is allowed, don't do anything unless bidden: mentally note your question and wait to inquire about it during the talk segment of the Cakes and Wine ceremony.

* *Minimize extraneous speech.*

Ecstatic yips or emotional utterances are appropriate, even expected. Otherwise, cultivate vigilance to enable yourself to note omens and miss nothing. Do this by refraining from making or allowing irreverent flippancies ("Dude, where's my cloak?") or confidence-deflating remarks ("Well, I guess I screwed *that* up!"): exercise the Witch Power to Be Silent. For the same reason, ritual leaders should not bark nerve-jangling orders during rites, such as "Chant, damn you, chant!" (an example of something we actually heard during a ritual). Rather, they should ring all to attention using the altar Bell tool, and then speak mellifluously.

* *Clean efficiently.*

It's astonishing how much mess folk can make while in the throes of spiritual ecstasy, so if you're in a group, help prepare the ritual room before circle, and help tidy up afterward. Handle fragile items and spell remains delicately, and take precise direction about where things go or what you can or shouldn't touch, because you never know what the Coven considers holy—a dried bug in the corner may be a an intentionally preserved scarab, a frayed fabric remnant a piece of ancient Egyptian mummy shroud kept for use in rites for the departed soul.

---

27. As with our use of God/dess to connote either or both a male and a female Deity, so we use "Priest/ess" to convey either or both a male and a female Initiate, its antecedent "High" to specify a Third degree leader of a Coven, and "HP/S" as a short abbreviation for "High Priestess."

If you practice alone, put all in order as soon as you can: practicing Solitary magic is hard enough to maintain without others spurring you on, and a lot easier to make a habit when your circling space is always prepped and ready to use at a moment's notice.

RITUAL TABOOS

Ritual taboos are rarely understood or taken seriously in the secular modern world, even though they are a common feature of religious practice. For example, If you're a male you don't approach Jerusalem's Wailing Wall without a head covering; bareheaded tourists are even given a paper *yarmulke* (skullcap) to wear.

People may abide by taboos from sheer politeness or respect for tradition, but the word "taboo" has taken on a decidedly negative connotation that conjures up cartoonish stereotypes of headhunters chasing hapless archeologists who inadvertently broke one of their unwritten rules: people tend to think dismissively of taboos as being no more rational than children's rhyming games like "step on a crack, break your mother's back," or the infamously arbitrary list of Biblical prohibitions in Leviticus against wearing mixed fibers, eating pork, etc.

Compared with ritual *etiquette*, which has a clear social-courtesy aspect to it, ritual *taboos* can seem obscure because they are purely magical in nature. A ritual taboo is a form of Saturn magic that—by imposing limits, boundaries, or separations—channels and amplifies a rite's power. Their specific magical purposes may not be overtly stated or even remembered anymore, but the strictures remain and still fulfill their sacred functions simply by merit of being faithfully observed, so that they continue to work magically.

Wiccan rituals have two important taboos that serve to maintain the integrity and potency of the magic circle:

> *Once circle is cast, never breach its magical bounds unless you "cut out" of it.*

Casting a circle surrounds the space and all within it in an encompassing force-field sphere of protective energy that amplifies your ritual intentions and spell actions. People visualize and describe it in diverse ways—a curtain which blocks prying eyes, an impermeable membrane, an impenetrable ring, a black hole that allows no light to escape, and so forth.

More than a mere mental construct, the magic circle is akin to the magnetic field a physicist uses to contain and direct plasma or subatomic particles—and you can easily learn to *feel* it as an instant change of state and a palpable boundary. Heedlessly blundering through this force field without repairing the breach you've made can potentially expose both the realm within and the realm outside your circle to the effects of disruptive forces and Beings who are naturally attracted to magical workings.

HOW TO CUT OUT OF CIRCLE

If you need to leave a circle in progress in order to use the bathroom, leave early, etc., walk quietly up to the invisible boundary where the circle was cast, and pause in front of the area where you were admitted to the sacred space. Symbolically cut an opening in it using your athamé or the *mano pantea* hand gesture.[28] Step through the invisible opening, and then turn around and close the cut—swipe the center of the space thrice horizontally, as described below. Should you return before the circle is properly closed, cut back in using the same procedure to re-enter and seal the breach again.

There are a variety of equally valid ways to cut out of circle. Here are some of the most popular techniques:

> * Arch: *Touch the ground on one side, and then draw your athamé or hand up to a point higher than your head and back down to the ground at the opposite side, all in a single fluid movement.*

---

28. Forefinger and middle finger straight, third and pinky fingers bent, with thumb either straight or bent across or under the latter two.

* *Porthole:* Touch the ground in front of you, and then trace your athamé or hand around in a circle higher than your head before retouching the ground.

* *Vesica Piscis (Marquise Cut):* Touch the ground in front of your exit, then trace the shape of a marquise-cut diamond: draw your athamé or hand in a thin arc upward to a point higher than your head, pause a split-second, then draw a symmetrically opposite arc back down to your starting point. (This traces out the space between two intersecting circles, as illustrated in The Goodly Spellbook, "The Qualities of Quantities: 2—The Dyad," symbolizing the intersection of the world within and the world outside the magic circle.)

* *Zipper:* Touch the ground in front of yourself, then draw your athamé or hand straight up as if opening a zipper.

Closing the cut: When you're on the other side of the circle boundary, seal the breach by slicing your athamé or *mano pantea* gesture thrice, side-to-side across the middle of the doorway space, reiterating the High Priestess's initial threefold circle casting. Do this quickly horizontally—first slice sunwise, second ayenward, third sunwise again.

> *Avoid moving ayenward unless bidden to do so by the High Priest/ ess, or it's appropriate to your spellwork.*

Most spells attract or conjure something, which necessitates sunwise movement (that is, deosil/clockwise in the Northern Hemisphere, widdershins/counterclockwise in the Southern), from casting and calling to a Cone of Power dance and passing around the Cakes and Wine.

The magic circle is a spinning generator of spiritual energy much like an electromagnetic dynamo, and it's important to keep its whirl of energy spinning consistently throughout.

If you absolutely have to walk ayenward in circle, try to walk backward so that you are still facing in a sunwise direction.

Of course, once a taboo is established, intentionally breaking it can raise an opposite kind of power. Witches typically use ayenward motions (that is, widdershins in the Northern Hemisphere, deosil in the Southern) to banish, undo, curse, and celebrate Samhain (in honor of death and darkness). And some take down their magic circle by retracing their set-up steps backwards when dismissing the Quarters. At rite's end, Coven Oldenwilde draws the Elemental pentagrams that we used to call the Quarters widdershins, as explained below.

OBSOLETE TABOOS

These days certain ritual taboos are rarely practiced, because many Wiccans view them as prejudiced. They reflect a time when the larger society to which Witches belonged was so pervasively segregated by race, gender, physical traits, and so forth that many did not even recognize these taboos for the stereotypes they represented.

For example, early Gardnerians were taught to use only their right hand for actions such as calling the Quarters during rites. This taboo derives from antiquity when the left hand was deemed the "sinister" one associated with cursing, uncleanliness, etc.

But a great many Witches are born left-handed, including Lady Passion. Indeed, recent studies have proven that left-handedness is associated with statistically higher levels of creativity such as artistic talent than right-handedness. Nowadays most Wiccan rituals, including the Oldenwilde Ritual Script, simply direct that you use your "power" or "dominant" hand for ritual actions unless otherwise directed for a particular purpose by a spell formula or the High Priest/ess.

Even so, some people still erroneously use the label "Left-hand Path" to describe so-called "black magic," "Satanic" practices. By such epithets, the listener is expected to infer that, in comparison, the speaker's *own* magical practices are virtuously "right-handed," "white," superior. All of these false dichotomies are meaningless: magic can be used for selfish or for noble ends, but only the intention of its user can determine which is which, not the particular spell or practice. Such labels reflect ignorance of magic.

Satan is, of course, a modern monotheist construct, not an ancient polytheist deity[29] or daimon (as we described in *The Goodly Spellbook*: "The Burning Times"). As for white versus black, magic can't and shouldn't be reduced to such a baseless—and racist—color stereotype. That hasn't stopped some folks from taking colors to an extreme, labeling whatever magical specialty they profess to practice or write about with practically every color in the crayon box. For instance, a "green Hedgewitch" is supposedly a healing herbalist, a "black hander" one who practices Satanism or "chaos magic," a "white Witch" only blesses, a "red Priest" is martial (or a sex-magic degenerate), a "blue boo" works weather magic, and so forth. These are modern labels for which we've never seen any traditional basis.

Similar ritual taboos now fallen into disfavor were originally gender-based and were once as common in Wiccan ritual as they were in mainstream society at the time. One of these is that the High Priestess had to be a heterosexual female, and the High Priest a heterosexual male: gay Witches were barred from Coven membership because most members were married couples—mainly to avoid suspicion, reproach, and consequent persecution. Gays were seen as very magical people, though, so because they could not belong to one single Coven, they often circled with many, and served in the role called "Messenger of the Gods," one who communicated news and fostered connections among besieged, secretive Craft communities during trying times.

These days, far fewer Wiccans are continuing such customs. In the Ritual Script for Covens and Groups, we refer to the High Priestess as "she" and the High Priest as "he," following Lady Passion and *Diuvei's personal practice, but these ritual roles should not be viewed as fixed in stone—their genders can be changed to any combination that reflects your identity or preferred practice.

In this regard, Witches take Nature as a truer guide than nurture, since both the heavens and the earth provide diverse examples of gender fluidity in the form of hermaphrodite God/desses, and animals that are interchangeably female and male or that change gender in order to adapt to conditions that threaten the continuation of their species.

---

29. George Orwell's political satire *1984* brilliantly captures the monotheist cult dynamic of God vs. The Devil in the rivalry between Big Brother and Emmanuel Goldstein that the Party manufactures and uses to manipulate the citizens of Oceania.

Pagans around the world have always recognized transgender magic—from cross-dressing men in European and American mummers' plays and transgendered *kothis* in India who embody Goddesses at Hindu festivals,[30] to the "two-spirit persons" who often serve as shamans in Native American cultures such as the Teton Dakota Sioux and the Zuni.[31]

Nevertheless, it remains important to preserve the magical *polarity* between the two ritual roles, whether the participant, High Priestess, High Priest, Covenmates, or students be heterosexual or LGBTQ. Both feminine and masculine energies coexist in each of us, but typically in a state of suppression or conflict: personifying them separately but harmoniously, as traditional Witch rituals do, helps activate, unify, and utilize the power of both energies within us. It also goes far toward healing the pain of eons of female-suppressive sexism and the separation of the sexes during worship characteristic of monotheism, and that even some Pagan groups still perpetuate (e.g. by insisting on being composed of only all females or all males).

Moreover, the HPS/HP polarity corresponds to the ritual balance between other pairs of opposites: "the Goddess" and "the God," the Moon and the Sun, the chalice and the blade, mercy versus severity, water/earth versus fire/air, and so forth. Whatever the HPS's and HP's personal gender identifications, a sexual tension felt between the two (even if their relationship remains perfectly platonic) fuels spell energy, just as negative and positive poles propel an electrical current.

Even today in Gardnerianism, many ritual actions are traditionally done "cross-sex," thus utilizing the between-the-worlds magic of sexual paradox and gender fluidity. For example, it is the HPS who casts circle with a masculine sword at the beginning of circle. It is also she who wields the "male" athamé to bless the Wine in the Cakes & Wine ceremony near the end of circle, but the HP who

30. "Mortal to Divine and Back: India's Transgender Goddesses," *The New York Times*, July 24, 2016, http://www.nytimes.com/2016/07/25/world/asia/india-transgender.html.

31. *Crossdressing in Context, Vol. 4:* Transgender & Religion, G.G. Bolich, Psyche's Press, 2008.

cradles the "female" cup as the HPS penetrates it with her blade. Similarly, the female High Priestess is traditionally primarily responsible for mentoring male students, and the High Priest for female students.

DRAWING THE ELEMENTAL PENTAGRAMS

When invoking each of the Four Quarters in turn, most Witches are taught to draw in the air just one form of pentagram (five-pointed star), starting at the top point, proceeding in a widdershins direction to the lower left point, then continuing widdershins to each remaining point until concluding back at the top. When dismissing each Quarter, they're likewise usually instructed to draw a single form of pentagram that reverses this action, starting at the lower left and going in a deosil direction to the top point and onward till returning to the lower left.

These two pentagrams are the invoking and banishing Earth pentagrams in the system of Elemental pentagrams popularized by the Order of the Golden Dawn. If this is already your or your Coven's accustomed practice, feel free of course to stick with it.

However, we find this practice magically arbitrary, since it violates Quarter correspondences by failing to differentiate the other three Elements, and it contradicts the deosil direction of every other motion made in setting up the circle by making a widdershins motion to invoke. We've therefore long used instead our more targeted and magically potent Oldenwilde system.

Here's why: the Oldenwilde system invokes each Element with a deosil motion as the ritual circle is being erected, and banishes each widdershins as the circle is being taken down. This consistency of direction reinforces the sunwise whirl of energy that every other step in erecting the circle is intended to establish (as explained in *Ritual Taboos*).[32] Our system also respects the distinct individuality of each Element, since it attributes to each a unique pair of invoking and banishing pentagrams.

By contrast, the Golden Dawn system draws half of the invoking pentagrams

32. If you live in the Earth's Southern Hemisphere, you will probably want to reverse these pentagram pairs and use the widdershins ones for invoking, the deosil ones for banishing.

OLDENWILDE PENTAGRAMS

	INVOKE	BANISH
AIR/ EAST		
FIRE/ SOUTH		
WATER/ WEST		
EARTH/ NORTH		

GOLDEN DAWN PENTAGRAMS

	INVOKE	BANISH
AIR/ EAST		
FIRE/ SOUTH		
WATER/ WEST		
EARTH/ NORTH		

widdershins, and half of the banishing pentagrams deosil. This muddling of the two directions violates the careful magical distinction that every *other* part of a traditional Witch ritual maintains between sunwise versus ayenward motions. The Golden Dawn system also draws the Air-invoking pentagram identically to the Water-banishing pentagram, and the Air-banishing identically to the Water-invoking; yet, inconsistently, there is no such parallel identity between the Fire and Earth pentagrams.

In all fairness, the Golden Dawn system is relatively easy to memorize, and it does have one ritual virtue: All of the Air and Water pentagrams start with a side-to-side motion, and all the Fire and Earth ones with an up-or-down motion. This horizontal-versus-vertical distinction links opposite directions together and helps tie microcosm to macrocosm: East and West (the directions of sunrise and sunset) are horizontal, South and North (the directions of noon and midnight) are vertical, just as they are in relation to the motion of Sun, Moon, and stars.[33]

As always, if you're not sure which system you want to adopt, experiment as a Coven or Solitary with both and see which you prefer. Fortunately, the two don't differ radically: of the eight pentagrams, both systems draw four—the invoking and banishing Fire and Water pents—in the same way.[34] And either system provides each Quarter-caller with an opportunity to draw their pentagram with Witchy aplomb: for example, by emphasizing the concluding stroke with a sweeping flourish.

---

33. Reference *The Goodly Spellbook*, "The Four Quarters."

34. There are also differences in drawing the rarely used fifth Element "Spirit" pentagrams. The Oldenwilde system invokes Spirit deosil from the top point and banishes widdershins away from the top point, in conformity with the rest of the system. (They are thus drawn the same as the Golden Dawn banishing Earth and invoking Earth pentagrams, respectively.) The Golden Dawn system, as we received it via the Gardnerian Tradition, posits invoking and banishing pentagrams for "Spirit—Active" (drawn the same as the Oldenwilde invoking and banishing Air pentagrams) and for "Spirit—Passive" pentagrams (same as Oldenwilde banishing and invoking Earth).

RITUAL PREPARATION

"You have to take obsession and pair it with discipline. . . . If you have complete control then you can go completely out of control."

—DIAMANDA GALÁS, AMERICAN PERFORMANCE ARTIST

REGARDLESS OF ITS FORMAL BEGINNING TIME, A RITE, LIKE A
SPELLCASTING, *TRULY* STARTS THE SPLIT-SECOND YOU BEGIN TO
PREPARE FOR IT—RESOLVING TO DO IT AND DECIDING WHAT IT WILL
ENTAIL; GATHERING NECESSARY SPELL COMPONENTS; ENSURING
THAT THE CIRCLING SPACE IS OPTIMALLY FUNCTIONAL (CANDLES
SET WITH WICKS STRAIGHTENED TO ENABLE EASY LIGHTING, WATER
AND SALT REPLENISHED IN THEIR MAIN ALTAR RECEPTACLES, ETC.);
AND BATHING AND DRESSING IN WAYS THAT SET THE MOOD, EVOKE
ANTICIPATION, AND CORRESPOND WITH YOUR MAGICAL GOAL.

In learning the traditional, orderly processes we explain here, you have already *begun* to bend reality. Indeed, the truism "You get out of Wicca what you put into it" springs to mind. The more precisely you prepare for rites, the smoother they will flow, for little is worse than feeling fully invested in a ritual only to break out in a panic sweat and all grind to a screeching halt when you—and, horrors! others—realize that you neglected to make available a crucial ritual component.

The first thing to consider is *what type of magic* you want or need to work, such as:

* Celebrating/Turning the Wheel of the seasons

* Praising/Giving a Thanks Offering to the God/desses

* Appealing to the Gods for a need, boon, insight, or inspiration

* Healing, hexing, summoning, or conjuring, etc.

* Attracting or banishing

* Ceremony, such as an Initiation, Elevation, Rite of Passage, Handfasting, or Rite for the Departed Soul, etc.

* A quick spell to solve a problem, or an intricate "long spell" for high stakes gain[35]

Another ritual consideration is *purity*—or, rather, deciding what type of purity that you feel the ritual deserves. Contrary to the modern stereotype that says our ancestors reveled in filth, they were quite insistent on the importance of meditative bathing and similar prior to rites.

A *ritual bath* prior to certain Gardnerian rites remains a key part of their ceremony. Like spurging and censing (detailed below), bathing is a calming way to purify mind and body, cleansing away as it does accumulated mundane muck to enable you to focus fully on magic. And at the very least, showering before you arrive is the polite thing to do if you're going to doff your clothes and circle skyclad with others.

Here are some other suggestions:

....

35. Often when a newly practicing Witch assumes that a spell they cast failed, they're simply unaware that the Gods have listened and deemed their plight worthy of prolonged support. This "long spell," can end up being some of the most satisfying magic that you are ever privileged to work. The risk to work it is to fully, humbly let the Gods resolve the matter in Their own sweet time—to stow your immediate ire about a thing and to trust that They will bring you justice to the degree that you strongly feel is required.

It doesn't happen as a result of what you do, as much as what you think, or the damage you feel on a heart level. Whether it happens inadvertently, or by intention, a long spell's magic is decidedly frosty, leaden, Saturnine—inexorable as an advancing glacier that grinds mountains to nubs. It's a chain of inescapable circumstances that, once you activate it, incrementally tightens around your target to yield cold revenge or hot justice. Exercise patience to the nth degree.

Like a line of dominoes stood upright on end, when the last piece that spells your target's downfall is finally in place, they suffer the Gods' justice in such full-circle fashion that the coincidences and synchronicities of their demise that you learn about later stretch credulity. Swiftly the high-and-mighty are laid low; you, their hard-beset victim, are vindicated, exalted. Indeed, a long spell's wicked-delicious fruition in effecting justice is so awe-inspiring that it's undeniable to even the most hard-boiled skeptic. Spell success is what makes all Pagans and Wiccans true believers in magic's efficacy.

SET A GOODLY DATE & TIME FOR THE RITE

Timing is everything, in life and love, as in magic. Therefore, timing a spell for maximum efficacy should, if possible, be based first of all on magical considerations, and only then perhaps adjusted to suit your or others' convenience.

If astrological timing is a key part of your spell—for instance, if you are consecrating a magical tool on a specific day and hour that a planet associated with the tool "rules" or has especial influence on—then that trumps all other timing concerns. For the annual Sabbats (see below) or the monthly Esbats (the New or Full Moon), however, any day within three days of the actual date is acceptable.

The main rite should not begin till after sunset, when the visible world makes way for the invisible. This magically effective practice also reflects a tradition from Celtic culture, which considered a holiday to begin on its eve—that is, with the preceding sundown—as evidenced in the olde English names "May Eve" for Beltane and "Hallows Eve" (eve of All Hallows' Day) for Samhain. And if at all possible, you should allow a minimum of three hours for it, for as Lady Passion oft reminds folks, "Real magic can't be rushed: it takes as long as it takes."

Friday night is a goodly time to schedule events such as a weekend-long Sabbat to commence; a one-night Sabbat circle to be conducted; students to meet weekly; or a New or Full Moon Esbat for a spellworking circle to be held. Friday is traditionally the Witches' special weekday, our equivalent of the Jewish Saturday or the Christian Sunday. Noted one nineteenth-century folklore scholar:

> According to a tradition current in Friesland, no woman is to be
> found at home on a Friday, because on that day they [Witches] hold
> their meetings and have dances on a barren heath.[36]

DETERMINING WHERE TO HOLD YOUR RITUAL

Where to hold your ritual is also an important consideration. The *Key of Solomon* advised pre-modern spellcrafters:

---

36. As cited in *The Folklore of Plants*, Thomas F. Thistleton-Dyer, Merchant Books, 1889, *Thorpe's Northern Mythology*, chapter 3, page 19.

The places best fitted for exercising and accomplishing Magical Arts and Operations are those which are concealed, removed, and separated from the habitations of men. Wherefore desolate and uninhabited regions are most appropriate, such as the borders of lakes, forests, dark and obscure places, old and deserted houses, whither rarely and scarce ever men do come, mountains, caves, caverns, grottos, gardens, orchards; but best of all are cross-roads, and where four roads meet, during the depth and silence of night. But if thou canst not conveniently go unto any of these places, thy house, and even thine own chamber, or, indeed, any place, provided it hath been purified and consecrated with the necessary ceremonies, will be found fit and convenient for the convocation and assembling of the Spirits[37]

This remains excellent advice; yet in these days of overpopulation, sprawl, and surveillance cameras, it's increasingly difficult to find a place outside that's securely "separated from the habitations of men," or a crossroads that's free of streetlight glare and late-night automobile traffic. And if you are confined to a prison or other institution, it is likely forbidden to circle in a "concealed" place.

In an institution, you may need to stand firm on your Wiccan religious rights and insist on being allotted a designated space and privacy for worship. A place that's adoors and unpaved is preferable, although an ecumenical "chapel" may have to suffice.

In a home, it's best to designate and reserve a room or space in an attic or basement apart from utilitarian daily life, to be used for naught but working Witchcraft. Otherwise, a living room will work if you can close it off with doors or portable room dividers and light-blocking, sound-dampening window curtains.

If you're a teen or tenant repressed by one or more intolerant monotheists in

37. *Key of Solomon*, tr. S. Liddell MacGregor Mathers, Book II, Chapter VII, "Of Places Wherein We May Conveniently Execute The Experiments And Operations Of The Art."

your realm, you may need to make and store in a trunk or lockbox a micro set-up of tools, etc. that you can use in a closet, or even work mental or natural magic that you can nonchalantly explain away if detected, or that flies beneath their radar entirely.

Ideally, *nine feet by nine feet* is the minimum amount of floor or ground space you will need to accommodate a conventional "nine-foot" magic circle (that is, nine feet in diameter). But this is only a minimum, and you will need more than nine feet for a group or Coven that's larger than four or five people.

Make yourself aware of the room's dimensions. If you're able to choose or construct a long-term ritual space, its length, width, and height should be demarcated according to *sacred proportions* explained in *The Goodly Spellbook*, "Sacred Proportions: Numbers of Life." For ritual structures, this is a very ancient and widespread tradition.[38]

The ritual room's walls or corners should be *oriented to the Four Directions*, or as close to them as you can manage. Avoid placing your main altar against the same wall as the main entrance to the room, to minimize disruption of the stable focus of energy that an altar is meant to provide.

ATTITUDE AND PREPARATION

Be proud and open about your intent to attend or conduct Witch rites. Acting furtive or secretive only piques people's suspicions, and can panic them if they happen to stumble on a ritual in progress.

---

38. Ancient sanctuaries were often laid out in harmonious whole-number ratios: for example, the remains of the important Isis sanctuary at Behbeit el-Hagar in the Nile Delta show that its inside width and length are in the ratio of 3:5, which would have resonated to the musical interval of a minor third or major sixth—appropriate to the Mysteries of "the Queen of Heaven." The Greek Parthenon is based on the more complex ratio 4:9, which is 2 squared to 3 squared. Rediscovering such mathematico-musical properties of ancient sacred spaces is a burgeoning branch of archeology known as "archeoacoustics."

The simplest and one of the most common sanctuary shapes other than a circle was a cube or square, often entered from another cube or open square as the sanctuary's "outer court." For example, the Temple of Solomon and the oldest Etruscan temples followed this 1:2 double-square design. The Ka'aba in Mecca—originally a shrine of the Great Mother Goddess Al'lat—is a cube whose corners point to the cardinal directions, with the silver-mounted Black Stone that once represented Al'lat inset in its Eastern corner.

Let non-participating family members, friends, guards, neighbors, etc., who might unwittingly interrupt you know about the time and space you have set aside for the ritual, and bid them not intrude. We accomplish this by putting out our own version of a "WITCHES CIRCLING: DO NOT DISTURB" sign on our Coven-stead's front door.

If you are planning a private ritual adoors at a site accessible to the public, such as a park or campground, pay a fee to reserve it in advance, or devise another way to ensure that no one but yourself or invited participants will be occupying it. When you leave, be sure to clean up all potentially eyebrow-raising traces of your presence such as bits of candle stubs, poppets, and other spell tools and ingredients to forfend prurient rumors of "Satanic sacrifice," etc. from erupting and thwarting your and other Witches' ability to later access the site.

If circling with a group, ensure that they agree beforehand about the details of the Cakes and Wine ceremony. Who will buy or prepare the Cakes? What food allergies need be avoided?

Will the libation be wine,[39] ale, or spirits? Being less rarefied, non-fermented drinks such as water, tea, and juice are not considered *as* goodly an offering to the Gods. But it's fine to have them available in circle for participants to drink after the Cup/chalice completes its first ritual round.

Who will bring this libation? Does anyone have a communicable illness, and thus need a separate Cup reserved for their use only? Some Wiccan groups always pass around separate cups instead of a communal chalice, especially in a public ritual. But these should all be filled with at least a drop or two from a single consecrated vessel.

Details about ritual foods and drinks follow in the material about Esbats and Sabbats later in this book.

Until group members can spontaneously and silently rise to the occasion during a ritual, you should probably also mete out roles ahead of time, such as who will call which of the four Quarter directions. If you're in the midst of circle and

---

39. Wiccan inmates have the same legal right to imbibe, say, an ounce of wine in their rites as Catholic inmates do sacramental wine.

realize you've forgotten this prep step, the High Priestess and High Priest should step up and call two Quarters each, or gesture one or more students or Initiates to spontaneously do so.

If you are following a degree-based Initiatory tradition such as Gardnerianism, Alexandrianism, etc., consider ahead of time each participant's magical rank order of precedence. In such traditions, female gender and magical rank seniority ("ladies and Elders first," as it were) determine the order in which participants take part in procedures that must be performed on or by one person at a time, such as when being spurged and censed, or when retrieving one's athamé from the altar prior to using it to call the Quarters.

The High Priestess is typically first in precedence (save for when she eats the last bite of Cake after it's made the first round during the Cakes and Wine ceremony), followed by the High Priest, then members of the Third degree or the next highest degree present, followed by those of lesser degree, and so on, down to non-Initiated students and interested participants.

Within each degree of magical rank, precedence is determined by the date each member attained the degree, with an earlier date outranking a latter one. Ritual precedence thus acknowledges each participant's presumed level of experience and understanding of the traditions being practiced.

CHECKLIST OF RITUAL SPACE PREP
◯ SWEEP AND CLEAN THE SPACE.

Unless the space is used frequently and exclusively for magic, it's also wise to purify it spiritually by sprinkling salt water on it, waving pungent incense around it such as sage or myrrh, or shaking a sistrum or rattle to dispel any lingering spirits, even though the circle will be more formally consecrated during the ritual.

When sweeping, move around the space either in an ayenwards direction to banish impurity, or from each Quarter toward the room's center to prevent sweeping your luck away from you.

◯ DETERMINE THE FOUR DIRECTIONS AND MARK THE CIRCLE'S BOUNDARY.

Use a compass if need be (beautiful silver compasses are available online), or directly observe the stations of the Sun or full Moon. Each orb rises in the East, culminates in the South (at noon for the Sun, at midnight for the Full Moon), and sets in the West.

When indoors, it's acceptable to designate the Quarters in accordance with the room's walls or corner alignments rather than insist on geomagnetic precision.[40] The Gods don't quibble about more-or-less East.

If you have no way of determining a room's compass alignment—for instance if you're in a windowless prison cell—define your Directions according to whichever wall or corner holds your main altar (even if your altar is the foot of your bed, or is not physical, but only visualized). Treat it as if it were the Eastern Quarter (or Northern if you prefer, as explained under "*Prepare your main altar*" below).

Or, you can base the Quarters on which direction the room's main entrance best represents for your magical purposes. Does it open onto hope like a new Sun rising in the East, or sorrow like a dying Sun setting in the West? Ancient temples were typically constructed with their main entrance in the East, so that the light of the dawning Sun would illuminate and help animate the Deity statue within. In contrast, Christian churches traditionally have their main entrance in the West and their altar/crucifix/pulpit opposite, in the symbolic direction of sunrise.

For most rituals, the circle doesn't need to be geometrically perfect—as long as it's roughly symmetrical, it can even be an ellipse (as are the circles we cast in our ritual room). Nor does the circle usually need to be physically marked out as long as the caster and participants are aware of where its general magical boundaries are.

If you are casting a *ceremonial* magic circle, however, it does need to be care-

---

40. Since the magic circle is a self-contained microcosm, we've seen and heard of rituals adoors that succeeded even though the Quarters were mistakenly oriented, so that North, for instance, actually faced east by the compass. The Quarters' symbolic order is more important than their precise orientation.

fully drawn and marked in chalk or similar material, using a cord compass (see "Circle-casting" in the "Options and Variations" chapter on page 108).

When adoors or in a large indoor space, you can follow this procedure to locate your Quarters: Gather five temporary markers—flags, stones, saplings, patient friends who will stand in place, whatever. Stand in the center of your intended circle space and mark it. Face the East direction, then pace straight forward a minimum of 4½ feet. (Whatever distance you choose will be the radius of your circle—that is, half the diameter or distance all the way across your circle. As noted above, your circle should traditionally be a minimum of nine feet in diameter, but it can be larger, especially if it needs to hold more than a small group of participants.)

Place a marker, then pace straight back toward the center; from there, continue to pace in a straight line for the distance of your radius, at the end of which place a marker to demarcate the West. (Adjust it as need be to align it with the Center and East markers.) Return to the Center and repeat this process for the South and North. Then, replace the markers with your Quarter lights (candles, torches), altars, or whatever decorations you want to use.

○ **PREPARE YOUR MAIN ALTAR.**

THIS SHOULD BE SITUATED IN THE EAST (OUR PREFERENCE), NORTH, OR CIRCLE CENTER.[41] FOLLOW THE ILLUSTRATED LAYOUT HERE.

....
41. Each of these altar placements has worldwide precedents stretching far back into archaeological prehistory. The Witch Tradition that Gerald Gardner inherited appears to have prescribed a Central altar, as can be seen, for example, in photos of Gardner's circle setup in his Witchcraft Museum. It's conceivable that this placement stems from the olde European Witch practice of circling around a sacred tree (typically an elder or walnut), giving rise to tales of mushroom fairy rings or discernibly trodden footpaths that were called "hag tracks" from the belief that "they are caused by hags and witches, who dance there at midnight." (Sources: *The Folklore of Plants*, Thomas F. Thistleton-Dyer, Merchant Books, 1889, *Grimm's Teutonic Mythology*, chapter 3, page 1052; and *Folkard's Plant Lore, Legends, and Lyrics*, 1884, page 91.) In Coven Oldenwilde's ritual room, our altars—one in each Quarter, with East as the main altar—are placed against the walls, allowing plenty of space in the center for group physical spellwork such as the Mill Dance, fire-leaping, circling round a spell focus, etc. If you are a Solitary Witch, however, you might find that a Central altar you can readily set up for a rite in the middle of a bedroom or living room and then take down afterwards is especially helpful for establishing a normally mundane space as temporarily sacred.

An altar is a kind of spiritual workbench—a flat, raised, generally square or rectangular surface used to support magical tools and ritual operations. (Central altars, however, are often round or elliptical.) It also acts as a lens or focal point for magical energy, which is why it's best kept clean and not used for mundane projects or purposes. Although you can buy specially made altars, most Witches re-purpose existing items such as a wooden box or footlocker, a chest or travel trunk, a shelf, or an end-table indoors, a stump or large stone outdoors. Coven Oldenwilde's main altar is a slab of marble laid atop stacked cinder blocks, whose square holes provide small shelves for storing items such as taper candles.

You may soon find your main altar's power so comforting that you want to erect more—perhaps three more to start, one for each of the Quarter directions in a circle. Soon you may be able to see a potential altar in most any flat surface that you see—a fireplace mantel, a car dashboard, a windowsill, a bookshelf, a cabinet top—and begin to arrange and use a variety of items atop it depending on your particular purpose and your personal magical affinities. Our Covenstead has little altars everywhere, featuring magical items and deity statues from cultures worldwide such as Japan and Egypt.

The main altar furnishings for a Wiccan circle, however, are well established by tradition. We list and illustrate them here, using our main altar as an example.[42] You don't have to have every single tool we show in order to perform the Ritual Script. Only the underlined tools are absolutely necessary; the others are important, but you can acquire or make them in due time. (Like a personal *Book of Shadows* that documents progress in prowess, your altar's look and the tools atop it will naturally change over time as you magically deepen.) The left side of the altar as you face it is the Goddess's side; the right side is the God's.[43]

---

42. Different traditions prescribe different altar layouts. Coven Oldenwilde's derives from the Gardnerian layout as adapted by Coven Trismegiston to reflect consistently the Goddess/God polarity.

43. For an altar that is situated in the East, left and right equate to the altar's northern and southern sides, respectively; for an altar in the North, its western and eastern sides; for an altar in the Center, either northern or western for the Goddess, and either eastern or southern for the God.

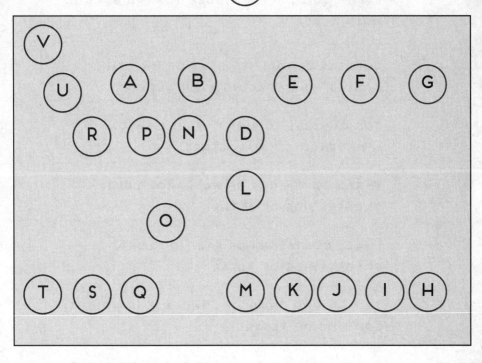

A Goddess representation
B Goddess candle
C Hecate representation (above altar)
D Maiden candle
E God candle
F God representation
G Censer
H Incense box
I HP athamé
J Incense tongs
K Candle snuffer
L Crystal ball

M Paten
N Water
O Anointing oil
P Bell
Q Wheel representation
R Salt
S Wand
T HPS athamé
U Mortar and pestle
V Scourge

Not shown: Chalice; Libation bowl; Lighter/matches; Taper candle.

ALTAR TOOLS

◯ *Maiden/Dryghtyn candle* (IN MIDDLE TOWARD BACK OF MAIN ALTAR)[44]

◯ GODDESS CANDLE (TO LEFT OF MAIDEN CANDLE WHEN FACING MAIN ALTAR)

◯ GOD CANDLE (TO RIGHT OF MAIDEN CANDLE WHEN FACING MAIN ALTAR)

◯ SMALL CONTAINER OF WATER (ON LEFT/ GODDESS SIDE OF ALTAR)

◯ SMALL CONTAINER OF SALT (ON LEFT/ GODDESS SIDE OF ALTAR)

◯ CENSER AND CHARCOAL/INCENSE (ON RIGHT/ GOD SIDE OF ALTAR)

◯ PATEN (IN MIDDLE TOWARD FRONT OF ALTAR)

◯ PRIESTESSES' ATHAMÉS (ON LEFT/GODDESS SIDE OF ALTAR)

◯ PRIESTS' ATHAMÉS (ON RIGHT/GOD SIDE OF ALTAR)[45]

44. Various Covens call this the Maiden Dryghtyn, or Fine Candle.

45. Alternatively, you can wear your Athamé on your Cord or cingulum during ritual rather than placing it on the altar. If you do not have an Athamé, substitute the mano pantea gesture. Some Witches sympathetic to fairies' disdain of iron substitute the Wand whenever an Athamé is called for, and indeed the olde grimoires tend to follow this practice, using the Athamé mainly to delineate the circle.

ON OR NEAR THE ALTAR:

○ ANOINTING OIL (BUT WE PREFER TO PLACE THIS NEAR THE CIRCLE ENTRANCE WHERE THE HPS CAN FIND IT IN THE DARK)[46]

○ WAND

○ CAKES (ON A PLATE)

○ CUP/CHALICE

○ WINE, ALE, OR SPIRITS (WINE MAY BE OPENED PRIOR TO CIRCLING)

○ LIBATION BOWL (UNNECESSARY IF ADOORS, AS OFFERING IS POURED ON GROUND)

○ SWORD

○ BELL

NEAR AT HAND BUT NOT ON THE ALTAR:

○ TAPER CANDLE

○ MATCHES OR LIGHTER

○ ASPERGILLUM (FOR SPURGING)

○ FEATHER (FOR CENSING)

---

46. In rituals other than Initiations and Elevations, the annointing oil can be any essential oil that the HPS or HP deems appropriate and that can be safely applied to the skin.

○ CARAFE OF DRINKING WATER

○ BOTTLE OPENER (IN CASE YOU FORGOT TO OPEN THE WINE!)

○ PLACE AT LEAST ONE QUARTER CANDLE IN EACH DIRECTION (AND, OPTIONALLY, INCENSE).

Do not light the candles yet. Generally, use green in the North, yellow in the East, red in the South, and blue in the West. If you lack these colors, you may substitute all red (a default Gardnerian color) or all white. Other candle color substitutions include black or brown for North, gold for East, pink or orange for South, and turquoise or sea-foam for West.

Near the altar, place a *taper candle*—a white or light-colored candle, preferably long and slender—to light the altar candles and then be carried around to light Quarter candles. If you follow the procedure described in "To Admit Participants into a Ritual Space" below, you will also need a *guide candle* in a holder that can be conveniently carried into the ritual space and then set beside the altar, where you can light the taper candle from it.

○ ARRANGE YOUR CAKES AND WINE MATERIALS.

Decoratively fan out or spiral your cakes on your cakes plate, and set this, your bottle(s) or carafe of wine, ale, or spirits, and your Cup/chalice together next to your main altar (we place them to its left), at the ready for the Cakes & Wine ceremony to follow spellwork.[47] You may also elect to include a carafe of drinking water near these, because magic can be thirsty work.

○ PREPARE THE INCENSE.

....

47. This part of ritual may be skipped during a Sabbat in which the feast is scheduled for after the circle.

If you're using a charcoal on which to burn powdered resin or dried herbal incense, light it and place it in the censer just before the rite so that it will be hot enough to emit a satisfying cloud of smoke when incense is first sprinkled on it during the rite. Charcoals for incense—unlike the briquettes you buy for a barbecue—come as small disks or squares with an indentation to hold the incense, and can be difficult to light even though they're typically impregnated with flammable saltpeter. We light them by picking up the charcoal with a pair of tongs and holding a section of its upper edge in the flame of an old candle—not one of the ritual candles, since the shower of sparks the saltpeter emits will stain it (and burn your fingers if you don't use tongs)—with a goodly portion of the coal's edge starts to glow red.

Use a charcoal if your rite will include the Consecration of the Elements, for more formal rituals, or when your spellwork specifies that a particular incense or herb be burned. On other occasions, it's acceptable to use more convenient stick or cone incense, or a Native American–style "smudge stick" of sage or braided sweet grass. Bear in mind that a burning coal often makes a censer very hot, so if the HP will be using it to Cense the circle or participants, he needs some way to carry it safely, such as a cauldron censer that contains insulating dirt or sand, or a censer suspended on a chain like those used in churches.

◯ CHECK THE AMBIENT TEMPERATURE.

If it's prohibitively cold, turn up your household heat or stoke your fire. Shivering is non-conducive to magical concentration.

◯ ENSURE NO DISTRACTIONS OR INTERRUPTIONS.

Silence phone ringers, message machines, TVs, rambunctious kids and pets, etc.; close curtains and lock doors.

Once you've fully prepared your space, don a robe, or doff your clothes if you've planned a skyclad rite. (Privacy permitting, solitary rites are always more powerful if performed skyclad, meaning ritually nude. In Traditional Covens, skyclad is usually optional depending on the season and the spellwork to be done, but mandatory for the most formal rites, such as Initiations and Elevations. Note that spurging is best done to skyclad folk to prevent saltwater or oil from staining their ritual garb, and censing is likewise ideally done skyclad to avoid stray sparks landing on flammable clothing.) Lastly, remove watches and shoes, the latter because, worldwide, it's traditional to tread sacred space with feet bared—to be in literal touch with the earth, and thus in Pagan paradox fashion, to be able to reach heavenly magical heights.

> *"Sacrifice and adore unshod."*
> —*The Symbols of Pythagoras*[48]

If the weather is too cold to go barefoot, the Gods will understand, and if you have Reynaud's disease (cold hands and feet), you can do as Lady Passion does against our ritual room's oft-chilly cement floor and wear flat, black leather, thigh-high boots or similarly Witchy footwear.

48. *The Golden Verses of Pythagoras and Other Pythagorean Fragments*, by Florence M. Firth, www.sacred-texts. com.

COVEN OLDENWILDE'S RITUAL SCRIPT

COVEN OLDENWILDE'S RITUAL SCRIPT DESCENDS FROM THAT IN
THE GARDNERIAN BOOK OF SHADOWS AND SCRIPTS USED BY COVEN
TOBAR BHRIDE, COVEN TRISKELL, AND COVEN TRISMEGISTON, THE
CALIFORNIA GARDNERIAN COVENS IN WHICH *DIUVEI WAS TRAINED,
INITIATED, AND ELEVATED, AND THE LAST OF WHICH INITIATED
LADY PASSION.

The Ritual Script we offer here is "Outer Court," meaning that it can be used in public and to teach students without breaking Gardnerian oaths of secrecy because it contains minor wording changes from the Gardnerian Book of Shadows. It also allows the High Priest and students more active role participation than does the traditional Gardnerian script.

We've found our Ritual Script to be as immensely effective as it is beloved by our students. Once students fully memorize it, they find it easy to perform even when they are physically spent from dancing a Cone of Power, or if they feel a bit "cupshotten" (a Witch Word for tipsy from drink) following the Cakes and Wine ceremony.

Magic benefits from balance—from cultivating structure *and* inspiration, constancy *and* change—to make it effective and extraordinary. Learning to do default ritual to perfection will give you the foundation of skill and confidence necessary if you ever want to compose your own rites.

You may, optionally, ring the Bell on your Main altar to mark transitions between parts of ritual, such as after spellwork and before performing the Cakes and Wine ceremony. Ring it consistently once, or thrice, each time.

Transitions at the end of each of the ritual's stages are shown by the dividing mark illustrated here.

))) ! (((   ))) ! (((   ))) ! (((

As you read the script for the first time, be excited and empowered, not daunted. Take heart that once you've memorized, practiced, and perfected it to flow like a river comfortable in its course, you *will* at long last be able to manifest the magic you have so long desired to wield.

We recommend that you read through it several times. Strive to memorize it verbatim. Our "do this, don't do that" tutelage regarding proper circle preparations, erection, etiquette, and cleanup is based on decades of experience, and you'll find our expert tips extremely valuable in helping you to craft your rites into vital and unforgettable experiences.[49]

Just relax. Don't drive yourself into a panic trying to remember and act on every single detail we give here during your first whack at bat: you can focus on the finer points in future rituals as you grow in mastering the basics.

When you recite script words, intone them with mellifluous resonance so they ring or reverberate in midair. Infuse them with your belly-will. Experiment with when it is best to pause for effect. Practice executing the ritual movements and gestures with intentional measure and control—assured grace and Witchy flair.

Keep the script close at hand while circling until you can perform it consistently flawlessly. If you circle with a group, rather than having each participant fumble awkwardly to follow along in their own copy of the script, you may prefer to designate one participant to be a "Scriptbearer" who will stand at the elbow of each person in turn who has a ritual role, and hold one copy in one hand for them to read from, and a candle in their other hand to illuminate its pages[50] so that each participant can easily refer to it as needed until this cheat is no longer

---

49. View video showing many of the parts of the Ritual Script at: oldenwilde.org, Ostara 2010 ritual ("Fox Carolina News Special Report: The Witches of Western North Carolina").

50. It would seem more convenient to use a mobile device with a lighted screen such as a tablet, but be warned: Ritual magic often affects electronic devices in unpredictable ways. It is possible to shield them, however, as we often do by means of a talisman imprinted with a three-legged triskelion or four-legged "fylfot" symbol when a TV camera crew films us from within the circle.

necessary. The Scriptbearer shouldn't become a fixed role comfortably defaulted to by the shyest person in your group, but instead should be circulated to a different attendee each time you meet.

A number of sections and actions included in the script are considered optional in practice, and we've labeled them as such. You need not use all parts of the circle script every time. For instance, Consecrating the Elements and Spurging and Censing each participant may be logistically impractical or tediously time-consuming if performed on a huge crowd, but they would be crucial inclusions during Initiation and Elevation rites and for important spells. So learn the script in its entirety, and then wisely choose which parts of the script to use or skip as necessary to enhance the experience for participants and onlookers alike; whenever your rite is being filmed; or to accord with your own beliefs, circumstances, and Deities that you plan to invoke; and so forth.

Frequently mentally review the words and script structure until you can readily recite all aspects of the format, and your circles flow like second nature. While relaxed and bathing or showering is a goodly time to review and test your memory's accuracy. Intone script portions aloud, or visualize them on the page.

Don't forget basics, such as ensuring that if you circle with others, you don't completely block their view of the main altar while you are lighting its candles or are Consecrating the Elements. Turn a bit sideways so that participants can see your actions in detail. Speak loudly enough that your words are always audible to every participant.

Sharpen your ritual skills often. The more times you cast a circle carefully and formally in a ritual space, the easier it becomes to cast a quick, *mental* circle around yourself for personal shielding when necessary—and conversely, the more you practice personal casting, the more effectively you can cast ritually.

Rely on our circle scripts to serve as the traditional underpinning scaffold for your spells; just ensure that the spell you work in the middle of them is creative and empowering. The circle you cast is the ring, your spell its center jewel, and the ritual script the setting that enhances the gem's gleaming.

To Admit Participants Into a Ritual Space

ALL PARTICIPANTS "FOREGATHER"—ASSEMBLE TOGETHER JUST
BEFORE THE RITE—IN A DARKENED AREA SEPARATE FROM THE
RITUAL SPACE WHERE THE CIRCLE WILL BE CAST. THEY HOLD
HANDS SILENTLY IN A CIRCLE, ALTERNATING MALE AND FEMALE,
AROUND THE GUIDE CANDLE (A SINGLE LIT CANDLE PLACED IN A
HOLDER THAT CAN BE EASILY CARRIED). THE HP STANDS ON THE
HPS'S LEFT. ALL CALM AND CENTER THEMSELVES—BREATHING
SLOWLY, RELAXING TENSE MUSCLES, AND LETTING GO OF THE DAY'S
CONCERNS BY FOCUSING THEIR ATTENTION ON THIS MOMENT OR
ON THE CANDLE. WHEN THE HPS FEELS AN EXPECTANT CURRENT
OF ENERGY CIRCULATING THROUGH AND BONDING THE GROUP, SHE
STOPS HOLDING HANDS, AND ALL FOLLOW SUIT.

The HP picks up the guide candle and, followed by the HPS, leads all single file toward the circling area. He motions for participants to stand in a line before its entrance, then stations himself last, facing outward as a guardian till all others have entered. The HPS stations herself within the entrance, picks up a container of anointing oil, and faces the participants.

The HPS puts a dab of anointing oil on the forefinger of her dominant hand, and asks each participant in turn:

HPS: *"How do you come to the circle?"*

The participant responds with the passwords[51]:

Participant: *"In Perfect Love, and Perfect Trust."*

The High Priestess then anoints their forehead with the essential oil, in an Earth-invoking pentagram pattern (shown at right), and says:

H P S: *"Blessed be!"*[52]

She hugs the participant, and then steps aside a bit to allow them to enter

---

51. Also called "watchwords."

52. This phrase is always pronounced as three syllables: BLES-sed BE.

the circling area. The next participant in line steps forward, and the procedure is repeated.

Each participant enters the dark space singly and stands facing the main altar. A drummer may play a steady beat at a slow or moderate tempo.

The High Priestess anoints and admits the High Priest last, and she both embraces and kisses him when he gives the passwords. She discreetly slips him the container of anointing oil. The HP enters the circling area carrying the oil in one hand and the guide candle in the other, and proceeds toward the main altar, followed by the HPS. The HP sets down the candle beside or on the altar. Both stand facing each other before the main altar, the HPS on the Goddess side (left), the HP on the God side (right).

The High Priestess extends her arms down at her sides in an inverted "V" shape, each hand forming the *mano pantea* sign. The High Priest anoints her forehead with a pentagram and an inward spiral, saying:

> *H P: "Thou art Perfect Love, and Perfect Trust.*
>
> *Thou art the circle.*
>
> *Blessed be!"*

The High Priestess and High Priest embrace and kiss again.

))) ! (((   ))) ! (((   ))) ! (((

To Invoke the Quarter Powers

THE HIGH PRIEST LIGHTS A TAPER FROM THE GUIDE CANDLE AND USES IT TO LIGHT THE THREE CANDLES ON THE MAIN ALTAR, IN THIS ORDER: CENTER (DRYGHTYN/MAIDEN CANDLE), LEFT (GODDESS CANDLE), RIGHT (GOD CANDLE).

Optionally as he does so, he recites the Dryghtyn Prayer:[53]

---

53. Also called the "Blessing Prayer," this is recited by some Covens at the end of a ritual instead of the beginning. It was first published by Gardnerian Elder Patricia Crowther in *Witch Blood!: The Diary of a Witch High Priestess*, House of Collectibles, Inc., 1974, pp. 39–40.

HP: *"In the name of Dryghtyn,*[54]

the ancient providence,

which was from the beginning,

and is for eternity,

male and female,

the original source of all things;

all-knowing, all-pervading, all-powerful, changeless, eternal.

In the name of the Lady of the Moon,

and the Lord of Death and Rebirth;

in the name of the Mighty Ones of the Four Quarters,

the Kings of the Elements,

Blessed be this place, and this time, and they who are with us."

Then he lights or renews the incense on the main altar.

The HP uses the taper to light one or more candles at the *East Quarter*. As he does so, he intones:

HP: *"Eko, eko Azarak,*[55]

the Power of Air—

the Power to Know."

The High Priest pauses briefly, then concludes:

HP: *"Blessed be!"*

Participants echo in unison:

---

54. Pronounced DRY-tun, DREE-tin, or DRIKH-tin.

55. Find the pronunciations of this and the following three Names in *The Goodly Spellbook*, "From Abracadabra to Zomelak: Barbarous Words of Power."

All: "Blessed be!"

Bearing the taper, the HP proceeds sunwise to the *South Quarter* and lights one or more candles[56] there, intoning:

H P: "Eko, eko Zomelak,

the Power of Fire——

the Power to Will."

The High Priest pauses briefly, then concludes:

H P: "Blessed be!"

Participants echo:

All: "Blessed be!"

He proceeds sunwise to light candles at the *West Quarter* and intones:

H P: "Eko, eko Gananas,

the Power of Water——

the Power to Dare."

The High Priest pauses briefly, then concludes:

H P: "Blessed be!"

Participants echo:

All: "Blessed be!"

He proceeds sunwise to light candles at the *North Quarter* and intones:

H P: "Eko, eko Arada,[57]

the Power of Earth——

the Power to be Silent."[58]

---

56. He can optionally also light incense at this and each successive Quarter.

57. Note that the word is not "Aradia" as many Witches assume.

58. Alternatively, "the Power to keep Silent."

At this last word ("Silent"), any drumming or other music being played abruptly ceases. The HP pauses briefly, then concludes:

HP: "Blessed be!"

Participants echo:

All: "Blessed be!"

)))! (((   )))! (((   )))! (((

To Cast Circle

The High Priest snuffs out the taper flame and resumes his previous position at right before the main altar.

The HP hands the HPS her casting staff, sword, athamé, or wand, saying:

HP: "My Lady, the Powers of the Elements have been summoned . . ."

The HPS holds the tool aloft and responds:

HPS: ". . . and the circle binds them all together."

The HPS wields the tool aloft while circling sunwise three times around the participants, visualizing the tool as forming an energy barrier. (There are many ways to visualize this. See "Circle-casting" in the "Options and Variations" chapter on page 108.)

As she proceeds, she chants the following conjuration, timing it to end as she concludes each circuit.[59] She sings solo the first time, and then all join in for the second and third repetitions. If using a staff, at the end of each round she strikes its bottom end on the ground in front of the main altar to punctuate the chant and encourage participants to sing increasingly loudly.

HPS, All, All: "I conjure thee . . .
a space between the worlds . . .
that ye be . . .

---

59. The conjuration contains eight lines, so pace yourself by reciting two lines per ¼ ambulation of the circle.

a Guardian . . .

of the Pow'r . . .

that we shall raise . . .

in the names of

Herne and Hecate . . ."

After she concludes, the High Priestess faces the High Priest in front of the main altar and hands him her casting tool while declaring:[60]

HPS: *"The circle has been cast."*

The High Priest then returns the tool to its place.

If the ritual will include Consecrating the Elements or Spurging and Censing, continue with the next step, "To Consecrate the Elements."

If the ritual won't include Consecrating the Elements or Spurging and Censing, skip forward to the section "To Call the Quarters."

))) ! (((   ))) ! (((   ))) ! (((

To Consecrate the Elements[61]

The HPS and then the HP each takes up her or his athamé in their dominant hand and holds it in the breast position—with their forearm diagonally crossing their chest and the blade held flat against their shoulder or upper breast. While performing the consecration, each holds her or his athamé in the consecration position—with the hilt between both hands and the blade pointing downward.

The *High Priestess* plunges her athamé into a container

---

60. You may substitute the God and Goddess names of your choice. (Words and music composed by Lady Passion, based on Gardnerian tradition.)

61. We usually include this step only if we plan to spurge and cense, or plan to use the Elements to consecrate a magical tool or use as spell components.

of *water* atop the altar. While swirling a Water-invoking pentagram in the water with the blade, she intones:

> **HPS:** *"By moon which rules, now tides be still.*
>
> *I conjure Thee to work my will."*

Next, she plunges the athamé into a container of *salt*.[62] While carving an Earth-invoking pentagram in the loose salt with her blade, she intones:

> **HPS:** *"This salt for all Earth stands in place . . ."*

She uses the point of her athamé blade to scoop up three measures[63] of salt and deposits each into the consecrated water. While doing so, she says:

> **HPS:** *". . . to cleanse and consecrate this space."*

The *High Priest* thrusts the point of his athamé into the container of *incense* (or, if using stick or cone incense, wields the point in the smoke of the incense). While inscribing an Air-invoking pentagram with his blade, he says:

> **HP:** *"Let Air in spiraling smoke take flight—*
>
> *to call the Spirits and shift the Sight."*

Next, he wields his athamé point over the censer's smoldering *charcoal* (or, if using stick or cone incense, thrusts the point into *candle flame*). While drawing a Fire-invoking pentagram in the hot glow with his blade, he says:

> **HP:** *"Fire's light, Refiner's flame—*
>
> *all is never more the same . . .*

---

62. Table salt works better for this than using Himalayan rock salt and similar salt.

63. A "measure" is simply the amount that can be held on the tip of an athamé blade.

He uses the point of his athamé blade to scoop up three measures of incense and deposits each onto the charcoal.[64] While doing so, he says:

HP: . . . so cleanse and light in the Old Ones'[65] name."[66]

If the ritual will include Spurging and Censing: The HPS and then the HP return their athamés to the altar or to the sheaths on their cingulums (waist-cords). Continue with the next step, "To Spurge and Cense."

If the ritual won't include Spurging and Censing: The HPS and HP hold their athamés in the breast position. Skip ahead to the section "To Call the Quarters."

))) ! (((   ))) ! (((   ))) ! (((

To Spurge and Cense

The Circle: The High Priestess and High Priest (or two designated participants) begin by proceeding sunwise once around the circle to cleanse and purify its boundaries by spurging and censing.[67] The HPS goes first, spurging the circle by carrying the container of consecrated salt water and lightly sprinkling it about the circle's circumference, dipping and flicking an aspergillum[68] or her fingers. The HP follows, censing the circle by carrying the censer and wafting the consecrated incense smoke along the circle's circumference by fanning it with a feather or his hand, or by means of a swinging censer on a chain.[69] When each returns to the main altar, they set the tools back down on it.

---

64. If the incense is not in powdered form and therefore can't be scooped up with the blade, he can deposit three pinches of resin instead.

65. Optionally, he may substitute "in the Lady's name."

66. Elemental consecrations composed by Niklas Gandr.

67. Although Witches commonly refer to this purification process as "censing and spurging," you're traditionally expected to reverse the order—to spurge the circle or participants with consecrated water first, then cense them with consecrated incense smoke: otherwise, according to oral tradition, you risk magically "putting the fire out" with the water, and thereby offending the Fire Element and negating your Power to Will.

68. A Witch's aspergillum is typically a fresh, soft-leafed twig or bundle of herbs. Its handle area may be decorated with ribbons. The tool is dipped in scented oil or consecrated saltwater and flicked around to "spurge" or purify participants or the ritual space.

69. Some witches use a whole dried bird wing.

The Participants: Recipients of spurging and censing stand in a semi-circle, each in a relaxed posture and, optionally, with eyes reverently closed. Taking up the consecrated *salt water*, the High Priest dips his index or first two fingers into it and anoints the High Priestess,[70] drawing or daubing on her the symbol of the lowest degree present (typically the First Degree symbol—an inverted triangle formed by touching the points just above the recipient's right breast, genitalia, left breast, and right breast again),[71] while saying:

H P: "Blessed be."

The High Priestess takes the salt water from him, spurges him in the same way, and then temporarily places the salt water back on the altar.

Taking up the consecrated *incense* (after adding more to the censer if need be), the High Priestess censes the High Priest, starting in front of him at his feet, and raising the censer upward to his head while waving the incense smoke toward him with a feather or her hand. When at his head, she taps his left shoulder, he turns sunwise halfway around, and she completes censing behind him from head down to heels, finishing with:

H PS: "Blessed be."

The High Priest censes her in the same way.

Then the High Priestess proceeds either sunwise or in order of rank precedence around the circle, spurging each of the other participants in the same way, followed by the High Priest censing each one in the same way. When finished, both return the tools to the main altar.

))) ! (((   ))) ! (((   ))) ! (((

---

70. Whoever will be spurging and censing the participants—be it the HPS and HP or their designees—should be spurged and censed first. Although there is no fixed Craft tradition governing this order of practice, the ritual rationale is that those who cleanse others should first be purified themselves.

71. Optionally, spurging can be done by sprinkling participants with an aspergillum instead of by anointing with a symbol of rank.

To Call the Quarters

Follow this procedure for each Quarter, starting with East[73] and continuing with South, West, and North:

The Quarter caller (who may be the HPS, the HP, or a designee, and may be different for each Quarter) steps forward to face the Quarter and raises her or his athamé aloft in salute, with arm and blade extended straight outward. All others turn toward that Quarter and salute likewise. The Quarter caller recites the Invocation, inserting the appropriate direction and Element and her or his magical name where indicated. During the phrase "summon, stir, and call you up," the Quarter caller draws the appropriate Element-invoking pentagram in the air, followed by a sunwise circle around the pentagram during the phrase "to guard our circle."

As a learning aid, we made and hung high on the wall of each Quarter in our ritual room a pentagram of dried mugwort stalks secured together with sinew, with a symbol of that Quarter's Element attached to the corresponding point—a feather for Air, a picture of aflame for Fire, a seashell for Water, a black wooden bead for Earth. The illustrations here show these. For each pentagram, start tracing it from the point next to the arrow toward the point bearing the Element's symbol; continue tracing deosil; and finish on the point bearing the Element's symbol. (This is the Oldenwilde way of invoking and banishing pentagrams. For others, see "Options and Variations" on page 108.)

---

72. HPS's and females' athamés on the Goddess side of the altar, the HP's and males' athamés on the God side, all in descending order of rank from the inner to the outer edge of the altar.

73. Some Covens prefer to call the Quarters in the order North, East, South, West. See "Options and Variations," below.

Coven Oldenwilde uses two methods of invoking the Quarters: the traditional Gardnerian default version with minor word tweaks, and a free-style, extemporaneous type we call "Oldenwilde style," described in "Options and Variations." Whichever method you choose, use it for all four Quarters. The Quarter Invocation given here is the Gardnerian default version, which we encourage students to learn by heart before branching out into Oldenwilde-style.

Quarter Invocation (Gardnerian default)

EAST / AIR   SOUTH / FIRE   WEST / WATER   NORTH / EARTH

"HAIL, YE GUARDIANS OF THE WATCHTOWERS OF THE (EAST/SOUTH/WEST/NORTH) . . . SPIRITS OF (AIR/FIRE/WATER/EARTH) . . . I, (YOUR MAGICAL NAME), . . .

Start to draw Element-invoking pentagram with athamé: . . .

"DO SUMMON, STIR, AND CALL YOU UP . . . TO GUARD OUR CIRCLE AND TO WITNESS THESE, OUR RITES. HAIL! AND BE WELCOME!"

All participants draw the same pentagram and repeat the final line:

All: "Hail! And be welcome!"

All then kiss their athamé blade, and then point it once more in salute before returning it to the breast position. Then they bow their heads, turn sunwise toward the next Quarter, and repeat the procedure.

After the last Quarter is called, all return their blades to their cords or atop the main altar, and the HPS optionally rings the bell to mark the transition to the rite's Middle section.

)) ! (((   )) ! (((   )) ! (((

Spellwork

ALL FACE THE MAIN ALTAR.

The HPS gathers everyone together to form an inward-facing, hand-to-hand circle. She welcomes all and explains the purpose of the ritual—the Witch reason for being there.

The type of Working to come varies according to need, season, etc. It often culminates with a spirited, empowering Cone of Power dance, followed by all participants dropping to the earth to "ground" their excess energy and prepare for the Cakes and Wine ceremony to follow.

OLDE SPELLS & RECIPES

Olde spells are preferable to new ones because they are tried and true—time-tested and renowned for being accurate and helpful.

If you find an olde spell that you'd like to work, ask a Craft Elder to evaluate it to ensure that it is not apocryphal—which is to say, a made-up modern spell designed to mimic an olde spell, but not based on real magical principles; or are truly olde, but incorrectly recorded by biased or ignorant writers.

Some genuinely olde spells contain intentional misdirection called a "Witch blind" that was deliberately inserted to try to prevent their misuse by dint of ill intention. For example, in *The Goodly Spellbook* we reproduced a list from the ancient *Greek Magical Papyri* grimoire of herbal spell ingredients disguised by gruesome names probably meant to dissuade the timid from attempting magic. In this book, we used a blind in one of the images to avoid revealing a Gardnerian secret.

Know that many olde spells are a product of the times in which they were written down. Try not to judge their inclusions harshly; and if you want to work these, substitute some difficult-to-find or ethically inappropriate ingredients, but avoid deviating from their formulas if at all possible.

Raising and Directing Spell Power

MOVEMENT FUELS A SPELL AS HEAT COOKS A MEAL IN AN OVEN.
RAISE PHYSICAL ENERGY TO HELP ELEVATE YOUR EMOTIONAL,
PSYCHIC, AND SPIRITUAL ENERGY AS WELL. START SLOW AND
BUILD IN SPEED TO FRENZY. THE AIR AROUND YOU MAY FAIRLY
REVERBERATE OR SEEM TO SIZZLE OR CRACKLE, BUT THE CAST
CIRCLE WILL CONTAIN AND AMPLIFY YOUR ENERGY UNTIL YOU ELECT
TO RELEASE IT TO MANIFEST YOUR GOAL.

Witches' Covens traditionally have both male and female members, rather than all-men or only-women meetings, in part because we appreciate that the platonic sexual tension that naturally occurs among us can also raise spell energy.

* *Verbally make and repeat your requests to the God/desses in regular words, in an archaic language, or by using Barbarous Words of Power, ancient hymns, chanting, song lyrics, words from a grimoire spell, etc.*

* *Stir up your emotions about the matter. Laugh, cry, hoot and holler! Dance, spin, stomp, spit, physically exert yourself—break a sweat during circle. Ululating or shrieking also helps intensify the power.*

* *Relish the vortex of energy you create. Feel the air seem to pulse, resonate, vibrate, whirl.*

* *Summon the Mighty Ones, the ancients, the Elementals, the Quarter Guardians, entities, daimons, Deities or your Ancestors—whatever appropriate forces you need to assist you to increase the power.*

* *When the energy becomes almost untenable in intensity, use the last of your physical reserves to give your spell intention a final mental boost. When the energy climaxes, aim and mentally shoot your bolt where you will it to go, such as by suddenly thrusting a wand or a pointing finger in a particular direction, or by raising your arms skyward, etc.*

* *Crouch down and put your hands atop the floor to "ground out" or give back any excess energy you have in gratitude to Mother Earth. Briefly relax and catch your breath.*

* *Practice raising and controlling spell energy until the process is smooth, and watch for omens that you see during rites; ponder their meanings afterward.*

* *Refrain from intentionally "zapping" other Witches when you feel electric with power; doing so is gauche and unwanted.*

* Regardless of what kind of spell you cast, once done, never "worry" it. Don't stress about spells—let the Gods work to bring it to fruition without having to be dinned by your self-doubt or doubt in Their abilities to enable you. If after three days to a week with no obvious results, re-impress the spell mentally, work a similar one with the same intent, or be patient and let the Gods resolve it in due course. Ever remember that Time is relative and that panic doesn't fuel spells—fortitude and trust does.

))) ! (((   ))) ! (((   ))) ! (((

Cakes & Wine Ceremony

Participants sit in a semicircle before the main altar. The High Priestess and High Priest sit facing each other in front of the altar, she on the Goddess and he on the God side.

The High Priest fills the Cup/chalice, then raises and holds it in front of the High Priestess. Wielding her athamé in the "consecration position"—hilt between both hands, blade point-down above the liquid in the Cup (wine, ale, or spirits)—the High Priestess intones:

HPS: "As the athamé is to the male . . ."

The High Priest replies:
HP: ". . . so the chalice is to the female . . ."
The High Priestess then inserts her athamé into the liquid and draws a Water-invoking pentagram as she and the High Priest say, in unison:

HPS & HP: ". . . and so, conjoined, they bring blessedness."

In offering to the Gods, the HP pours some of the liquid into an empty libation cup atop the main alta[74] and proclaims:

HP: "To the Gods!"

All repeat in unison:

....
74. A "libation" is drink poured out in sacrifice or thanks to the Gods. "Oblation" is the act of offering food and drink to a Deity or Deities.

All: "To the Gods!"

The High Priestess says:

HPS: "Blessed be."

All repeat in unison:

All: "Blessed be."

The High Priest offers the first sip to the High Priestess with a blessing:

HP: "May you never thirst."

The High Priestess responds:

HPS: "Blessed be."

She drinks from the Cup and then passes it back to the High Priest with the same blessing:

HPS: "May you never thirst."

The High Priest responds:

HP: "Blessed be."

He drinks, then passes the Cup to the next participant sunwise[75] and repeats the blessing; the participant responds, drinks,[76] and then passes the Cup sunwise to the next person in circle while repeating the blessing. Each person in turn responds "Blessed be," drinks from the Cup, then passes it on sunwise with the blessing "May you never thirst." When the Cup reaches the last person, she or he does not pass it to the High Priestess, but instead sets it in the center of the semicircle for later sharing.

While the Cup is being passed around, the HPS and HP bless the Cakes. Cakes, bread, crackers, or cookies of some kind having been artfully arranged on a designated Cakes plate such as a silver platter or similar,[77] and set down to the left

---

75. In the Northern Hemisphere, this means pass it to the left-hand side.

76. Even if someone is a recovering alcoholic, traditionally they should take a token sip or at least respectfully raise the Cup to their lips during the first round before passing it on to another.

77. An inexpensive way to make an awesome Cakes plate is to buy a large ceramic platter or plate and

of the main altar, the HPS retrieves the paten tool from atop the altar and places it beneath the Cakes plate. She holds up the Cakes plate and paten by supporting them with both hands in front of the HP.

The HP retrieves a wand (such as a priapic wand[78]) from the right of the main altar and wields it in the consecrating position, point-down above the Cakes. He uses it to draw an Earth-invoking pentagram while intoning:

HP: "O Queen most secret, bless this food unto our bodies, bestowing health, wealth, peace, strength, joy—and that perfection of love which is eternal happiness."

The HPS responds:

HPS: "So mote it be!"

The HP puts the wand back. The HPS passes the Cakes plate and paten to the HP. He holds up the Cakes plate and paten by supporting them on his upturned left hand and steadying them with his right. The HPS takes a cake and breaks it in twain with both hands, raising it aloft and declaring:

HPS: "To the Gods!"

All repeat in unison:

All: "To the Gods!"

The HPS places the broken cake in the libation cup, then concludes with:

....

a large ceramic cup or bowl from a thrift store, resale shop, or garage sale. Invert the cup or bowl and use clear epoxy to glue the bottom center of the platter or plate to the cup or bowl's base.

Neither piece has to match, but the end result should be pleasing, impressive, or stately and, thus, goodly to use in your circles' Cakes and Wine ceremonies. (This also makes a great Initiation, Sabbat, or birthday gift!)

78. This is a traditional ritual wand made of a fennel stalk topped with a pinecone. This tool confers fertility because it resembles a virile penis. Like many Witch traditions, the priapic wand, also known as a *Thyrsus*, originated with the ancient cult of Dionysus.

HPS: "Blessed be."

All repeat in unison:

All: "Blessed be."

The HPS then takes another cake and hands it to the HP's right hand (or places it in his mouth) while saying the blessing:

HPS: "May you never hunger."

The HP responds (or the HPS responds for him[79]):

HP: "Blessed be."

The HP hands the paten off to the HPS, who replaces it on the altar. The HP passes the Cakes plate to the participant next to him sunwise, while saying the blessing:

HP: "May you never hunger."

The participant responds:

Participant: "Blessed be."

The participant takes a cake from the plate, passes the Cakes plate sunwise to the next participant while repeating the blessing, and then eats their cake. The next participant in turn repeats the response, takes a cake, passes it sunwise with the blessing, and so forth.

When the Cakes plate reaches the last participant, he or she passes it to the HPS while repeating the blessing. The HPS repeats the response.

The HPS is the last in the semicircle to get a cake. She then sets the plate in the center of the semicircle for later sharing and says:

HPS: "Now we may all speak freely."

Relaxed banter and camaraderie follow. Participants' magical questions are answered, upcoming Sabbat plans are discussed, etc. The Cup continues to be refilled and passed, and individual cups or bottles may optionally be distributed, and all participants share the remaining Cakes.[80]

---

79. Because saying "Blessed be" with your mouth full of cake is only funny the first time.

80. The Cakes and Wine ceremony is also sometimes colloquially called "Cakes and Ale," which is

When the HPS senses that the time is right, she rises and rings the Bell. Participants stow their fabric pallets while the HPS puts the Cakes plate and Cup to the left of the main altar. Participants then reassemble standing in a semi-circle facing the main altar.

))) ! (((   ))) ! (((   ))) ! (((

Rite's End

All cease talking.

The HPS retrieves her athamé from the altar and raises it aloft, pointing it at the HP and each participant in turn, while saying:

HPS: *"Witches all—our rite's now at an end. I charge you to lock up our secrets in your hearts. And may the Gods preserve the secrets of our Arts."*

She pauses briefly, then raises her athamé higher and proclaims strongly:

HPS: *"May the Gods preserve the Craft!"*

All repeat strongly in unison:

All: *"May the Gods preserve the Craft!"*

However, all's not over, for as the circle was carefully erected, it needs now be no less carefully dismantled. . . .

))) ! (((   ))) ! (((   ))) ! (((

Dismissing the Quarter Guardians[81]

AFTER CLEARING THE RITUAL SPACE OF CAKES PLATE, CUP, CUSHIONS, ETC., PARTICIPANTS REMOVE THEIR ATHAMéS FROM THEIR CINGULUMS/CORDS OR, IN DESCENDING ORDER OF RANK,

....

the older version according to Gardnerian lore. Owing to its sexual symbolism, the conjoining of the chalice and athamé in the blessing of the wine is called "the Great Rite in token" when it is performed in lieu of the most sacred (and secret) rite of Traditional Wicca.

81. The term "dismissing" should not imply any negative connotation here. Since you have summoned the Guardians to witness the rite, you should politely dismiss Them so They may go and do as They will until you need Them again.

FROM THEIR PLACES ATOP THE MAIN ALTAR. AS BEFORE,
ANYONE WHO DOES NOT HAVE AN ATHAMÉ CAN HOLD THEIR
DOMINANT HAND IN THE *MANO PANTEA* GESTURE. ALL HOLD
THEIR ATHAMÉ OR HAND IN THE BREAST POSITION.

Follow this procedure for each Quarter, starting with East and continuing sunwise South, West, and North (or, optionally, starting with North and continuing ayenward West, South, and East[82]):

The person who originally called that Quarter steps forward and raises her or his athamé aloft in salute, as before. All others turn toward that Quarter and salute likewise.

The Quarter caller recites the following Dismissal, inserting the appropriate direction. Toward the end of the Dismissal, she or he starts drawing the Element-banishing pentagram for that Quarter.

QUARTER DISMISSAL

"HAIL, YE GUARDIANS OF THE WATCHTOWERS OF THE (E/S/W/N): WE THANK YOU FOR ATTENDING UNTO THESE OUR RITES, AND ERE YE DEPART FOR YOUR PLEASANT AND LOVELY REALMS . . ."

Start to draw Element-banishing pentagram with athamé: *". . . we do bid you hail, and farewell!"*

In response, the other attendees draw the same pentagram, and repeat the final line:

All: "Hail, and farewell!"

---

82. See "Options and Variations: Quarter Invocations/Dismissals and sequence," below.

All kiss their athamé blade, and then thrust it out in salute once more before returning it to the breast position. (Optionally, they quickly touch the flat of their athamé blade diagonally atop their breast, then thrust it out in salute, then bring it back toward them and kiss the blade before replacing it back atop their breast.) Then they bow gracefully to the Quarter, turn toward the next Quarter, and repeat the procedure.

))) ! (((   ))) ! (((   ))) ! (((

SNUFFING THE CANDLES
BEGINNING AT THE MAIN ALTAR, THE HP USES A CANDLE SNUFFER[83] TO PUT OUT ALL THE FLAMES EXCEPT THAT OF THE MIDDLE, MAIDEN CANDLE.

The participants turn sunwise to witness the HP as he proceeds to each Quarter in turn.

The HP begins in the *East* and snuffs its Quarter candle(s) while saying:

HP: *"Fire fade—the circle, still . . ."*

In the *South* he snuffs the candles while saying:

HP: *". . . let all things be as we will . . ."*

In the *West* he snuffs the candles while saying:

HP: *". . . dark, the secrets of our Art . . ."*

In the *North* he snuffs the candles while all say in unison:

HP & All in unison: *". . . since the beginning of Time."*

The HP returns to the East Quarter and replaces the snuffer atop the main altar, to the right.

))) ! (((   ))) ! (((   ))) ! (((

---

83. Many consider it bad luck to blow out a candle, because both breath and candle-fire are symbols and carriers of spirit. If you do not have a snuffer, you can clap or pinch the candles out. For information on types of Witch candle snuffer tools and how to acquire, make, and use them, see Lady Passion's book *Candle Magic: Working with Wax, Wick, and Flame.*

HPS: "We have been the worlds between—and magic's Mysteries we have seen."

She pauses briefly, then continues:

HPS: "Merry Meet, Merry Part . . ."

All raise their arms and hands high skyward and say loudly in unison:

All: ". . . and Merry Meet again! Harrahya!"

All hug and depart the circle area at leisure.

The HP or a designee lingers to extinguish the Maiden candle and any remaining flame or incense. Then, or at a later time, he removes the libation bowl from the main altar and returns its contents reverently to the Earth adoors.[84]

To Dedicate Yourself to the Craft

One of the first spells that Solitary Witches typically perform in circle is a one-time formal self-dedication to the Olde Gods and a vow of devotion to studying and practicing the Olde Ways. They declare to the Gods their intention to master magic, defiant of consequence (such as being denounced by intolerant relatives) and excuse (such as lack of time or personal inconvenience).

Originally, to "dedicate" something was to proclaim it set apart for a sacred purpose, as in consecrating a shrine to a Deity. By dedicating yourself to the Olde Religion, you are formally committing yourself to your true nature as a magical being, a proud adherent of this perennial philosophy.

Self-dedication is a voluntary promise, not a magical rank or status. The words you use for this type of spellwork should be primarily personal and composed by yourself instead of being borrowed from someone else's book or blog.

---

84. *Diuvei sets our offerings adoors on a stone-slab altar in our backyard wildlife habitat, turns or walks away for a few minutes to allow the spirits to sup, then casts the contents out in the corresponding direction for the Wheel of the Year. Then he brings the bowl inside to clean and a-ready it for the next rite.

Here are some components that you should include in such a rite:

* **Timing:** *During a New Moon is appropriate for starting a new enterprise such as a commitment to the Craft, and during a Full Moon while bathed adoors in the glow of the Goddess is powerful and moving, so either time is fine. Traditionally, Friday night is associated with Witch rites.*

* **Skyclad:** *You should do this rite naked as a newborn babe to show trust and openness.*

* **Purification:** *It's important to cleanse and purify yourself spiritually for this working, so bathe prior to the ritual, optionally in water with scented essential oil or herbs added, and cleanse yourself further by including the Spurging and Censing step in this rite.*

* **Abjuration:** *You may elect to renounce verbally any or all previous religious affiliations[85] using words such as the following: "I, (insert your Craft name), do solemnly renounce and negate any previous vows I have taken before any church or body. I dissolve all previous religious loyalties, fealties, and obligations. Henceforth, my allegiance is to the Craft of the Wise."*

* **Oath:** *Vow aloud to the Goddess and God, or to all the Gods, that you dedicate yourself to heeding Divine guidance, to practicing Witchcraft, and to striving to embody compassion, service, wisdom, courage, perseverance, and whatever other goodly qualities to which you aspire.*

* **Presentation:** *Formally present yourself to each of the Four Quarters. Face the East, South, West, and North in turn, and introduce yourself by your adopted Craft name to the Elements, Guardians, and Deities associated with each direction. Ask for Their protection and power. For instance, you might ask the East for foresight; the South for vitality; the West for aplomb; and the North for persistence.*

* **Identity:** *Pick a unique magical name that connotes your fundamental character or highest ideals. Don't choose a Deity name, for you'll have to live up to it, or end up living it down. Avoid common names like "Raven," "Moonwolf," "Rhiannon," "Merlin," and clichéd agglomerations of such like "Silver Bloodclaw": instead, consider drawing your name from such fertile but oft overlooked troves as Latin herb names (say, "Salvia") or mottos (such as "Nunquam Desisto," meaning "I never quit"). Connote dignity befitting a reverent representative of the Craft.*

))) ! (((   ))) ! (((   ))) ! (((

---

85. If you don't abjure during self-dedication, you'll have another opportunity to do so during a traditional Gardnerian Initiation rite. Abjuration is not a rejection of any wisdom you've gained through another religion, but rather an acknowledgment that you no longer follow that faith.

OPTIONS AND VARIATIONS

"Vocatus atque non vocatus deus aderit."
(Called and even not called, the God approaches.)

—ORACLE OF DELPHI

WRITING YOUR OWN RITES

IN EVERY RELIGION, RITUAL LANGUAGE BINDS ITS FOLLOWERS TO
EACH OTHER AND TO THOSE WHO HAVE ADHERED TO THE FAITH
BEFORE THEM—WHICH IS WHY MANY CATHOLICS, FOR EXAMPLE,
STILL INSIST ON RECITING THE MASS IN LATIN EVEN THOUGH THEY
NOW RISK EXCOMMUNICATION.

Yet many newcomers to the Craft spurn traditional magical scripts and itch
to compose their own ritual script from scratch. As artistically stimulating as this
may seem, we strongly advise that you start with a song before you tackle a sym-
phony: write your own Quarter Callings or Spellwork invocations, or a version of
one of the short sections in the closing part of the Ritual Script.

If certain traditional words or phrases bother you, change them as slightly as
possible in order to preserve tradition. For example, most Witches nowadays substitute the word "rebirth" for the older "resurrection" in the Dryghtyn Prayer (as
we've done in the Ritual Script). In time, however, the language and rhythms of
the traditional script will engrave themselves on your bones, and you'll likely find
yourself increasingly reluctant to alter the mystical recitations that have trans-
ported generations of Witches into "the worlds between."

In composing your own rituals, use the techniques of magical speech that we
teach in *The Goodly Spellbook* chapters "Chants and Charms—The Power of Words"
and "Witches' Secret Language." Intone the lines you write aloud to feel how they

ping, ring, affect you, and would sound to others. And, please, if you're determined to use archaic pronouns such as "ye," "thou," and "thee" to lend an affectation of antiquity, don't sprinkle them in arbitrarily as uneducated writers do. Look them up to make sure you're using them in grammatically correct ways—lest ye be marked anon for a fool.

ATHAMÉ ALTERNATIVES

If you don't have—or prefer not to use—an athamé when Consecrating the Elements, Calling the Quarters, etc., you can substitute the *mano pantea* gesture as illustrated here. There is also plenty of Craft precedent for using a wand instead of an athamé for such ritual operations, as likewise preferred by some Witches who consider blades to connote violence, or who avoid iron tools as being repugnant to fairies. In a pinch, a raised forefinger, pencil, or other sharp will suffice as a substitute.

DISTRIBUTING ROLES

If working in a group, you may elect to take turns performing the different parts of the Ritual Script so everyone gets a chance to perfect diverse ritual roles and functions. Over time, participants will naturally reveal their magical talents, ranging from resonant voice to infallible musical beat to preparation perfectionism, etc. When they do so, encourage them to impart their secrets to other in the group in a class or tutorial: this will help them refine their talents, since teaching a skill to others is one of the best ways to learn more about it oneself.

OMITTING STEPS

Once you learn the Ritual Script thoroughly, you can elect to omit certain steps if doing so enhances the flow or feeling of the rite. For instance, if you're confined to a small space and have to foregather in the same room in which you will conduct the ritual, you can skip the *Admitting* stage, or tweak it: the HPS can walk inside and around the circle of participants, anointing their foreheads and asking for the password phrase.

Coven Oldenwilde may omit *Spurging and Censing* if we have a large crowd of participants; are being filmed; don't feel that prolonged ritual cleansing would enhance our planned spells; or have Sabbat feast-foods distractingly tantalizing us from the dining room. The more participants a ritual has, the more time-consuming Spurging and Censing each of them becomes. If overused, this rite can feel tediously rote, which defeats its purificatory purpose. But as a Coven and in our Solitary spellworkings, we do often Spurge and Cense during a skyclad ritual, or prior to working a markedly important or tricky spell—not only because it's traditional, but also because performing this rite primes Witches' subconscious to mark a special occasion or to perform a fantastical feat of magic.

Minus Spurging and Censing, the *Consecration of the Elements* is not really necessary either, unless saltwater and incense will be needed for a tool consecration or during the spell working. We keep consecrated water, salt, and incense atop our main altar at all times to enable us to work individual magic at a moment's notice; but we always begin a group ritual with fresh water, salt, and incense. Over time, we've observed, salt migrates out of its open-topped bowl and can rust, discolor, or strip metal, pit marble, and permanently bond with certain types of container. Water attracts bugs and algae, and will turn foul or evaporate if left too long. Incense can mold or desiccate with exposure to air. Keep your Element representations tidy and replenished to ensure best spellwork results.

CIRCLE-CASTING

Experiment with different ways of casting circle, such as using *various tools*—sword, athamé, staff, wand, sistrum, your hand. What distinct feeling or power does each inspire in you? What omens does each provoke during spellwork? Which tool do you feel most comfortable and adept using?

In the same vein, experiment with varying the *protective boundary visualization* that you use while casting, such as envisioning an iron ring; a reflective silver sphere; a curtain of invisibility; an impenetrable, hoary hedge; a thick fog, primordial mist, etc.

One of Lady Passion's favorite techniques is to catch the light from the Maiden candle in her casting staff's smoky-quartz topper stone, and then proceed by wielding the staff in a confusing pattern while visualizing it forming a barrier such as a thorn bush or an electric fence. Just bear in mind that it *matters* what you visualize here: for instance, fire jetting from the floor like a ring of blowtorches is a dangerous thought-form, thus is *not* a recommended visualization—as we can attest from singeing experience!

The circle should be cast *thrice around*, but there are various ways to do this. For example:

* **Gardnerian-style circle-casting**: *The Consecration of the Elements is performed immediately before the circle is cast; then, the HPS or Solitary Witch circles once while reciting the conjuration, a second time while spurging the circle with salt water, and a third time censing it with incense (or the spurging and censing may be done by two participants who follow her as she circles just once). This sequence emphasizes cleansing and purifying the circle and participants as soon as possible.*

* **Oldenwilde-style circle-casting**: *The caster circles three times while wielding a tool and chanting a conjuration, with optional Consecration of the Elements and Spurging and Censing both performed after the circle-casting. Our preference is to prioritize protection over purification by casting the circle as soon as possible, before performing any magical operations such as consecration or further purification.*

* **Ceremonial or "high magic"–style circle-casting**: *Because this kind of circle is traditionally used for summoning and interacting with a variety of sometimes-capricious daimons, entities, or Spirits, the circle-caster fortifies the circle's role as a form of magical seal (see* The Goodly Spellbook, *"Making Sigils and Seals") by using chalk, paint, or another substance to draw its components physically.*

A classic technique for drawing a ceremonial circle is passed down in Wiccan oral lore and handwritten in the oldest surviving English translation of the *Key of Solomon*, the so-called *Clavicle of Solomon*.[86] It requires a cord compass made from an athamé and a 9-foot cord—the same cord, we believe, as the 9-foot silken *cingulum* that many traditional Gardnerians earn at Initiation and wear tied around their waist. We were taught that this cord should have four knots tied in it: one at each end, one at is midpoint, and a fourth offset one foot from the middle knot.

The *Clavicle* instructs you to stick your athamé into the ground at the center of your intended circle in a cleared outdoor ritual space.[87] Then, lay out the cord straight from the East to the West, with its midpoint adjacent to the athamé blade. Mark the ground where the endpoints of the cord fall—these will be your East and West Quarters. Repeat the procedure from North to South and mark those Quarters. Next, retrieve your athamé and use it to draw a circle through the four directional marks, leaving a small gap or gate at the North, for entering and exiting during preparations, that you'll close later.

You should use your cord's middle and offset knots to make another set of four directional marks one foot outward away from the first set, and draw a second circle through those, again leaving a temporary gate. Finally, the *Clavicle* directs you to mark and draw a third circle a "demi-foote" (half a foot) out from the second one, and leave open a third North temporary gate. You'll end up creating three concentric circles (or the closest things to a circle that you are able to draw free-hand) with diameters of 9, 11, and 12 feet.

....

86. Also known as *The Clavicle of Solomon*, revealed by Ptolomy the Grecian, Book 2, Chapter 9, "How the Circles Be Made." British Library, Sloane 3847, dated 1572. Transcription by Joseph H. Peterson, http://www.esotericarchives.com/solomon/sl3847.htm.

This is the only surviving manuscript of the *Key* that describes a specific technique for measuring and drawing the circle. It also contains clear attestations of the origin of the term *Athamé* in *Artavus*, an obscure medieval Latin term for a pen knife with a curved blade, which *The Clavicle's* scribe translates variously from his Latin source as "Arthany," "Arthano," "Artanus."

87. The *Clavicle* also instructs you to stick the athamé into the ground in front of him when you call each of the Quarters. The magical intent behind this may be similar to Tibetan shamans' practice of plunging the phurba, the three-sided ritual knife said to be derived from nomads' tent pegs, into the ground or a bowl of raw rice at a ritual's commencement in order to pin the energy raised by the rite in place for its duration.

Inscribe appropriate protective and powerful magical names and symbols[88] in the space between the 9-foot and 11-foot circle. (If you intend to summon a daimon or Spirit during such a Ceremonial magic working, a common practice is draw a triangle outside just outside the outermost circle in which to manifest and contain It.) Then, after ensuring that you and all participants and needed magical tools and spell components are inside the 9-foot circle, draw the closing segments across the three open gates in the North. Cast the circle by carrying a consecrated candle around its inner perimeter. (The Maiden candle would be appropriate for this.) Spurge and cense yourself, any participants, and the circle itself; call the Quarters; and begin your rite.[89]

If your circle is indoors, use chalk or masking tape, etc. to mark out the circle and symbols instead of your athamé. If you want the circle permanently inscribed, paint it on the floor. Lady Passion has used discreet glow-in-the-dark paint barely visible in daylight for this; if you want to be bold, you could use fluorescent day-glow paint, or paint visible in black light.

Be warned, however, if you elect to flaunt your Ceremonial circle for all and sundry to see. After the Burning Times, this kind of magic circle became so closely associated with popular stereotypes of "black magic" that modern Hollywood horror-movie set designers appropriated it as their stock image of a "Satanic" circle, thereby misleading many who happen upon its traces to leap to falsely lurid conclusions.[90]

....

88. These differ in nearly every version of the Key, leaving you free to decide for yourself what inscriptions to use.

89. This is a simplification of the full technique in the *Clavicle*; other versions of the Key call for one or two swords and an incense burner at every Quarter, drawn squares enclosing the three circles, and a lantern to hold the candle. The *Clavicle* seems unique among olde grimoires in specifying an athamé for drawing the circumferences of the circles, rather than a sword or the separate knife with a single-edged blade that was the original "black-handled knife" before this term became synonymous with our modern double-edged athamé.

90. To learn how to use a ceremonial circle to summon daimons, see *Spirit Conjuring for Witches: Magical Evocation Simplified*, Frater Barrabbas, Llewellyn Publications, 2017.

Coven Oldenwilde uses either of two methods when *invoking the Quarter Guardians:* the traditional, memorized Gardnerian Outer Court version we call "Gardnerian default," and an extemporaneous, freestyle form that is poetic and replete with magical correspondences or seasonal references appropriate to the rite, which we've come to call "Oldenwilde style." Gard default is beautifully haunting in its antique simplicity, but Oldenwilde style can be tailored to the particular spell-work you'll be doing in the ritual, the kind of weather your community needs at this time of year, and so forth.

Both methods begin and end with the same *"Hail . . ."* formula, but in Oldenwilde style the Quarter caller does not draw the Elemental pentagram until the concluding phrase, *"Hail, and be welcome!"*

Whichever method is used to call the first Quarter should be used to call the remaining three—if you mix the two techniques, your circle's Quarter-calling may feel inconsistent and imbalanced. Usually the HPS or HP decides ahead of time which method to use, but sometimes whoever calls the first Quarter establishes the choice.

Quarter Invocation Oldenwilde Style (Example 1)

"HAIL, YE GUARDIANS OF THE WATCHTOWERS OF THE (EAST)[91]—
SPIRITS OF (AIR)[92]—"

Fill in the rest with appropriate words, such as:

*"Winds waft seeds
to feed our kind.
Warn of what's to come,
and make us wise."*

---

91. Caller inserts whatever Quarter direction they're facing (East/South/West/North).
92. Caller inserts whichever Element they're addressing (Air/Fire/Water/Earth).

Start drawing Invoking Air pentagram and surrounding sunwise circle with athamé: *"Hail! And be welcome!"*

Quarter Invocation Oldenwilde Style (Example 2)

"HAIL, YE GUARDIANS OF THE WATCHTOWERS OF THE EAST,
SYLPH ELEMENTALS, SPIRITS OF AIR . . .
WARM SPRING WINDS
WAFT OUR SPELL TO THE GODS TONIGHT.
I CONJURE YOU TO GUIDE, GUARD, AND AMPLIFY OUR POWER.
BRING US NAUGHT BUT UNDERSTANDING.
HAIL! AND BE WELCOME!"

Participants echo in unison the last line, *"Hail! And be welcome!"* while drawing the Invoking Air pentagram and surrounding sunwise circle with their athamés. All kiss their athamé, point it again at the Quarter in salute, and then bow their head while replacing it atop their breast and turning sunwise to repeat the process in the remaining three directions.

Our *Quarter-calling sequence* starts in the East and moves sunwise around the circle to complete, because we find that starting in the North feels heavy, associated as it is with Earth, midnight, winter, fixity and solidity, etc. So, we "start light" in the direction of dawn, East/Air,[93] and continue sunwise to conclude on a firm foundation in the North/Earth Quarter.[94]

For simplicity, our Quarter-dismissing sequence is the same as our Quarter-calling sequence, starting in the East and moving sunwise through

93. Lady Passion usually calls the South and North, and ⁺Diuvei the East and West, because the HPS can drown a mountaintop when she summons Water.

94. Note that many Witches invoke the fifth Element, Spirit, in the center of the circle; and others also call the directions Center, Above, and Below, emphasizing the three-dimensional, spherical nature of the magic circle. Following Gardnerian and older tradition, we feel that calling the Goddess and God during the circle-casting duly invokes the Element of Spirit. We also feel that introducing three further directions, for a total of seven, would erode the ritually crucial Wiccan correspondence between four Quarters and four Elements, and would therefore necessitate a whole different system of correspondences involving the Seven Planets.

South, West, and finally North. For polarity's sake, however, many Witches prefer to undo the circle by dismissing the Quarter Guardians ayenward, starting with North and moving through West, South, and finally East.

SPELLWORK

The Working section of the circle script need not always be exclusively devoted to casting spells. Depending on the season, your whim, or your need, you may elect to perform:

* *Cyclic seasonal Sabbats such as the Crone's Lament of the Dead or a Dumb Supper at Samhain; the Maiden birthing the Sun God or the mock battle between the Oak King and the Holly King at Yule; the making of a Bridhe's bed at Imbolc; dancing around a Maypole at Beltane; reenacting a second mock battle between the Oak and Holly Kings at Litha; holding a communal bread/grain feast at Lammas, and a communal fruit and veggie feast at Mabon. (See "The Eight Sabbats," below.)*

* *Deity-centered ceremonies such as Drawing Down the Moon or the Charge of the Goddess.*

* *Traditional myth reenactments such as the Eleusinian Mysteries.[95] By physically reenacting a myth, you are retelling and perpetuating its mythos—the larger pattern of attitudes, beliefs, and insights to which it belongs. Depths of its meanings are revealed as you explore and ponder its symbols and word origins, and as you experience and relive its stories—especially when performed as part of an Initiatory ceremony. Enactments can range from elaborate productions replete with costumes, props made like those in antiquity, and florid script parts that each character participant recites, to rustic skits featuring quatrain rhymes and improvised asides.*

* *Other Craft activities such as making magical tools; perfecting your pronunciation of Barbarous Words of Power; practicing olde chants; learning how to play a new musical instrument; being taught a new skill by one of your group's members; meditating; doing spiritualist table-tipping experiments . . . truly, there are trillions of possible permutations!*

---

95. The NROOGD Tradition, on the United States' West Coast, is known for its well-researched public reenactments of the Eleusinian Mysteries, the classical world's most influential Initiatory rite. (For one such performance, *Diuvei set the invocations to music in authentic Greek modes.)

LUNAR ESBATS & SOLAR SABBATS

"So here are you, and here am I,
Where we may thank our gods to be;
Above the earth, beneath the sky,
Naked souls alive and free."

— George Orwell, *The Pagan*

Sabbats (pronounced "SAB-buhts") occur at the four astronomical beginnings of the seasons—the equinoxes and solstices—and at their four peaks when each season is in its full glory: winter's depth, spring's flower, summer's lushness, and fall's leaf drop. *Esbats* ("EHZ-buhts") traditionally occur once a month when La Luna is either Full ("moonbright") or New ("moondark"), although they can also be held weekly. Despite generations of guessing, the origins of both terms are so olde and obscure that they remain a mystery.

Sabbats are celebratory affairs featuring a seasonal rite and communal feast, and are spaced every six to eight weeks or so year round. Esbats are usually work-oriented meetings at which Witches learn and practice core magical skills and perform spells to accomplish goals.

Pagans refer to "the Sabbats" as a whole, and by their specific names as each one's time approaches and when they occur. Four of them are called "Lesser Sabbats," and they represent the four pivot-points of the Earth's yearly orbit around the Sun: the Earth's axis is exactly perpendicular to the plane of this orbit at the spring equinox (Ostara) and the fall equinox (Mabon), and it is at its maximum degree of tilt in one direction or the other at the summer solstice (Litha) and the winter solstice (Yule). The other four Sabbats are called "Greater Sabbats," and are timed to be at or near the midpoints between the equinoxes and solstices. The terms Lesser and Greater don't mean that half the Sabbats have diminutive status, but simply derive from the fact that Witches traditionally celebrate the Lesser Sabbats with their individual Covens, and the Greater Sabbats at larger gatherings of multiple Covens.

Nowadays, the year is usually divided into four "astronomical seasons," which begin at the Lesser Sabbats: Spring at Ostara, Summer at Litha, Fall at Mabon, and Winter at Yule. This is the system we use here because it's the most familiar to us. Originally, though, each of the four seasons was considered to begin at one of the Greater Sabbats. Imbolc was the first day of Spring, Beltane the first day of Summer, Lammas of Fall, and Samhain of Winter. Seasons reckoned this way are called "solar seasons," and this arrangement is still the norm in Ireland, China, and some other countries.

This older solar-season system is in some ways the more magical, since it paradoxically summons the renewed warmth of Spring and Summer at the coldest time of the year (late January/early February, according to meteorologists), and propitiates at the hottest time of the year (late July/early August) the Fall harvest that will sustain us through Winter's chill. On the other hand, the astronomical-season system reflects an "as above, so below" correspondence between the cycle of the year and the cycle of the day—it matches Spring-Summer-Fall-Winter with Morning-Afternoon-Evening-Late night.

Asking which system is the "right" one may be as pointless as asking where a circle "really" begins and ends: For instance, when Winter climaxes at Imbolc and begins to decline toward Spring, do you want to call that the "end" of Winter, or its "peak?" The answer can affect only some wording and symbolism in your Greater Sabbat's weather spells—not their effectiveness, which is all that really counts.

In ancient times, the Greater Sabbats were undoubtedly dated according to the exact midpoints between the equinoxes and solstices, as they still are in the Chinese calendar. Nowadays, each is tied to the beginning of a calendar month, a little more than a week before each exact midpoint, for reasons we explain below under "Origins of the Sabbats." But some Pagans do prefer to celebrate the Greater Sabbats on the actual seasonal midpoints, which can be determined for a given year from an astrological ephemeris. The Sun is at one of these points when it reaches 15° of a fixed sign: Scorpio for Samhain, Aquarius for Imbolc, Taurus for Beltane, or Leo for Lammas. In the Southern Hemisphere, these sign/Sabbat correlations are reversed: Samhain is in mid-Taurus, Imbolc in mid-Leo, and so forth.

The Greater Sabbat of Samhain ("SOW-wen") is the "Witches' New Year," the start of the Wiccan sacred year. This is why our Sabbat tables begin with this celebration. This tradition is yet another oft-overlooked indication of the unbroken continuity of the Witch religion in Europe, since it goes directly back to the Pagan Celtic and Germanic tribes (as we explain further below).

In contrast to the Sabbats, the monthly Esbats continually change dates in accordance with the Moon's mutable cycles. For example, the twelve or thirteen Full Moons that occur in a given year[96] will not fall on the same dates again for another nineteen years—and even *this* so-called "Metonic cycle" of Full Moon recurrences gradually drifts out of sync with the civil calendar in such a way that calculating Full Moon dates is a complex mathematical process that medieval monks appropriately termed *computus*.

Because Esbat times are so fluid and variable, they don't bear the kinds of fixed traditions associated with each Sabbat, making them ideal for adapting to Coven, group, or Solitary needs and circumstances. Just as the Moon's influence is oft deemed more subjective than the overt, in-your-face Sun's, so Esbats can feel more privately intimate than publicly shared Sabbats—which explains why observing both in tandem yields balance to every magical life.

Covens may let non-Initiate guests attend their "open" Sabbat celebrations, but typically reserve Esbats for only themselves and their students. Since Full and New Moons occur at the same time for every Witch world-wide, we all share basic Esbat meeting times—yet as our table illustrates, the dates we celebrate Sabbats on differ radically depending on whether we live in the Northern or Southern hemisphere, because the seasons are diametrically opposite each other on either side of Equator. Thus, Witches in Asheville, North Carolina, may be circling around a balefire during a fall Samhain while Witches in Adelaide, Australia, are dancing around a Maypole during a spring Beltane. Working such opposite-season rites helps keep the planet balanced.

---

96. It's a common but false assumption that every year has thirteen Full Moons. In fact, only seven out of every nineteen years contain a thirteenth Moon.

SUN SIGNS & SABBATS

DATES	SUN MID-SIGN/ ENTERS ZODIAC SIGN	GREATER, LESSER SABBATS (NORTHERN HEMISPHERE)	GREATER, LESSER SABBATS (SOUTHERN HEMISPHERE)
OCT. 31	MID-SCORPIO	SAMHAIN	BELTANE
NOV. 21*	SAGITTARIUS		
DEC. 21*	CAPRICORN	YULE (WINTER SOLSTICE)*	LITHA (SUMMER SOLSTICE)
JAN. 21*	AQUARIUS		
FEB. 1	MID-AQUARIUS	IMBOLC	LAMMAS
FEB. 21*	PISCES		
MAR. 21*	ARIES	OSTARA (SPRING EQUINOX)	MABON (FALL EQUINOX)
APR. 21*	TAURUS		
MAY 1	MID-TAURUS	BELTANE	SAMHAIN
MAY 21*	GEMINI		
JUN. 21*	CANCER	LITHA (SUMMER SOLSTICE)	YULE (WINTER SOLSTICE)*
JUL. 21*	LEO		
AUG. 1	MID-LEO	LAMMAS	IMBOLC
AUG. 21*	VIRGO		
SEP. 21*	LIBRA	MABON (FALL EQUINOX)	OSTARA (SPRING EQUINOX)
OCT. 21*	SCORPIO		

*Date may vary between 19th and 22nd of the month.

DARK HALF, LIGHT HALF OF THE YEAR

In keeping with a pervasive focus on the balance of opposites, Pagans divide the year into a "dark half" and a "light half" of time—basically, fall/winter and spring/summer. Our brains and bodies react naturally to this divide: our moods, appetites, libido, and energy levels differ noticeably during cold, dark months versus warm, bright ones—so much so that some people become depressed with Seasonal Affective Disorder (aka SAD).

Now, you might think that the dark half of the year should begin at the autumnal equinox, the Mabon Sabbat, when night starts waxing longer than day, and the light half of the year should commence at the spring equinox, the Ostara Sabbat, when the day starts overtaking the night.

For Wiccans, though, the "dark half" starts at Samhain during mid-fall, and the "light half" begins at Beltane during mid-spring. This way of bifurcating the year accurately reflects the Earth's actual meteorological temperature cycle, which lags behind night/day cycle changes by an average of a month and a half. In temperate climes, cold weather doesn't really take hold till Samhain, and (as we noted earlier) the average coldest day of the year occurs around Imbolc, at the midpoint of the dark half of the year. Conversely, Beltane is usually the earliest Sabbat that one can celebrate adoors without needing to wear a cape, and the average hottest day of the year happens around Lammas, at the midpoint of the light half. Since both sunlight and temperature affect how people subjectively experience the seasons, the succinct phrases "dark half" and "light half" aptly describe how the year *feels*.

Dividing the year into dark and light halves along the axis of Samhain and Beltane is another ancient European Pagan tradition, known to have been practiced by both Celtic and Germanic peoples. Samhain is a very old Gaelic word that many scholars believe means "summer's end," for summer and winter were once the only two seasons reckoned in the year. For many Germanic tribes, according to ancient and medieval sources, this long continued to be the case—such as in the Old Norse calendar, which calls the dark season *Skammdegi* ("short days" or "dark days") and the light season *Nóttleysi* ("nightless," which is literally true for part of the year in the northernmost lands the Vikings settled).

Some modern authors wrongly shift the dark/light dividing line to Yule and Litha, starting the dark half of the year at winter solstice and the light half at summer solstice. But this is actually a completely different division of the year: the "waxing half," which comprises winter and spring, when the days grow increasingly long and the nights short; and the "waning half," summer and fall, when nights lengthen and days diminish. The twice-yearly ritual re-enactment of the battle between the Oak King and the Holly King commemorates these waxing and waning Sun shifts.

It's easy to twist yourself in knots trying to understand these differing ways of keeping Pagan time and the diverse Goddess and God correspondences that various traditions assign to the Wheel of the Year. For example, some say, reasonably enough, that the Sun God rules the light half of the year and the Moon Goddess the dark half—yet the Gardnerian tradition accords rulership of the dark half to the Horned God of Death and Rebirth and the light half to the Great Mother Goddess, doubtless in acknowledgement of nature's winter dormancy and summer's fruitfulness.[97]

In many magical traditions, the Earth Mother Goddess never "dies" during a season of the year. Conversely, many have myths about a sacrificed and reborn Sun God, grain God, or vegetation God. Does His death and rebirth or resurrection derive from ancient agricultural tradition? Is it a nineteenth-century Christian-influenced invention of folklorists? Or is it a simple yet profound metaphor for reincarnation? The answer may be all or none of the above—or it may lie in the beauty and potency of your own ritual interpretation of this mythological meme.

Many Wiccan authors trying to promote a generic theological scheme for the Wheel of the Year propound a maddeningly complex oedipal relationship between the Triple Goddess and the Sun God, in which She as Crone bids the

---

97. This may also be a perpetuation of olde Celtic religious belief. Until recently, cattle-herding was central to Irish and Scottish life: at Samhain, the herds were brought down from pasture and culls were slaughtered to feed the tribes over the winter (which would correspond to the Horned God of Death and Rebirth); at Beltane, they were driven back to fertile green fields for the summer (which would correspond to the Great Mother Goddess).

dying Sun God farewell at Samhain, then as Mother births Him anew at Yule, returns to Maiden form while cradling Her infant Sun at Imbolc, dates the adolescent God at Ostara, mates with Him and is impregnated anew at Beltane, then marries Him at Litha. Finally, even though pregnant, She reverts to Cronehood to oversee Her husband's death during harvest time at Lammas and Mabon.

This convolution seems to have originated with several speculations about cross-cultural mythology that the poet Robert Graves put forth in 1948 in his *The White Goddess*. Janet and Stewart Farrar assembled and expanded on these in their introduction to the Sabbats in *A Witches' Bible Compleat*, 1981, and many other subsequent authors have passed this awkwardly mechanistic myth forward as if it were ancient Witch tradition instead of a relatively modern invention.

In fact, polytheism never exhibits a single "theologically correct" dogma—only different facets of a deeper truth, which in this instance is cyclical change. In our "Guide to Sabbat Rites," we describe various olde God/dess customs for particular Sabbats that you can work or adapt, but we don't try to prescribe an unavoidably arbitrary selection of ethnic God/desses for each Sabbat: rather, we encourage you to explore your own or your tradition's Deities and Their relationships to the seasons, the God/desses Who are appropriate to your spell purpose at a given time, or whichever mythos will best help you mark, navigate, and influence the ever-changing tides of time.

MORE IS BETTER

Some Witch groups eschew meeting for monthly working Esbats and only celebrate the eight annual Sabbats. We have seen, however, that restricting meetings to only eight times in twelve months affords no time to explore and perfect spell skills. In the same vein, meeting for Esbats only during moonbright is not more innately "Witchy" than holding moondark Esbats: Lady Passion's experience is that Esbats held when the Moon seems sky-invisible can be the most affecting for the very reason that these nights' overt darkness tends to foster feelings of *extra* intimacy.

Consider the merits of all these Craft traditions and meet early and often so you can learn fast and consistently rather than slowly and sporadically. You can often best utilize these merits by taking into account their seasonal context. For instance, New Moons that occur during fall and winter are goodly times to cultivate the mind, such as by scrying a magic mirror, regressing to past lifetimes, traveling astrally, inscribing talismans, etc.; whereas spring and summer Full Moons are optimal times to cultivate the body, such as by leaping a fire, assuming a magical persona, reveling at Pagan gatherings, making herbal medicines and inks, and mastering energy-raising via traditional Witch dances whose steps we illustrated in *The Goodly Spellbook*.

We and many other Witches believe that celebrating both the eight annual Sabbats and mixed monthly New and Full Moon Esbats is the best of all worlds. Marking the Sun's seasonal trajectory on Sabbats and observing varied lunar Esbats provides a magical balance between sacred fun and spiritual work. Meeting so frequently requires the commitment necessary to master magic; it may not be for the faint of heart, but it aids the devoted to learn deeply. You'll find that both kinds of rituals become a beneficial addiction when they reveal their creative, inspiring, and enabling joys.

For Solitaries, performing your own even small-but-appropriate ritual actions each Sabbat and seizing every chance you get to hone old skills and practice new ones during Esbats will keep you attuned with nature, the Gods, and Craft ways. In a Coven context, Sabbats and Esbats serve best in tandem to nurture students, bond Covenmate Initiates, and enable the success of short- and long-term magical activism, plans, and projects.

WITCHES & HOLIDAYS

Many Witches don't celebrate most conventional religious and national holidays, other than as an excuse to relax, feast, and commune with Covenmates, friends, or family. As Pagans, we literally give more credence to the Easter bunny than Jesus's resurrection. Thus, you won't find us in sunrise service sporting white patent leather shoes, but rather tripping the Sun fantastic in a nearby public park at a community Easter-egg hunt helping our child bury carrots to thank the March hares for all the treasure.

Witches tend to be peaceniks—including those of us who regret having joined the military in youth because we didn't realize there were wiser ways to "see the world." We consider ourselves to be more citizens of the Earth than nationalistic partisans, and therefore consider patriotic celebrations—such as, in the U.S., Flag Day, Veteran's Day, Memorial Day, and Independence Day—too warrioresque to be inspiring. We may elect to observe Thanksgiving as an autumnal Pagan Native American feast of turkey, pumpkin, and cranberry, but certainly won't send our kids to school costumed as Pilgrims—that cult of Puritan zealots who waged genocide against the indigenous Pagan population and hypocritically persecuted their fellow nonconforming immigrants.[98]

Many other countries have established official holidays that Pagans and Wiccans deem similarly objectionable. Too often these have been invented or are manipulated by Church, State, or Corporation in an effort to instill blind piety, patriotism, or consumerism in folks. This doesn't mean that we reject all outright, but rather that we each choose whether or how we want to participate in any one of them.

Most typically, Witches celebrate, when we will, the most obviously magical parts of each holiday. For example, Lady Passion and *Diuvei routinely join in the secular American New Year's Eve rites of making noise and toasting with champagne at midnight.

Though this isn't *our* ancient Pagan New Year, we appreciate it from the stance that *many* cultures recognize the magical importance of a year's threshold, whenever they deem it to occur. We know that celebrating it with percussive noises is meant to drive off ill entities and break up the previous year's stagnation. It's common to offer up and consume foods or drinks with special meanings for this time of year in hope of goodly luck and to remember far-flung friends and lost loves. It's also universally a time for divinations about the year to come. So we keep rattles and whistles at the ready, and pop the champagne cork while standing at our front entrance, to divine our mundane New Year from the length and

98. See *The Goodly Spellbook*, "Magical Movement and Gestures: Mystical Dance."

trajectory of its flight across the street in front of the Covenstead: the longer and straighter, the more auspicious; the shorter or more hooked, the more ominous.

The Pagan holidays most Witches celebrate are universal, ancient, and pur-poseful. Contrary to monotheist holy times primarily based on male exploits and historic "events" that can rarely be proven to have really happened, our holy times are eternal, seasonal ones that everyone planet-wide can see and experience year in, year out: spring, summer, fall, winter, and the transitional times in between. Throughout the history of humankind, the Wise have cast potent spells during these junctures and crossroads of time.

Around the world, countless popular holidays continue to perpetuate, under the veneer of folk tradition, the same mystical seasonal rites of "turning the Wheel of the Year" that Witches and Pagans perform consciously in our Sabbats.

For example, Chinese New Year, Mardi Gras, Carnival, Fastnacht, Groundhog Day, and Imbolc all help us push past mid-Winter's cold and dearth toward the rebirth of Spring. Halloween, *Día de los Muertos* (Day of the Dead), and Samhain all help us remember and see beyond mortality as Summer's last kisses die away in mid-Fall.

Because we celebrate the cycles of Nature for their own sake, Witches and Pagans are the keepers of Time's mainspring, the natural calendar of Sun and Moon that drives the man-made one. Knowing this, we feel not only obligated, but proud to turn the Wheel in the Olde Way—and are willing to defy repressive authority in order to do so.

ESBATS

Whenever ye have need of anything,
Once in the month, and when the moon is full,
Ye shall assemble in some desert place,
Or in a forest all together join,
To adore the potent spirit of your queen,
My mother, great Diana. She who fain
Would learn all sorcery yet has not won

Its deepest secrets, them my mother will
Teach her, in truth all things as yet unknown,
And ye shall all be freed from slavery,
And so ye shall be free in everything . . .

—CHARLES G. LELAND, *ARADIA, OR THE GOSPEL OF THE WITCHES*

Esbats are typically Witches' study and working meetings, during which we practice a skill, make or consecrate a new tool, perform a needed spell, Initiate or Elevate a Coven member, etc. They are usually closed to new Seekers and non-Witches—if any of these want to attend a Witch ritual for the first time, most Witches invite them as guests to a Sabbat instead.

Witches prefer to gather for monthly Esbat rites held when the Moon is Full (fat/round, bright in the sky). But if it's appropriate to our spell intention, we'll gather for our Esbat when the Moon is New (seems absent in the sky).

Full Moon Esbat spells typically conjure or attract what a Witch wants, and New Moon Esbat spells are meant to repel or banish what a Witch *doesn't* want. However, some Witches reverse this, utilizing the New Moon as the beginning of the Moon's increase, for attraction magic, and the Full Moon as the beginning of Her decrease, for repulsion magic, so that as the Moon waxes or wanes, so will the spell target be attracted or repelled. Both ways have their merits, and in practice you can use either one as long as you make your intention clear while casting the spell.

For the sake of spell correspondences, it may be simpler to remember that the Full Moon is the peak of "moonbright," the lighter half of the lunar month, and the New Moon is the peak of "moondark," the darker half of the lunar month. Each provides, in its own way, a powerful boost to your spellworkings. In Nature, both the Full and the New Moon cause each month's *spring tides*—the greatest difference between high and low oceanic and terrestrial tides because both the Sun and the Moon at the time are reinforcing each other's gravitational pull. *Neap tides,* by contrast, show the least difference, because they occur when the Sun and

Moon are astrologically square (90° apart) and thus, cancel out each other's gravitational influence. Experience will show you that this Half Moon is weak and makes spellcasting challenging.

You can schedule an Esbat for any evening within three days of the exact date of the Full or New Moon, and schedule them months, even a year, in advance because Moon phases are widely published in calendars and online.

But if your Coven or group prefers to meet weekly, it's traditional to do so each Friday after sunset. A weekly—rather than monthly—meeting still keeps you connected with the Moon's rhythms, because the seven-day week is one quarter of Her sidereal cycle.[99] Friday, the day of Venus, is astrologically appropriate for friendship and bonding. Such Friday meetings are also often loosely referred to as "Esbats."

Some books and calendars provide evocative-sounding names for each of the Full Moons—"Wolf Moon," "Harvest Moon," "Sturgeon Moon," and so on. Most of these are inspired by Native American names for each lunar month. The trouble is, there are *hundreds* of such lists of Moon names—each very local and specific to the tribe that used or uses them, or the author or website that promotes them. (In practice, therefore, you can adopt or make up any list you like; you just can't assume that your "Snow Moon" or "Lawnmower Moon" is shared by anyone else.)

One of the few documented pre-Christian European lists of Moon names is the Germanic-derived Anglo-Saxon calendar that the Venerable Bede described in the eighth century C.E. It, too, contains culturally specific names—such as "Mud Month" (*Sol-mðnaþ*), for the lunar-month equivalent of February, and "Month of Three Milkings" (*Þrimilce-mðnaþ*), for the equivalent of May. This well-known calendar directly inspired the "Shire Calendar" used by the Hobbits in J.R.R. Tolkien's *The Lord of the Rings*.

There is no standard traditional Wiccan list of Moon names, but this doesn't mean that every Full or New Moon is interchangeable: each one is colored by its

99. Reference *The Goodly Spellbook*, "Table of the Seven Planets: Moon."

timing in the seasonal cycle—that is, by the Sabbat to which it is closest in time and by the Sun sign in which it occurs. It's therefore quite traditionally acceptable to schedule Sabbat celebrations on the nearest Esbat, to combine the energies of both Lunar and Solar peaks—and if you're planning to hold an outdoor overnight Sabbat, you may prefer to schedule it for the nearest Full Moon Esbat so that your rite will be bathed in moonlight. (Conversely, if you want to keep your gathering concealed from hostile eyes, schedule it for the nearest New Moon Esbat.)

You can use the following guides to plan Esbat spells and rituals that take advantage of seasonal Sabbat and astrological Sun-sign factors. The "Esbats near Sabbats" table divides the Sabbats into the traditional "dark" and "light" halves of the Sabbat year.

In the "Esbats in Sun Signs" table, bear in mind that on a Full Moon Sabbat, the Moon will be in the opposite sign from the Sun (that is, six signs away). To help drive this Pagan paradox home with a bit of magical mischief, the table's spell suggestions proffer magical challenges to the zodiacal signs' usual inclinations. Recognize that the table encourages you to consider acting *oppositely* from your normal learned habits, and work opposite magic according to the power of the astrological time. You'll discover thereby the hidden unity in such oppositions.

More generally, there are many astrological correspondences you can make use of in a given zodiacal sign's Esbats. For example, Pisces fins equate with (rule) the feet,[100] so it's appropriate to stomp to empower spells during March when the Sun is in the fishes' sign—which in this case also happens to fit with our Pisces spell suggestion of "grounding." Of course, you can *always* Pisces-stomp to emphasize spell intention, but a fish avoids the hook by showing some restraint, and the same principle applies to all the signs above.

....

100. See *The Goodly Spellbook*, "To Promote Wellness," which gives the correspondences between astrological signs and anatomy.

ESBATS NEAR SABBATS

DATE RANGE (NORTHERN, SOUTHERN HEMISPHERE)	HALF OF THE WICCAN YEAR	NEAREST SABBAT	SPELL WORKINGS
N: MID-OCT.–MID-NOV. S: MID-APR.–MID-MAY	DARK HALF	SAMHAIN	DIVINING THE FUTURE, HONORING ANCESTORS, APPEASING RESTLESS SPIRITS, GRIEVING FOR RECENT DEAD
N: EARLY DEC.–EARLY JAN. S: EARLY JUN.–EARLY JUL.		YULE	GENEROSITY/GRATITUDE, FIRE-SCRYING, MEDITATION, SALUTING THE SUNRISE
N: MID-JAN.–MID-FEB. S: MID-JUL.–MID-AUG.		IMBOLC	ASTRAL TRAVEL, PAST-LIFE REGRESSION, PSYCHOMETRY, REMOTE HEALING
N: EARLY MAR.–EARLY APR. S: EARLY SEP.–EARLY OCT.		OSTARA	EGG-ON-SPOON RACE; DIVINING THE FUTURE BY SCRYING EGG LIPID DRIPPED IN WATER
N: MID-APR.–MID-MAY S: MID-OCT.–MID-NOV.	LIGHT HALF	BELTANE	FERTILITY/PROSPERITY SPELLS, COLOR CORRESPONDENCES, PLAYING INSTRUMENTS, PAGAN DANCES
N: EARLY JUN.–EARLY JUL. S: EARLY DEC.–EARLY JAN.		LITHA	GROUNDING, PROTECTION OR HEALING MAGIC, FIRE-LEAPING
N: MID-JUL.–MID-AUG. S: MID-JAN.–MID-FEB.		LAMMAS	BAKING/CONSUMING BREAD IN MAGICAL SHAPES, BATHING IN OATS
N: EARLY SEP.–EARLY OCT. S: EARLY MAR.–EARLY APR.		MABON	HARVESTING, HERBAL MEDICINE-MAKING, LUCK SPELLS

ESBATS IN SUN SIGNS

DATE RANGE	SUN SIGN	SPELL SUGGESTIONS
MAR. 21–APR. 20*	ARIES	SPURN IMPULSIVENESS
APR. 21–MAY 20*	TAURUS	RESIST STUBBORNNESS
MAY 21–JUN. 20*	GEMINI	PRACTICE THE POWER OF SILENCE
JUN. 21–JUL. 20*	CANCER	WORK SPELLS WITH OTHERS
JUL. 21–AUG. 20*	LEO	DITCH EGO, LISTEN TO WISDOM
AUG. 21–SEP. 20*	VIRGO	BE LAZY AND MESSY A WHILE
SEP. 21–OCT. 20*	LIBRA	BE FAIR TO YOURSELF
OCT. 21–NOV. 20*	SCORPIO	SELF-SOOTHE; AVOID SEX
NOV. 21–DEC. 20*	SAGITTARIUS	AVOID GROUPS; FEEL WITHIN
DEC. 21–JAN. 20*	CAPRICORN	DON'T HERMIT; MAKE FRIENDS
JAN. 21–FEB. 20*	AQUARIUS	SEQUESTER YOURSELF
FEB. 21–MAR. 20*	PISCES	GET GROUNDED

*Sun-sign starting & ending dates vary by 1 or 2 days each in different years.

SECRETS TO ESBAT SUCCESS

Here are some insider tips for Pagan groups and group leaders, to help ensure that every Esbat you organize is a rewarding experience for everyone. Although our advice is phrased for Wiccans, it applies to any Pagan path.

Since Paganism is currently among the fastest-growing religions on the planet, chances are you'll have one or more relative newcomers or new students at any given Esbat. Most will be sincere spiritual Seekers, but there are two troublesome types you may encounter who rarely reveal their stripes until after they've passed your initial interview or participated in one of your open Sabbat celebrations.

Many an "IRAB" ("*I read a book*") seeks training already convinced that they know a lot—maybe more than *you* do. These often try to show off their sense of superiority in not-so-subtle ways, such as by trotting out an obscure mystical minutia inapt to the situation in the hope you don't know it. They are annoying and test your patience.

In fact, their certainty is unearned and depends on the quality of magical training that the author they parrot received or did not. The content of reading material they prize is usually specious, shallow, or erroneous—but since this is all they know, they tend to defend its veracity vociferously. They may insist that you should incorporate it into the Coven or group's practice, or may want to teach it to your students themselves.

Such people are prone to demanding magical shortcuts, such as credit toward getting Initiated for the amount of time they claim that they've spent reading or practicing Solitary (*sans* witnesses of course, with the onus on you to take their word for it). They may boast a string of titles and degrees from other sources—most of which you'll never have heard of, and for which they can't provide contact information to confirm. And they oft try to dominate discussions and decisions. They may have developed ineffective and resistive ritual habits, or may instinctively revert to magic that they view through a comfy lens of New Age, Buddhist, or other non-Pagan spirituality they've previously explored.

Remind them of the Craft truism that "thou must suffer to learn"—that mastering anything as worthwhile as traditional Witchcraft necessitates effort over time. Despite their know-it-all façade, they are just very insecure folks who try to project the appearance of occult expertise in order to bolster their ego. They are unaware of the irony that they seek teaching while already claiming to understand everything. They may come to realize that they have much to learn if they simply quiet down, listen, and collaborate. If not, they'll move on and try to peddle their self-centered bluster to some other group.

Another type of Seeker you'll frequently encounter is the "spiritual consumer"—people who are trying on different brands of spirituality as if they were shopping for a pair of pants. These are attracted to the concept of practicing magic and the image of being a Witch, but they want their spirituality to be convenient—minimal commitments, few challenges, and free 24/7 counseling from you for as long as they choose to dabble in your religion and spottily attend your meetings. They won't openly acknowledge it, but they are typically looking for something specific—nothing so transcendent as wisdom or enlightenment, but a spell, a skill, a soulmate, or (surprisingly often) validation of their personal sexual perversity. As soon as they either acquire it or realize they can't extract it from you, they'll huffily pretend that you've offended them somehow, and use that as an excuse to take their business elsewhere.

For funny-but-true descriptions of more Pagan types, see *The Flake Filter* at: http://www.oldenwilde.org/oldenwilde/teaching/flakefil.html.

Such ilk aside, most newcomers to the Craft truly do yearn to learn. Yet often, lacking life experience in a culture deeply steeped in magic—since "developed" countries tend to value only utilitarian ways—they initially find the occult's intricacies and wide-ranging topics challenging to comprehend.

So make working magic sacred fun. Alternate skills that you teach or practice: shuffle making tools, using magical inks, working poppets and brewing potions, etc. with other techniques such as Past Life Regression, breath and body work, or discussing Witch ethics so that none get bored or overly frustrated by exploring a single magical skill for six months in a row until it loses its cachet, or they feel bewildered by too much minutia about the subject.

Group leaders should avoid resentment or getting burned out from supplying all the ritual supplies themselves. Groups fare best when everyone pitches in to enable rites. Any who routinely plead poverty and don't even donate so much as free labor to support the joint venture telegraph their disdain of a core Wiccan tenet—communalism. Their peculiar refusal reveals that they don't value Pagan collectivism and collaboration. Should they arrive with naught to offer but their own need, send them to a store posthaste to rectify their *faux pas*, or instantly put them to a task that you deem crucial for the class's or rite's success, such as prepping the ritual room or Cakes and Wine. If they *still* balk, encourage them to reconsider their choice of religion, and to move on of their own free will.

Christian, Jewish, and Muslim services may last about an average of two hours, but never rush an Esbat to conform to a quick in-and-out time frame. Ease into working magic by chatting about mundane matters for a while first, such as work, kids, who feels ill or just got a raise. Accentuate the positive versus endless complaints, and don't let someone use the meeting like a therapy session and dispirit folks prior to ritual. Once the ice is broken, circle leisurely, focusing on the experience rather than the clock.

Make working Esbats as soul-stirring, memorable, and lively as Sabbat celebrations. Intersperse circling with scheduling group field trips to a planetarium, museums that feature bizarre exhibits, or local haunted places or decrepit cemeteries where they can photograph ghost orbs hanging around tombstones. Walk woods, circle near running water. Sure, you could dryly explain the rudiments of astrology in circle, but the subject will impact them more deeply if you take them adoors to physically adore the Moon, planets, and stars.

Follow the Ritual Script during circles, but always have a trick up your sleeve—something magically enchanting and unexpected planned for the spellwork portion of the ritual. Motivate participants' perpetual surprise by keeping all the spell components under wraps until it's time to reveal them, such as inside a lid-covered cauldron.

Spurn prudery and infuse Esbats with audacious experimentation as long as Working meetings don't suffer from a lack of concentration or focus. Exemplify Witches' balanced work-hard/play-hard ethic by incorporating irony, paradox, experimentation, and raw emotion. Challenge and cajole students or Covenmates to banish self-doubt, hesitancy, and fear of failure. Cheer them on to succeed by trying every kind of magic that comes their way with an open heart and mind. Applaud uptight, un-rhythmic men who dare dance exuberantly, women who bravely play an unfamiliar musical instrument, and kids and teens who best their parents in the strength of their willing spirit and creative approaches to Esbat meeting topics.

After consecrating Cakes & Wine, talk about spiritual subjects or current events that affect spirituality or threaten or support Paganism. The High Priestess or High Priest may inform participants that a new law will give them more religious freedom. A Covenmate may share a supernatural experience, and another might ask how to use an obscure magical ingredient. Having discussed general life matters prior to circle enables the ceremony conversation to remain spiritual until Rite's End, and for participants to emerge satisfied that both their personal and spiritual life has been nurtured.

ESBAT FOODS

Cakes and Wine (aka Cakes and Ale) are consecrated by word and deed to the pleasure of the Gods, and a portion of both put in a libation bowl atop the main altar, to be placed adoors later. Then they are passed around until all have taken a token bite and sip, at which point they are placed in the center of the circle. All sit around the plate and cup and can nip at will from them and any other refreshments on hand.

The traditional recipe for Witch Cakes calls for honey, salt, and raw or boiled oats to be shaped into crescents and baked. But neither this nor a literal "cake" is required: seasonal foodstuffs are always a goodly Esbat choice, although you should try to choose edibles that somehow connect with or support the evening's spellwork. For instance, if you worked a spell to conjure rain, you wouldn't negate it by serving *nopales* (desert cactus), but rather a platter of sliced, juicy cucumber or celery. You can serve and consume anything you can afford, from crackers to fried pickles and more. The best Cakes and Wine foodstuffs are hand-held, non-flaky, non-sticky, non-greasy, bite-sized morsels that make napkins unnecessary and minimize crumb cleanup—an ideal that is hard to attain, since food is an inherently messy affair.

Some Esbat participants may have legitimate allergies to consider when making your ritual food choice. Others may try to burst onto the scene with long lists of psychological food issues best diagnosed as orthorexia, which manifests as an obsessive aversion to consuming particular foods. Orthorexics tend to provide florid rationales for their choices, which smack to most ears of being extreme diets based on dubious theories. For instance, they may refuse to eat "members of the nightshade family" such as potatoes and tomatoes—not because they have a rare auto-immune disorder that might actually be triggered by such foods, but because they read a book, blog, or tweet that persuaded them to automatically add the ominously classified plants to their ever-growing watch-list of feared physical impurities.

Picky people can be quite demanding, and they often display other body issues as well that can impede their spiritual growth, such as claiming intense self-consciousness that precludes them from working magic skyclad.

The "Wine" in the ceremony can be bottle-straight, or mulled (heated with herbs, spices, and similar natural additives). It can also be liquid "spirits" such as liquor, spiked punches or herbal teas, and liqueurs. Or it can be mead or ale—just never cheap "beer," as the latter often contains additives that tend to foment strife. The properties of some herbal-based wines directly promote bonding, such as damiana wine. And we've made our own bottles of ritual wine by fermenting local muscadine grapes with champagne yeast.

"God is in the grape,"[101] so those who refuse to take so much as a token sip during the ceremony are resisting learning the spiritual components of ingesting sacred substances and thus, should be discouraged from future participation. Alcohol is a traditional component of magical drink in almost every culture, and respecting it means neither abusing nor abstaining absolutely from it—for the true meaning of the Cardinal Virtue of Temperance is the power to avoid either extreme.

101. Bacchus, Dionysus, etc.

To aid your planning, we provide two tables of traditional Esbat Cakes and Wine suggestions: "Eightfold Esbat Menus" gives examples of dishes and drinks based on the nearest Sabbat to each Esbat, and "A Year of Esbat Flavors" offers food and drink suggestions appropriate to the calendar month in which an Esbat occurs. Both tables are categorized by the Dark and Light Halves of the year, and the months are listed for both the Earth's Northern and Southern Hemispheres.

All these suggestions operate on magical correspondences to support your seasonal spellwork. For example, since Beltane marks the time that colorful spring flowers bloom, it's appropriate to eat jambalaya, which is replete with colorful vegetables and spices. The twelve months are closely tied to the twelve Sun signs, but correspond in a more down-to-earth way to the rhythms by which we shop, cook, eat, and drink in modern lives scheduled by the mundane year. Thus, each of these flavors can help your Esbat's Cakes and Wine rite bridge the transition from the timeless back to the temporal realm as your ritual approaches its conclusion.

Of course you'll want to tailor these suggestions to your own personal tastes and regional foodstuffs available to you. If our suggestions betray an American Southern twang, it's because we've made and enjoyed each of these treats for Esbats that we've celebrated at our Covenstead in North Carolina's Blue Ridge Mountains.

Both Esbat and Sabbat foods should feature seasonal fare. Since Witches aim to work *with* the cyclical astrology of the seasons rather than fight this natural flow of time, go with what's growing, being harvested, and thus is on sale—what food-stuffs *most* extol the virtues of the season you're enjoying at the moment.

Think medieval, whimsical, outside the box: it's not blasphemous to try cheese or onion straws, pâté, or tapenade. Coven Oldenwilde doses day-old bread to within an inch of its life by painting it with olive oil and sprinkling atop it parmesan and romano cheese, cracked red pepper, smoky paprika, and dill. Lady Passion often provides balanced "half 'n' half" options to suit folks' tastes, such as by making half a batch of non-salted buttered croissants savory with herbs and spices, and the other half sweetened with basil, mint, oregano, or lemon honey spice.

The one food taboo that our Coven feels really passionate about is: no added

EIGHTFOLD ESBAT MENUS

NEAREST SABBAT	DISHES & DRINKS
SAMHAIN	NUTS AND SEEDS; BEEF STEW; CINNAMON SCHNAPPS OR SHINING PUNCH (PULPY LIME JUICE AND MOONSHINE)
YULE	RICE CHEX® OR DILL-ENCRUSTED BREAD; GOLDSCHLÄGER,® WARM DR. PEPPER® WITH LEMON SLICES, OR EGGNOG; SUNRISE MIMOSAS
IMBOLC	WHEAT CHEX®; WARM CINNAMON MILK OR VODKA BITTERS
OSTARA	DEVILED EGGS; CARROTS; HERBED SOUR CREAM OR RANCH DIP
BELTANE	JAMBALAYA; APHRODISIAC DAMIANA HERB WINE OR LIQUEUR
LITHA	CHILLED POTATO SOUP; LEMON ICES; MIXED HERBAL SUN-TEA OR ICY ALE
LAMMAS	PORK, PEPPERS, AND ONION SKEWERS; GRAPES; DINNER ROLLS; OAT ALE
MABON	HAM SANDWICHES; APPLES; WHEAT ALE

A YEAR OF ESBAT FLAVORS

MONTH (N)	MONTH (S)	FLAVOR BY MONTH
OCTOBER	APRIL	SWEETS
NOVEMBER	MAY	BITTERS
DECEMBER	JUNE	DARK CHOCOLATE
JANUARY	JULY	FIZZY DRINKS
FEBRUARY	AUGUST	SPIKED DRINKS
MARCH	SEPTEMBER	FISH OR EGGS
APRIL	OCTOBER	SPRING SALAD
MAY	NOVEMBER	EDIBLE TREE SHOOTS AND FLOWERS
JUNE	DECEMBER	SAVORY MEALS
JULY	JANUARY	HERBAL TEA
AUGUST	FEBRUARY	BREAD AND VEGGIES; SACRED SUBSTANCES
SEPTEMBER	MARCH	BREAD AND PROTEINS

salt or sugar. Willful indulgence in these is proven to cause, or contribute to, high blood pressure, obesity, and diabetes. Scientists and nutritionists rightly warn us that corporate food manufacturers saturate most of the processed foods they sell us with unhealthful amounts of salt and sugar—even though they're aware that these substances' crystalline structures pierce holes in cells that ultimately break down their customers' brain, organ, and skin processes, unnecessarily enabling many a degenerative condition, and generally accelerating the aging process.

Make your foods spice-rich instead. We advocate replacing salt and sugar in recipes with herbs, peppers, onions, etc. These are not only common magical components (burned as incense in rites, or used in diverse ways as spell ingredients and potion components), but are also inexpensive and work internally on us when we ingest them in food or medicinal form. Explore their virtues by using them in Esbat Cakes and Wine and Sabbat feast foodstuffs. Smoky paprika is one of our favorites: it has the almost unique property of fooling the brain into feeling satiated, thus thwarting over-indulgence.

Here is a true Coven Oldenwilde story that illustrates spices' magical importance and many uses: As Lady Passion was writing this very section, she received an e-mail from a female client who'd phoned her for a consult to fix a family problem. The client has two young autistic children, two young unaffected children, and a closetful of Witch tricks, but felt unable to banish a ghost haunting her home.

Lady Passion agreed to her descriptions of events: the mother *was* experiencing genuine signs of a true haunting. The client requested a spell to dispel the entity, which she credited with having given her family a run of bizarre bad luck and setbacks. While Lady Passion encouraged her to communicate with It and reach a détente toward harmonious coexistence, the client felt strongly that the whole experience was like having one kid too many with which to contend.

So, knowing busy mothers' needs and restrictions, Lady Passion recommended that she treat everyone with a one-two punch by cooking with and having them ingest common, inexpensive dill-weed spice and then later bathing in it as well. Dill's teensy, soft green needles are renowned for being able to break a curse. The e-mail expressed her client's delight that she'd fed each person in the household dilled chicken sandwiches they'd greedily gorged on, then got each one to soak in a dill bath. We liked her paradoxical play on the word "chicken" to become brave; *she* felt deeply relieved that a single grocery-store herb could be quickly used two ways to stop the chaos and end the ghost's aggression.

Because we stack up spell correspondences higher than a fat deacon piles his plate at a pancake breakfast, Witches consider aesthetic *presentation* equally important with ritual *content*. We often arrange our Esbat Cakes in a magical way on a typically circular ceremonial Cakes plate, which we then cover with a cloth or fabric placemat and place near the altar just prior to ritual. (In Coven Olden-wilde's ritual room, we keep it raised above the floor on a beautifully glazed hand-thrown ceramic cake stand donated to us by the artist.) The Cakes plate needs to be light enough to pass around, and might be made of wood, ceramic, or metal. One of our favorites is a silvery round aluminum pizza pan from a family pizzeria that stood for many years on the present site of Apple Computer headquarters when *Diuvei was growing up in Cupertino, California.[102]

Anyone can pile chips on a plate, but Witches appreciate aesthetic detail—layers upon layers of symbolic magical intention that combine to overwhelm the status quo and achieve what we want. Take a few extra minutes to arrange your foodstuffs in an artistically pleasing fashion that furthers your ritual focus.

Pattern options include:
>An outward or inward spiral
>Concentric circles
>A vertical diamond shape
>The Greater Cross-quarter Sabbat symbol
>The Lesser Quarter Sabbat cross symbol
>A smiley face
>A pentagram
>A planetary orb
>A lunar crescent
>An 8-spoked Wheel of the Year

---

102. Cicero's Pizza, now doing a thriving business in San Jose, California.

An exclamation point
A question mark
A yin-yang symbol
A horizontally or vertically sliced circle
A circle with a center dot (the astrological Sun symbol)
A triangle or pyramid
A stacked square

All such ways of displaying your Esbat Cakes visually convey a silent magical message or Craft tenet, reinforce the current season, or support the spellwork just performed. For example, a square stack equates with Earthen stability because the square was the ancients' symbol for Earth (rather than the quartered circle we associate with it today, which itself is originally a Sun wheel). It can make even meager fare seem more substantial—more like "a square meal." An exclamation point can warn participants that the food is on the spicy side; a question mark, that there are surprising ingredients in morsels baked inside puff pastry.

You might also consider adding a wee bud vase of flowers in the middle of your arranged Cakes, a drawn sigil, or a vine wreath. Or you might change the design of your plate to reflect seasonal or Sabbat color correspondences.

Considering that many Pagans feel too excited to eat before working spells, and students about to attempt Initiation or Elevation in magical rank traditionally fast for twenty-four hours beforehand, such precise attention to detail gives participants something special to look forward to after working magic.

Except for Initiations and Elevations, pre-ritual fasting is an individual choice, never a requirement or expectation, and it can be as simple as eating lightly for a day or so before the rite. This is not some modern watering-down of ancient austerity: unlike monotheists who promote frequent and long-lasting fasting to mortify what they consider the body's innate pollution (as exemplified by Lent and Ramadan), the Pagan Greeks practiced the benefits of quick fasting to foster spiritual focus, and then rewarded participants in such rites as the Eleusinian Mysteries with a raucous feast once they'd completed the processional and ritual. Similarly, medieval and Renaissance grimoires such as the *Fourth Book of Agrippa* recommended pre-ritual periods of abstaining from food, sex, and "all perturbation of minde" not for puritanical reasons, but for the magical purpose of preparing to conjure spirits, which is easier when you're somewhat detached from everyday physical and emotional distractions.[103]

The Cakes and Wine Ceremony remains a vital aspect of Witches' rites for many reasons—among them that, after working wicked cool, intense magic, everyone's rightly deserving of rejuvenation by merit of ingesting and imbibing; its ingredients serve to loosen tongues during the only time during ritual that participants are allowed to speak freely; and the experience bonds disparate people gamely trying to spiritually deepen.

Don't be haphazard about what you offer to the Gods and participants during Esbats, or treat the ceremony as an afterthought. Use it as yet another means to educate and inspire others. Attendees will go home with their impressions of the Mysteries they witnessed, and reaching them through their bellies can cement these impressions on yet another level—becoming delicious food memories that they prize for life. Neuroscience tells us that food is closely linked to memory and emotion via the sense of smell, so the Cakes and Wine you share at the end of your ritual are as important in their way as the incense you light at the beginning.

Over time, folks may so rave about what you serve during your magical rites that you decide to embrace the dish or menu as a tradition for that month each year. Just avoid getting into a rut, and generally strive to keep your ritual food offerings as interesting as all your Esbat rituals.

103. Heinrich Cornelius Agrippa: his *Fourth Book of Occult Philosophy*, Esoteric Archives digital edition by Joseph H. Peterson, 2000.

THE EIGHT SABBATS

*"Forget not
that the earth delights to feel your bare feet
and the winds long to play with your hair."*

—KHALIL GIBRAN, *THE PROPHET*

Honoring the Sabbats is the best way to stay connected in time with Mother Earth's cyclic changes. Consistently celebrate them year in, year out, and you'll see how well they help keep you stable and productive—grounded in lively and comforting spiritual routine.

Pagan Sabbat rites are held eight times a year and are primarily celebratory in nature—intended to mark the changing of the seasons, to praise the Gods, to cement Pagan community bonds, and to rejuvenate Witches. They're spread out every forty or fifty days (six to eight weeks or so apart) over the course of the year, and are traditionally held either on the exact date or within three days of it—which allows them to be celebrated on the weekend closest to the date with which the Sabbat is associated—or else on the closest New or Full Moon Esbat. In practice, though, Nature is flexible in this respect, and the last two thousand years' worth of fluctuating Sabbat calendar dates (some of which we'll look at in "Origins of the Sabbats") show that keeping up the annual rhythm is more important than hitting each season's turning-points exactly on the beat.

As with Esbats, never rush a Sabbat. Magic takes as long as it takes—and when Witches meet, there's all manner of it to enjoy. Perhaps this is why it is Pagan policy to hold three-day weekend gatherings. Should your family or employer think this excessive, tell them it was longer than this in olden days: for example, the twelfth-century *Serglige Con Culainn* ("Sickbed of Cúchulainn") documented that Samhain celebrations lasted a full week—the day of, and the three days before and after.

Each Sabbat has traditional meanings, as well as potentially limitless ways to perpetuate them. It takes a while to memorize when each Sabbat is, and to learn how to pronounce its name properly, because most are in an olde or foreign tongue and appear in various spellings (for example, "Imbolc" is sometimes spelled "Imbolg" or "Oimelc"). The pronunciations we give are the ones most English-speaking Wiccans use, not necessarily the ones used in most of these names' original Gaelic and Germanic languages.

The Greater Sabbats are also called "the Cross-Quarter Days," and are symbolized by an "X" (see *The Goodly Spellbook*, "Making Sigils and Seals")—the shape they make when mapped on the circle of the zodiac. The Greater Sabbats fall on the same day each year, as listed in the table to follow. They are Witches' high holy days of:

     SAMHAIN (pronounced *sow-in*)[104]
     IMBOLC (*im-bolk*)
     BELTANE (*bel-tain*)
     LAMMAS (*lahm-us*)

The Lesser Sabbats are called "the Quarter Days," and are depicted as a plus sign, often inside a circle (see *The Goodly Spellbook*, "The Four Quarters"). These mark each year's two equinoxes and two solstices:

     YULE (winter solstice; pronounced *yool*)
     OSTARA (spring equinox; *oh-stah-rah*)
     LITHA (summer solstice; *lee-thah*)
     MABON (fall equinox; *may-bun*)

All Eight Sabbats together are symbolized by the Eightfold Wheel of the Year, depicted at the head of the accompanying table. For convenience, we'll reiterate here the dates of the Sabbats in both the Northern (green) and the Southern (red) Hemispheres:

---

104. SOW as in "now." However, many sorely misinformed Christian fundamentalists are convinced that "Sam Hain" is the name of the God of the Witches!

THE 8 ANNUAL SABBAT DATES

SAMHAIN	OCT. 31	MAY 01
YULE	DEC. 21 *	JUN. 21 *
IMBOLC	FEB. 01 *	AUG. 01
OSTARA	MAR. 21 *	SEP. 21 *
BELTANE	MAY 01	OCT. 31
LITHA	JUN. 21 *	DEC. 21 **
LAMMAS	AUG. 01	FEB. 01
MABON	SEP. 21 *	MAR. 21 **

* Dates may vary by one or two days each year.
** Some celebrate Imbolc on Candlemas, February 2.

SABBAT CELEBRATIONS

Sabbats can be celebrated as Solitary rites, together with Covenmates, or at a "gathering" or "festival" of hundreds of Pagans. If one is held in a Covenstead, clean up after yourself as you go along. If you're asked to call a Quarter or fill some ritual role during the main rite at a Covenstead or gathering, give it your all.

Large Sabbat gatherings can be so exceedingly liberating that you can easily find yourself tempted to dance, schmooze, trip, or play musical instruments non-stop for three or four days and nights in a row. Experience will help you realize the value of pacing yourself to match the fest's ebb and flow—to avoid over-imbibing the first night so that you feel up to the following day's festivities. Remember to eat to keep up your stamina, and to nap or take some alone-time when you need it.

Witches typically camp out or share rooms during Sabbat gatherings. Some groups charge a hefty fee to attend, unless they "comp" you in for free in exchange for helping them cook, clean, or teach a magical workshop or whatnot during the weekend.

When using the Internet to elicit participants for their Sabbat, many groups post tedious disclaimers such as "No alcohol or substances allowed." Such are laughable, however, for we've never been to a gathering that wasn't rife with both! (Our disclaimer: You didn't hear that from us. . . .) Peace is supposed to prevail at such times, and Pagans respect the sacred purpose of Sabbat fun too much to abuse it. Event insurers sometimes require organizers to declare such a blanket denial, so the insurer won't have to pay on the off chance that a friend of a friend someone unwisely invited has to be airlifted to a hospital from a drug overdose, or downs a gallon of scotch and starts swinging a sword at others in a drunken rage.

Many attendees don't like being constantly accosted by dogs at gatherings, but snakes, big birds, and other magical familiars abound.

Kids are allowed to run as naked and free as any adult, but all watch out for their welfare, particularly if the gathering is large and replete with unknown people.

Treat any gathering site as if it were your own campsite: toss all trash in receptacles before you crash, or return home with it if need be.

Most Pagans like to "rough it," preferring natural surroundings to posh amenities. So resist complaining about composting toilets or cold showers, because at least you don't have to dig a hole for your own waste, and there *is* running water.

All Sabbats feature a *main rite*. If a Sabbat will be a three-day, weekend-long affair at a gathering or Covenstead, its central ritual is usually scheduled for the peak of the event on Saturday night.

Participating skyclad in the main rite is often an option. If clothed, black is a default color to wear, in honor of our Witch Ancestors. Anything's oft acceptable: robe, sarong, cape, costume, loincloth, chain mail, woad or madder body paint, what have you.

Sabbats include a *communal feast*. In lieu of the usual Cakes and Wine ceremony, a large meal is held either before or after the main rite. The meal may be potluck, or provided for an extra fee in addition to the gathering ticket price. Food types can run the gamut from raw fruits and vegetables to pit-roasted pork.

For Pagans, no matter what our diet is—be it vegan, vegetarian, omnivorous, carnivorous—we revere what gives us sustenance. As animists, we believe strongly that even a grain of rice has sentience, and that we should honor the sacrifice of all life we consume. However costly or humble our meal, we relish all that comes our way, and strive to waste neither its substance nor its spirit.[105]

Thus, when the Sabbat feast is ready and all attendees are assembled, one of the Priest/esses gives grateful tribute to the Gods with libations and offerings of "first fruits"—some of the best pickings of the feast—just before the humans set to drinking and eating. The Priest/ess may perform this brief but indispensable rite by using recitations and consecrations from the traditional Cakes and Wine ceremony, or by making another prayer or toast appropriate to the occasion.

Lady Passion includes ideas for each Sabbat's Traditional Food and Drink and Traditional Magic With Food and Drink in the "Guide to Sabbat Rites," below. For complete, detailed Sabbat feast menus and recipes, see Lady Passion's *Simply Savory: Magical & Medieval Recipes* at smashwords.com or oldenworks.org.

Searching the Internet is the best way nowadays to find Pagan Sabbat gatherings/festivals near you. Because festival organizers come and go more quickly than websites, however, you need to make sure that the information you find is up to date, not merely describing a gathering that was last held several years ago. Currently in the U.S., the most reliable resource for finding Sabbat festivals is The Witches' Voice, at www.witchvox.com, which allows you to search "local events" by Sabbat and by state or country. (If you're organizing a gathering, whether in the U.S. or elsewhere, be sure to publicize it there if you want lots of Pagans to find it.)[106]

ORIGINS OF THE SABBATS

"[E]very civilization reinvents the festivals it may inherit."

—Philippe Walter, medieval scholar[107]

....

105. For more on this topic, see *The Goodly Spellbook*: "On Sacrifice and Blood."

106. some books give comprehensive listings of u.s. and international pagan festivals, although the information is only as current as the book's latest edition: for example, drawing down the moon, 3rd edition by margot adler, penguin books, 2006; and dancing the fire: a guide to neo-pagan festivals and gatherings by marian singer, citadel, 2005.

107. Walter, Philippe, *Christianity: The Origins of a Pagan Religion*, tr. Jon E. Graham, *Inner Traditions*, 2006, p. 183. Walter, a French professor of medieval Christian mythology, demonstrates the origins of the Christian cycle of holidays in the Pagan eightfold Wheel of the Year.

Witchcraft's rapid rise in modern popularity and visibility has helped bring to light what our Eightfold Wheel of the Year truly preserves and maintains: the original, underlying framework on which most, if not all, sacred and secular calendars of the year are woven, as the lists of "Related Holidays" in our *Guide to Sabbat* Rites indicate. Of course, the precise historical lineage of the "Eight Ritual Occasions" (as traditional Wiccan writings sometimes call the Eight Sabbats as a group) will probably always be shrouded in uncertainty because of their great age, and because it's only since the 1950s that Witches have been free to write and speak openly about our traditional, non-oathbound practices—so exactly how long we've been donning our black cloaks and traveling discreetly to mountaintops and forest clearings to keep the ancestral seasonal rites may never be established to the satisfaction of academics who refuse to certify the antiquity of a magical tradition unless it can present a tidy paper trail of documentation.

But we can follow clear traces of this Eightfold Wheel backward through time. One set of tracks not only suggests how it became integral to modern Wiccan and Pagan practice, but perhaps more importantly can help us discern the root meaning of each of the Sabbats. This trail leads from modern Britain through medieval England, Scotland, and Ireland, and back to older Germanic and Celtic cultures, as well as to the Italian civilizations of ancient Rome and Etruria.

Our first way-post is the uncanny resemblance between the crosses and X's in our diagrams of the Lesser and Greater Sabbats and the national flags of England, Scotland, and Ireland as combined in Great Britain's Union Jack. Officially, the red cross of England is the "Cross of St. George" and originated as a Crusader cross eventually adopted for the fourteenth-century Order of the Garter. Also officially, the white X of Scotland, called a "saltire" in heraldry, is the "Cross of St. Andrew" and originated in the twelfth century when the Scots sought independence from the Archbishopric of York by claiming St. Andrew's relics. Ireland's red saltire was declared the "Cross of St. Patrick" only in the late eighteenth century (quite inaccurately, according to Catholic traditionalists[108]), and most

---

108. The traditional Cross of St. Patrick is a cross *pattee*, an upright cross whose arms flare outward in curves, effectively giving it an eightfold appearance.

historians associate it with the coat of arms of the politically powerful Fitzgerald dynasty.

The connection of such shapes with certain saints was always arbitrary, however—for example, the Bible nowhere suggests that Andrew the Apostle was crucified on an X-shaped cross—and didn't even become standardized until later times. The paper trail for these national badges is vague, and fails to explain *why*, of all possible symbols, a cross and a saltire would take such firm hold as the standards of the Kingdoms of England and Scotland, respectively, or why the saltire would be depicted so often over so many centuries as the emblem of Irish political entities that had nothing to do with the Fitzgeralds.

Their psychological magnetism begins to make sense only when you recognize that the cross has been a well-recognized symbol for the stations of the Sun since prehistoric times. The Cross of England depicts in graphic form the solar turning-points that are the basis of the English "Quarter Days"—a term also oft used in Wicca for the Lesser Sabbats. Since Anglo-Saxon times,[109] the Quarter Days have marked out the English secular year, rather as "fiscal quarters" do in modern America. They occur on four Church feast days that are each within a few days of a solstice or equinox: *Christmas* (Dec. 25, close to the Winter Solstice), *Lady Day* (March 25, the Feast of the Annunciation, close to the Spring Equinox[110]), *Midsummer Day* (June 24, St. John's Day, close to the Summer Solstice), and *Michaelmas* (Sept. 29, St. Michael's Day,[111] close to the Fall Equinox). To this

109. As documented in the writings of the Anglo-Saxon monk-scholars Bede and Byrhtferth.

110. March 25, the olde Roman date for the spring equinox, was the beginning of the year for much of medieval Europe. William the Conqueror reset England's New Year's Day to the Julian calendar's date of January 1, but in the twelfth century the English returned New Year's to Lady Day. March 25 remained New Year's in England and its colonies until 1751–1752, when the modern Gregorian calendar was adopted (against popular protest). As it happens, the Earth is currently at Perihelion (that is, closest to the Sun) a day or two after Jan. 1, although this point in the Earth's orbit continues to advance by one day every 58 years—which the astrologically astute will recognize as a "double Saturn return."

111. In mystical Christian angelology, each of the seven astrological planets corresponds to an archangel. Michael is the archangel of the Sun.

day, the Quarter Days still determine the timing in England of taxes, law courts, and so forth. It's because of this English Quarter-Day calendar that the intervening Greater Sabbats are often called "Cross-Quarter Days." (We've also heard them called "corner days.")

Scotland, too, has always based its civil calendar on four "Quarter Days"—but for the Scots, these directly derive from the saltire of the Greater Sabbats, essentially corresponding to the English Cross-Quarter Days. (We'll use the English definition of cross-quarter days here, to avoid confusion.) Up until 1990, when the Scottish civil calendar was altered to be more uniform, the payment of quarterly rents, the hiring of servants, and the opening of law courts were scheduled for *Martinmas* (Nov. 11), *Candlemas* (Feb. 2), *Whitsunday* (May 15), and *Lammas* (Aug. 1).

These dates were based on the pre-Christian Celtic feast days that Witches call the Greater Sabbats—Samhain, Imbolc, Beltane, and Lughnasadh (a Gaelic name for Lammas). These four holidays continue to be celebrated throughout the Celtic world. In Ireland, most people still divide the year by the olde solar seasons, commencing on the Celtic cross-quarter days: Winter begins on *Samhain* (Nov. 1), spring on *Lá Fhéile Bríde* (St. Brigid's Day, Feb. 1), summer on *Bealtaine* (May 1), and autumn on *Lúnasa* (Aug. 1).

And in Wales, the third Celtic-dominant British nation, the cross-quarter days likewise begin the solar seasons, but under the names *Calan Gaeaf* (Nov. 1), *GĐyl y Canhwyllau* (Feb. 2; the name means "Festival of Candles"), *Calan Mai* (May 1; also called *Calan Haf*), and *Calan Awst* (Aug. 1). *Calan* means "the first of," and is a significant clue to the antiquity of the Welsh holidays, as we'll explain below.

THE GERMANIC YEAR-CROSS

Both Quarter and Cross-Quarter days are depicted in the famous and influential cosmological diagram created around 1000 C.E. by the Anglo-Saxon monk Byrhtferth of Ramsey, titled *De concordia mensium atque elementorum* ("On the concord of the months and the elements"). At the four points of a diamond, colored circles labeled with the Four Elements correspond to the solstices and equinoxes. Byrht-ferth assigns them to the same average[112] dates we know—Dec. 21, March 21, June 20, Sept. 20. Halfway along each of the sides of the diamond is another set of four circles, each bearing a date that's halfway between the preceding and following solstice or equinox: Feb. 7, May 9, Aug. 7, Nov. 7.[113]

In Byrhtferth's cross-quarter-day circles is another clue to the Wiccan Wheel of the Year's origins: Each is labeled as the beginning of one of the four seasons. His diagram confirms that the Anglo-Saxons—just like their Germanic cousins on the Continent, and their Celtic neighbors in Scotland and Ireland—considered each season to begin at a cross-quarter day, rather than at a solstice or equinox as we commonly do today. (It's in line with that tradition that Shakespeare's play is titled *A Midsummer Night's Dream* and not *A Night-before-the-first-day-of-summer's Dream*.) Likewise, the Chinese calendar times the beginning of each season according to the date when the Sun is halfway between the preceding and following equinox or solstice[114]—as did the ancient Romans, according to Varro.[115]

For example, the Anglo-Saxons and other Germanic peoples celebrated a holiday called *Winterfylleth*—roughly meaning "winter full moon," and nowadays often called "Winter Nights"—as the start of Winter. Since the original Germanic calendar was lunisolar, meaning that its months were literally "moon-ths" timed according to the New and Full Moons, Winterfylleth was the Full Moon that occurred near the cross-quarter day the Celts called Samhain. This seasonal feast day also began the Germanic New Year, just as with the ancient Celtic and modern Wiccan Samhain.

On the opposite spoke of the year-wheel, the holiday many still call *Walpurgisnacht* ("Walpurga's Night," apparently so named because St. Walpurga's canon-

---

112. That is, given that they range from year to year between the 19th and 22nd of their respective months.

113. For a translation and exploration of Byrhtferth's diagram, see BabelStone, "Byrhtferth's Ogham Enigma," at http://babelstone.blogspot.com/2008/12/byrhtferths-ogham-enigma.html.

114. See *The Goodly Spellbook*, 2nd ed., "Three-Bean I Ching" in "Omens and Portents."

115. Varro, *De Re Rustica* ("On Agriculture"), I.1.28.

ization on May 1, 870 C.E. was the only plausibly Christian excuse for perpetuating an important Pagan Sabbat) marked the beginning of Summer for most
Continental Germanic peoples. By historical times, Walpurgisnacht was being
celebrated on the fixed date of April 30, the eve of May 1, at the same time as the
Celtic Beltane.

As the year, so the day: just as Celtic and Germanic peoples shared the custom
of beginning the year with its dark half, so they also shared the practice of reck-
oning a given day as beginning on its preceding night. This is why "Hallowe'en"
is celebrated on Oct. 31, the eve, or "e'ening," preceding All Hallows' Day on Nov.
1. It's also why a period of two weeks is called a "fortnight" (from Anglo-Saxon
fÐowertÐene niht, "fourteen nights"). This latter practice may have originated with
the olde custom of beginning each lunisolar month with the first visual observation of the New Moon, which can only occur when She is a slender "cup-up"
crescent in the evening sky, hovering just above the setting Sun like the horns of
an underworld God.

But there was one way in which the Germanic feast-year differed significantly
from the Celtic: it placed a much stronger emphasis on the Lesser Sabbats. With
one exception, it's hard to find evidence that the Celts celebrated the cross-like
solstices and equinoxes with major feast days before the advent of Christianity.
For example, there seems to be no known, authentically pre-Christian Irish holiday equivalent to St. Patrick's Day, which has become the default spring-equinox
celebration in Ireland and much of the world because it occurs on March 17. The
exception is the summer solstice Litha, later Christianized as St. John's Day, June
23, whose eve the Welsh consider one of the mystical, triangular *Teir Nos Ysbrydion*,
"Three Spirit Nights," along with Samhain and Beltane.

By contrast, the lunisolar Pagan Anglo-Saxon calendar that Bede described
revolved around Yule and Litha, the winter and summer solstices, the "vertical
axis" of the year like a World Tree: The lunar month preceding Yule was *Aérra
GÐola* (Preceding Yule) and the one following it was *Æftera GÐola* (Following
Yule). Similarly, Litha was bracketed by *Aérra LÐtha* and *Æftera LÐtha,* with a third
LÐtha inserted between them every few years as a leap month. Halfway between

was *ÐastremÐnath*, which suggests that the Spring Equinox—which other Germanic peoples called *Eostre* or Ostara—was also an important holiday in Anglo-Saxon England. It was said to be named for the Goddess of the Dawn—cognate to the word "east"—which indicates that they saw this date as the yearly equivalent of the day's sunrise. Its opposite month, called *HÐlígmÐnath* ("Holy Month") and later *HærfestmÐnath* (Harvest Month), seems to refer to the traditional autumnal equinox holiday called "Harvest Home" in modern English, and Mabon by Wiccans.[116]

This Germanic year-cross of solstices and equinoxes might be the real reason for the equal-armed cross emblazoned on the flags not only of England, but of many other Germanic-influenced nations to this day. Starting from the very beginnings of heraldry at the time of the Crusades, this originally Pagan cross—distinct from the specifically Christian "Latin cross" with its extended lower limb referencing the the Crucifixion—spread through Germanic Europe as the white-on-red *Reichsfahne* ("imperial flag") of the medieval Holy Roman Empire, whence it was adopted into the flags still flown by Switzerland and the Scandinavian nations. A black-on-white version became the emblem of the crusading Teutonic Order of Knights, and thus of Prussia after they conquered it; thereafter it gained infamy during World War II as the *Balkenkreuz* ("bar cross") insignia painted on the airplanes of the Luftwaffe.

Just as modern Wiccans wear a pentagram in a circle as a symbol of religious identity, so some Heathens (a term of identity adopted by modern Pagans who practice Germanic/Norse/Anglo-Saxon magic) wear the year-cross inscribed in a circle—a symbol commonly called a "sun cross" or, rather loosely, a "Celtic cross" after its resemblance to the ringed stone crosses early Christians erected in Ireland. Because this symbol has also been notoriously appropriated by some Nazi-inspired groups such as the Aryan Nations and Stormfront, many Hea-

---

116. The Pagan Slavs shared the Germanic emphasis on the solstices and equinoxes, as evidence from Baltic, folk Russian, and other olde Slavic sources makes clear. Some scholars believe Germanic *Litha* derives from the same Indo-European source as Russian *lyeto*, "summer." Today, *Koliada* and *Kupala*—equivalent to Yule and Litha—are still major folk holidays in many Slavic countries, as is *Maslenitsa* ("Butter Day"), which was Christianized to be equivalent to Mardi Gras and Imbolc, but was originally celebrated at Ostara.

thens prefer to wear a symbol such as the Hammer of Thor that can't be mistaken for either a Christian cross or the logos of cults whose racist ideologies they despise.

Most Heathens celebrate the same Wheel of the Year as Wiccans, but many call the Sabbats by the Old English term "Holy Tides." Our table "Sabbats and Holy Tides" gives the equivalencies between these two versions of the Wheel.

Not all Heathens celebrate the Tides on the same dates as the Sabbats, however: many times their religious holidays are celebrated according to the "Old Norse calendar," a popular name for a calendar that was instituted and probably invented in Iceland around 930 C.E. and has continued to be used there up to the present day (albeit now unofficially). In its authentic form, it's an intricately ingenious solar calendar that contains thirteen months: twelve that contain thirty-day months, plus an annual four- or eleven-day leap month.

Each month's starting date approximates the Sun's entry into each zodiac sign (thereby framing this calendar on the equinoxes and solstices), but falls on the same day of the week each year, cycling through the ancient Chaldean Order of planets[117] twice during the year. For example, the month *Mörsugr* always begins on a Wednesday (Mercury's day—called *Óðinsdagr*, "Odin's day," in old Icelandic); the following month, *Þorri*, on a Friday (Venus's day—*Frjádagr*, "Frigg's day"); the month after that, *Góa*, on a Sunday (Sun's day—*Sunnudagr*, "Sunna's day"); and so forth through ten more months, till Mörsugr begins on a Wednesday again the following year. In 2016, for example, these three months began on the equivalent Gregorian calendar dates of Dec. 21, Jan. 20, and Feb. 19, respectively—approximately when the Sun entered Capricorn, Aquarius, and then Pisces.

Since the equivalent Gregorian dates vary by up to eight days from one year to the next, it's difficult to use this calendar correctly without the aid of a reliable conversion table for each year. Another confusing aspect of the Old Norse/Icelandic calendar is that it marks "Midsummer" and "Midwinter" in the literal middles of its two six-month seasons—on the approximate days when the Sun

---

117. The Chaldean Order is a very important series in traditional magic. See *The Goodly Spellbook*, "The Seven Planets and Their Properties."

enters Leo and Aquarius, shortly before Lammas and Imbolc, rather than on the summer and winter solstices as English speakers would expect from the terms Midsummer and Midwinter. Thus, this calendar's Midwinter falls at the start of Þorri, rather than of Mörsugr, because its six-month Winter begins shortly before Samhain on October 21–28 with the month *Gormánuður*, approximately when the Sun enters Scorpio.[118]

The Old Norse/Icelandic calendar cleverly binds together the planetary week and the astrological Sun signs—two independent cycles that are very important in magic, but are difficult to reconcile together. The downside to this feat is that this calendar is as labyrinthine as an Viking knotwork carving. Doubtless this is why many modern authors on Heathenry have peddled oversimplified versions of it. They often reduce the Old Norse calendar to twelve months—omitting the crucial leap month—and usually begin each of the months about twelve days too soon, on the 9th to the 14th of their corresponding Gregorian months.

In reality, these earlier dates were this calendar's equivalent dates in the old Julian calendar, and were corrected to the current ones when Iceland adopted the Gregorian calendar in 1700 C.E.—joining the worldwide reform that was instituted because the Julian calendar had drifted too far out of sync with the seasons.

Some authors also mistakenly interpret the peculiarly timed Icelandic Midwinter as the "true" Yule, leading them to disdain the winter solstice—despite the weight of Yuletide history and tradition surrounding the longest night of the year everywhere else in Germanic-descended Europe. Despite the implications of Aryan purity that might draw some misguided seekers to its "Old Norse" moniker, the Icelandic calendar is actually a medieval Germanic synthesis of several Western and Eastern magical traditions, and its structure allows for the Tides to be celebrated at times that aren't significantly different from the Sabbats.

....

118. See "The Old Icelandic Calendar," *Time Meddler's Calendarium*, http://www.time-meddler.co.uk/icelandic.html; "Do you know your old Icelandic months?," *Iceland Monitor*, Wed., Oct. 21, 2015, http://icelandmonitor.mbl.is/news/news/2015/10/21/do_you_know_your_old_icelandic_months/; and Janson, Svante, "The Icelandic Calendar," http://www2.math.uu.se/~svante/papers/calendars/iceland.pdf.

On the other hand, it's important to note that even if the Heathen Tides and Wiccan Sabbats share dates, the celebrations aren't completely interchangeable: ceremonial and feast practices differ in some respects between Tides and Sabbats, as they do between Heathenry and Wicca, although there are also a great many in common. For example, Heathen rites at these times typically follow the same ritual structure as Wiccan rites, but their central focus is usually on the *blot*—sacrificial offering of food, drink (ale or mead), or both to the Gods, spirits, and ancestors, equivalent to the Wiccan Cakes and Wine Ceremony—rather than on spellwork. We stress this distinction between these two closely related branches of modern Paganism to counter the tendency among institutional officials to force Heathens, Odinists, and Wiccans to be lumped together for religious-services times as if all Pagans worshipped our diverse Gods in exactly the same way.

SABBATS & HOLY TIDES

WICCAN SABBATS	HEATHEN HOLY TIDES*
SAMHAIN	WINTER NIGHTS OR WINTERFYLLETH
YULE	YULE OR GÉOL
IMBOLC	SOLMONAÞ
OSTARA	EOSTRE
BELTANE	WÆLBURGES OR WALPURGISNACHT
LITHA	MIDSUMMER OR LITHA
LAMMAS	HLÆFMÆST OR FREYFAXI**
MABON	HARVEST HOME OR HÁLIGMONAÞ

*Principal source: Wodening, Sward, Hammer of the Gods: Anglo-Saxon Pagarusm in Modern Times, *Anglesaxisce Ealdríht, 2003.*
**These names are modern reconstructions.

THE CELTIC SALTIRE OF THE SEASONS

In contrast to the upright Germanic cross, the obliquely oriented saltire has often carried Celtic connotations—at least since it first became associated with medieval Scotland, and probably before. For example, even though the red *raguly* (ragged-edged, like rough-cut boughs) "Cross of Burgundy" that the Kingdom of Spain later used as its emblem in the New World officially originated in the early 1400s as a symbol of the Duchy of Burgundy's patron St. Andrew, the Spanish diplomat Pedro de Ayala asserted in the 1490s that it originally commemorated the Scottish troops that an early Duke of Burgundy recruited when he sided with England against France in the Hundred Years' War. (It survives today in the flags of several Southern U.S. states once claimed by Spain.)

And even if Ireland's saltire mirrors the Fitzgerald family's coat of arms, as noted above, such hereditary symbols were never arbitrarily adopted, even if their original intent was unwritten in the heralds' rolls or forgotten by later heirs. It's possible that this originally Norman/Welsh dynasty—whose medieval Hibernian scions were oft described as "more Irish than the Irish themselves"[119]—could have adopted the saltire as a sign of their Celtic realms, which they ruled as practically autonomous viceroys of the English crown.

The timing of the four Celtic seasonal feasts that correspond to the Greater Sabbats must have originally been tied directly to the midpoints between the equinoxes and solstices. Since the Celtic calendar was lunisolar, they could well have been celebrated on the closest Full Moon (just like the Germanic Winterfylleth), which coincides most closely with Nature's cycles of fertility—and, in the absence of electrical lighting, is the best way to enable a big outdoor gathering to go on late into the "eve."

Why, then, are the Greater Sabbats all now held on or just before or after the first of the month, a week or more *before* the astronomically accurate "corner days?" Contact with the Roman Empire and, later, the conversion of political and cultural elites to Christianity brought the imposition of the strictly solar Julian cal-

---

119. See, for example, https://en.wikipedia.org/wiki/FitzGerald_dynasty.

endar on Ireland and Scotland, just as it did on the rest of Europe. In this Roman predecessor to our Gregorian calendar, the first day of each month was called the *Kalends* or *Calends,* from a Greek word meaning "to call out, proclaim"—because in Rome's earliest days this calendar was lunisolar, and the first day of each month was announced to the public by an official when he observed the New Moon.

At some point in late Roman or early medieval times, the Greater Sabbats throughout Roman-dominated Europe appear to have been permanently rescheduled to the Kalends of the Julian month in which they fell (just as the Icelanders tied their Germanic equivalents to the first day of their months). Thus, for example, the title of the well-known troubadour song "Kalenda Maia," which dates from about 1200 C.E., means "May Day"—it's the Provençal name for the first day of May, known to Wiccans as the Beltane Sabbat.

In Wales, three of the Greater Sabbats' names still reflect the Kalends—for example, Samhain is called *Calan Gaeaf,* meaning "Kalends of Winter," and Beltane is called either *Calan Mai* ("Kalends of May") or *Calan Haf* ("Kalends of Summer"). The fact that this name is similar in other ancient Gaelic regions—*Kalan Gwav* in Cornwall, *Kalan Goañv* in Brittany—suggests that all the Kalends-based Sabbat names could date as far back as the period when all these areas were under the rule of the Roman Empire. When former Imperial lands were conquered by Christianity, popes, bishops, and missionaries strove with indifferent success to channel the Greater Sabbat feasts into Church holidays established on or close to the Kalends.[120]

Because our modern Gregorian calendar is simply an upgrade of the Julian calendar, most of us continue to celebrate the Greater Sabbats on the first day of the month. One significant exception is Imbolc, which some Wiccans and Pagans follow the Irish custom of celebrating on Feb. 1 (the date of St. Brigid's Day), whereas others follow the English/Scottish/Welsh custom of celebrating on Feb. 2 (the date of Candlemas).

It might seem magically inappropriate to celebrate the Greater Sabbats a week

120. See Walter, op. cit.

or more ahead of their astronomically correct dates. But Nature is as forgiving as the Gods—these are, in effect, just a very early "eve" of the exact dates—and one of the most important factors with respect to these rituals is their annually repeated fourfold rhythm. The principle is the same as we mentioned earlier about orienting a circle to the Four Directions—in practice, its power isn't diminished if they only roughly approximate the compass directions, or even if they are accidentally off by 90° or 180°.

Ritual magic focuses on the archetypal Idea of principles such as the Cross-quarters and the Directions, rather than their precisely measured physical manifestations. That's why you can make even a distorted calendar, such as an inaccurate version of the Old Norse calendar described above, work as a magical calendar—as long as it's not so far disconnected from the astrophysical reality it's intended to reflect that you find that you're obeying an arbitrary schedule more than you're interacting with Nature's cycles.

THE BRITISH WITCHES' SYNTHESIS

The Wiccan Wheel of the Year unites the saltire of the Celtic calendar with the cross of the Anglo-Saxon one—a kind of calendrical parallel to the flag of Great Britain, the Union Jack. As generally practiced today, the "Eight Ritual Occasions" derive mainly from British Traditional Witchcraft, of which the best-known branch is what we nowadays call Gardnerianism after Gerald Gardner, the mid-twentieth-century Witch Initiate who was the first in modern times to publicize and popularize the Olde Religion as it was being practiced in secret.

According to oral lore passed down among Gardnerians, the British Covens from which Gardnerian Covens descend originally held the Greater Sabbats on the Cross-Quarter Days, but celebrated the Lesser Sabbats on the Full-Moon Esbats closest to the equinoxes and solstices. The Greater Sabbats provided (as they still do) an opportunity for descendant Covens to circle with their "Mother" Covens, those in which the daughter Covens' High Priest/esses were Initiated or

GREATER SABBATS & CROSS-QUARTER DAYS

WICCAN GREATER SABBATS	CELTIC CROSS-QUARTER DAYS		
	WELSH	IRISH	SCOTTISH
SAMHAIN (OCT. 31)	CALAN GAEAF (NOV.1)	SAMHAIN (NOV. 1)	MARTINMAS (NOV. 11)
IMBOLC (FEB. 2)	GWYL Y CANHWYLLAU (FEB. 2)	LÁ FHÉILE BRÍDE (FEB. 1)	CANDLEMAS (FEB. 2)
BELTANE (MAY 1)	CALAN MAI OR CALAN HAF (MAY 1)	BEALTAINE (MAY 1)	WHITSUNDAY (MAY 15)
LAMMAS (AUG. 1)	CALAN AWST (AUG. 1)	LÚNASA (AUG. 1)	LAMMAS (AUG. 1)

Elevated; but the Lesser Sabbats were (and still are) often celebrated more privately, in individual Covens.

Some say it was Gardner who began the practice of celebrating the Lesser Sabbats on the actual dates of the equinoxes and solstices, in order to add four more occasions for circling together for his rapidly growing Coven, although Gardner himself may have felt he was just restoring a lost tradition.[121] One of his High Priestesses even asserted that no specific Lesser Sabbat rites were passed down, although Gardner does in fact give a description of his initiators' Yule rite in his first nonfiction book, *Witchcraft Today*.[122]

In his even more revealing later book, *The Meaning of Witchcraft*, Gardner describes the Greater Sabbats as his Elders passed them down to him:

---

121. In his description in *Witchcraft Today* of a Yule rite he witnessed, Gardner wrote, "This in theory should be on December 22, but nowadays it is held on the nearest day to that date that is convenient for the members."

122. Ibid.

> [T]he four great festivals the witch cult celebrates are Halloween,
> May Eve (the old "Walpurgis Night"), Lammas, and Candlemas,
> February 2nd. (It is noteworthy that, being a moon cult, they
> celebrate the night before the day of the festival.)[123]

He goes on to compare the Candlemas Sabbat to "Oimelc, the festival of the moon goddess Bride among the ancient Celts and Gaels, [which] was February 1st." But he doesn't conflate this with the Candlemas Sabbat that he inherited from his Witch Elders. And Bride—who is still central to Irish celebrations of St. Brigid's Day, on Feb. 1—plays no role in the traditional Imbolc rite in the Gardnerian Book of Shadows.[124]

Another indication that Gardner was an honest chronicler of ancient but still-suviving tradition and did not invent these Witchy ways—as people determined to denigrate Wicca's antiquity claim—is his inaccurate guess in the above passage at the real reason the Sabbats are celebrated on their eves. If he had done enough research to be able to forge or reconstruct as plausibly ancient-looking a calendar as the Eightfold Wheel of the Year, he would have had to know about—and surely would have singled out here as "noteworthy"—the olde Pagan Celtic/Germanic custom of beginning the day at sunset that the "four great festivals" preserve.

Given all the evidence we provided here about olde European calendars, it seems clear to us that the British Traditional Witch calendar that Gardner inherited was mainly a continuation of the Celtic Cross-Quarter framework—the Greater Sabbats—but adapted to include the Anglo-Saxon Quarter Days, the more so after Gardner separated the Lesser Sabbats from the Esbats.

---

123. See http://www.sacred-texts.com/pag/gbos/gbos08.htm. In this published version of one of Gardner's early *Books of Shadows*, the Greater Sabbat rites are titled simply "November Eve," "February Eve," "May Eve," and "August Eve." The Imbolc ritual in traditional unpublished Gardnerian liturgy is very similar.

124. Gardner, Gerald b.,T*the Meaning of Witchcraft*, magickal childe, inc., 1959, p. 82.

The BTW calendar's Greater Sabbats place particular emphasis on the ancient solar seasons, which might still allow for it to be a modern import from Ireland (where these are still customary) were it not for its Candlemas Imbolc, which is a Welsh and Scottish practice. Indeed, its dates for the Greater Sabbats are identical to the Welsh dates, whose Romano-British "Calan" names prove their great antiquity. You could call it, in other words, an Anglicized Celto-centric ritual calendar.

To us, this way of truly attuned time-keeping simply doesn't have the artificially arbitrary or poetic look and feel of a typical eighteenth-, nineteenth-, or twentieth-century reconstruction like Robert Graves's thirteen-month "Beth-Luis-Nion Tree Calendar" or the four "Alban" holidays that Iolo Morganwg invented to fill in the year-cross for his Welsh Druid Revival movement.[125] Among the evidential proofs that this British Witch calendar is indeed a magical tradition passed on from very ancient times are its lunisolar character, marking holidays on their eves, reverence of the solar over the astronomical seasons, and Samhain New Year's—all of which the pre-Julian Celtic and Germanic calendars shared.

Our researches have turned up no pre-1950s modern occultist who put *all* these factors together to manufacture and popularize a similar calendar—indicating that it's not the product of a reconstructionist author. Further, its irregular Imbolc and de-emphasized, originally lunisolar Lesser Sabbats seem idiosyncratic enough to have developed in a genuinely organic way over time. (The specific collection of Celtic and Anglo-Saxon names that modern Wiccans apply to the Sabbats, on the other hand, was not standardized until relatively recently.)

In short, the preponderance of internal, circumstantial, and historical evidence favors the "Eight Ritual Occasions" as an authentically olde, long-practiced British Witchcraft calendar.

------

125. These are *Alban Eilir* (spring equinox, usually translated as "The Light of the Earth"), *Alban Hefin* (summer solstice, "The Light of the Shore"), *Alban Elfed* (fall equinox, "The Light of Water"), and *Alban Arthan* (winter solstice, "The Light of Arthur"). For more on the influence of Iolo Morganwg (aka Edward Williams, 1747–1826), see, for example, Powell, Dean, *Dr. William Price: Wales's First Radical*, p. 48 et seq. Morganwg's forgery of this and other supposed Druid manuscript traditions was revealed after his death.

THE ETRUSCAN WHEEL

It should go without saying that, despite modern Pagans' rightful focus on perpetuating the holidays of our ancestors, insisting on racial or nationalistic purity is absolutely alien to the Craft. The Gods don't care what side of a border the names and practices by which we honor Them came from: magic has always been stateless. For example, just because Wiccans and Heathens call the spring-equinox holiday by the Old Germanic name "Ostara" doesn't mean that we believe that all of its rites derive, or should derive, from northern Europe, and that we should therefore disdain decorating eggs for spring because the custom apparently originated in prehistoric Africa.[126]

All peoples on Earth share the cycles of the Sun. The eight points that anchor the flow of the year have always been the basis of holidays worldwide (although not everyone celebrates all eight of them). In our discussion of each Sabbat under "Guide to Sabbat Rites," we give examples of other well-known holidays linked to it. These help illustrate each seasonal turning point's core meaning just as a collection of etymologically related words can help illuminate the meaning of their common ancestral root word.

Historical evidence points to at least one ancient schema that ties all eight Sabbats together with their core meanings. The Etruscans—the original *streghe*, mysterious settlers in the region of modern Florence—were famous for their skill at divining accurate omens and portents from such natural phenomena as the direction of lightning strikes and bird flights. The Romans—who credited the Etruscans with teaching them religion—embraced Etruscan directional magic to such an extent that they not only adopted it for their divinations, but also used it to lay out newly founded towns such as Colchester, the first capital of the Roman Empire's colony in England.[127]

....

126. "Egg Cetera #6: Hunting for the world's oldest decorated eggs/University of Cambridge." Cam. ac.uk. 2012-04-10. Cited in *https://en.wikipedia.org/wiki/Easter_egg*.

127. Jones, Prudence, "Celestial and Terrestrial Orientation: The Origins of House Division in Ancient Cosmology," note 11, in *History and Astrology: Clio and Urania Confer*, ed. Annabella Kitson, Unwyn Hyman Ltd., London, 1989.

The framework that the Etruscan diviners used to interpret their divinations was the cardinal directions, from which they divided the horizon into sixteen regions, each ruled by a God/dess.[128] The meanings of the regions can be simplified into eight, one for each of the four cardinal and four inter-cardinal directions.

These divisions of space are also divisions of time, since they mark the stations of the Sun in His daily and—by correspondence—annual path through the realm above and the realm below the disc of the horizon. East corresponds to dawn and, thus, the spring equinox, Southeast to mid-morning and Beltane, South to noon and the summer solstice, etc.[129]

The accompanying table comparing the two systems of the Etruscan directions and the Eight Sabbats reveals that they correspond well. The capsulated meaning of each Etruscan direction that we give[130] summarizes the meanings of the pairs of God/desses that the Etruscans assigned to each direction. Indeed, the Etruscan directions match up *so closely* with the meanings of the Sabbats—as experienced Pagan ritualists understand them, and as non-Pagan holidays tied to these seasonal turning points express them—that they even shed light on Sabbats that are not always well understood in our modern post-agricultural times, such as the two harvest festivals Lammas and Mabon.

128. It's possible that this sixteen-fold division of the horizon was influenced by the astronomical observation that the plane of the ecliptic is tilted from the plane of the equator at an angle that, at about 23.5°, is approximately 1/16th of a circle.

129. See *The Goodly Spellbook*, "The Wheel of the Year."

130. From Jones

ETRUSCAN WHEEL OF THE YEAR

DIRECTION	ETRUSCAN MEANING	SABBAT
NORTH	NIGHT	YULE
NORTH-EAST	WEATHER	IMBOLC
EAST	FIRE, LIGHT, VICTORY	OSTARA
SOUTH-EAST	HUMAN ACTIVITY*	BELTANE
SOUTH	SUN	LITHA
SOUTH-WEST	NATURE DEITIES	LAMMAS
WEST	FATE, CONSEQUENCE	MABON
NORTH-WEST	UNDERWORLD SPIRITS	SAMHAIN
* Commerce and sex are two examples		

These Etruscan directional meanings are a useful guide to the primal focus of each Sabbat, and they succinctly indicate the natural and spiritual forces to propitiate at each.[131] You can also make ritual use of each Sabbat's directional correspondence as given in this table (reversing South and North and their related inter-cardinal directions if you live in the Southern Hemisphere). For example, after Coven Oldenwilde has concluded a Sabbat ritual and *Diuvei has politely allowed the Gods and spirits some time to sup from the libation bowl that he's carried adoors and set on our backyard altar, he casts the bowl's contents away in the direction corresponding to that Sabbat.

....

131. For more information on this people's ancient magical ways, read *Etruscan Roman Remains in Popular Tradition*, Charles Godfrey Leland, 1892, widely available in reprint/facsimile version from diverse publishers and sources.

* *A description of its significance* (using the modern astronomical seasons)

* *Alternative names for the Sabbat*

* *Forces to propitiate* (based on the Etruscan directional meanings)

* *The palette of colors it is associated with it, which you can use in decorations, ritual clothing, etc.*

* *Related holidays in other religious and cultural traditions*

* *Suggestions for spell and ritual activities for Coven, Solitary, and public celebrations—these are not mutually exclusive, and you can adapt many of these suggestions to any of the three types of celebration, as well as to a family celebration*

* *Traditional foods and drinks for this Sabbat, drawn from a variety of historical and modern Pagan practices*

* *Traditional magic you can perform using food and drink on each Sabbat*

When planning your Sabbat ritual, we recommend that you pick one of the many focal spells or themes suggested below at a time. Don't use *all* the goodly customs at once—save something for the sequel!

For the date of each Sabbat, see the tables for the Northern and Southern Hemispheres given above in the table "Lunar Esbats and Solar Sabbats."

GUIDE TO SABBAT RITES

Samhain

Autumn's peak; Witches' New Year. The origin of Halloween; when fall starts to turn toward winter,[132] vegetation dies, and the night outlasts the day. When the

---

132. As noted earlier, older traditions consider Samhain the beginning of winter.

veil between the worlds is thinnest; when spirits and hungry ghosts roam, seeking appeasement. A time of mourning and honoring the beloved dead, and doing divination to foresee the coming year's events.

Alternative names: Halloween, Hallows, Calan Gaeaf (Welsh).

Propitiate: Underworld spirits.

Color palette: Autumnal (red, orange, brown); black, representing creeping winter darkness.

Related holidays: Day of the Dead (Mexican), All Souls' Day (Catholic).

IF CELEBRATING AS A COVEN

Honor your Ancestors or Beloved Dead by conducting a Dumb Supper—an elaborate table setting without food, meditated on in silence; or a supper held silently, one place-setting *sans* food, to cultivate the good will of those who have Crossed Over into the Summerlands.

IF CELEBRATING AS A SOLITARY WITCH

Reclaim stereotypes by attending parties in full Witch garb. Or do any of the following:

Leave a midnight offering for mighty, mighty Hecate at a three-way crossroads (see spell recipe below); carve jack-o'-lanterns out of radishes or turnips (more traditional than pumpkins); play spooky music while baking Witch cakes; divine the future regarding how you'll fare throughout the New Year.

IF PLANNING TO LEAD A PUBLIC SAMHAIN RITUAL

Select a theme such as Gothic Romance; Romany Gypsy Dance; Haunted Woods; Day of the Dead, etc. Find additional inspiration in Coven Oldenwilde's Samhain Chronicles at http://oldenwilde.org/oldenwilde/samhain/intro.html.

TRADITIONAL FOOD AND DRINK

* *Serve apple wine or cider during the Cakes and Wine ceremony.*

* *For the feast, include meat, egg-drop soup, apples, or nuts. Many Witches traditionally burn a balefire, and it's appropriate to barbecue or smoke this feast's foods. As previously noted, autumn was the traditional time of year when livestock were brought down from high summer pastureland and some culled to consume for family thrival through winter.*

This was humane, since animal fodder had ceased to grow, threatening weak animals with starvation. Practical folk, Pagans sought to honor their beloved animals' sacrifice by internally incorporating their spirit.

TRADITIONAL MAGIC WITH FOOD AND DRINK

* Burn the meat bones, and use the ashes as a spell ingredient. Slice an apple horizontally and meditate on the pentagram within.

* Use autumn's fallen nuts to answer Yes/No questions. Toss a nutshell half on the ground or a flat surface: If it lands cup-side up, it bodes well; if it lands flat, it portends ill. (For deeper divination using three nutshell halves, see The Goodly Spellbook.)

* Predict the number of children you will bear by performing oomancy divination: drip the white of a raw egg into hot water and scry the number that appears as the albumen cooks.

* Or, predict events in the coming New Year for ritual attendees: Have each querent (person for which you divine/read) rub a raw, unbroken egg on their body, then crack its contents into a glass of water labeled with their name or initials. Wait until the egg white bubbles and congeals, and then scry each recognizable shape. A plane, car, or ship portends travel, a wedding bell marriage, etc. If the future looks goodly, have the querent drink it down for luck.[133]

* Appease many a hungry, roaming ghost by propitiating the Goddess Hecate Who rules the sky, the land, and sea, and the Underworld: find a triple crossroads[134] and, after sunset, leave food and drink offerings behind without a backward glance. If you have no food or drink, She likes katharmata (ritual remains), as well.

Yule

Winter solstice: The end of autumn and beginning of winter; the longest night of the year. The origin of Christmas, honoring the annual rebirth of the Sun God during the depths of darkness.

Alternative names: Winter Solstice, Midwinter.

....

133. To read how this is done in Colombia, for example, see "Oomancy: Food for the New Year" at Good Day, Regular People, http://www.gooddayregularpeople.com/2015/01/oomancy-its-thing.html.

134. Three roads that converge to resemble the English alphabetical "Y."

Propitiate: Night.

Color palette: Holly green, berry red, solar gold.

Related holidays: Christmas (Christian), Hannukah (Jewish), MÉdraniht ("Mothers' Night": Heathen), Kolyada (Slavic), Yalda (Iranian), Inti Raymi (Quechua), Saturnalia (Roman).

IF CELEBRATING AS A COVEN

* *Hand-make magical gifts in advance, and exchange them after the rite and feast. Really stretch yourself to extend your skills in order to show your love of your fellow Pagans/ Wiccans. Reenact the rebirth of the Sun God by having a Maiden or female Initiate "deliver" Him in the guise of a Yule log, then have participants divine how long the winter will be by scrying how the log burns: the brighter, the stronger the Sun babe, and therefore the shorter the winter will be. (Some say it's goodly luck to let the Yule log burn to ashes; others save a sliver to light the next year's Yule log.)*

* *Or, have two males wield decorated blunt wooden swords to reenact the twice-yearly solstice battle between the Oak King (symbolizing the waxing Sun, who rules while the days grow longer, from winter solstice till summer solstice) and the Holly King (symbolizing the waning Sun, who rules while the days grow shorter, from summer solstice till winter solstice). Each wears a crown indicating their role: the Oak King, a circlet of strung acorns; the Holly King, a wreath of holly sprigs. The battle is highly stylized and choreographed, with the High Priestess and female participants feigning to try to prevent the battle, while the two Kings mock and insult one another, clash, and struggle until the Oak King—who is destined to win at Yule—"slays" the Holly King. The Holly King is briefly mourned, then the new King celebrated. In olde Saturnalia tradition, Coven Oldenwilde has the winner don a golden, bejeweled "emperor" necklace, and he "rules" the group for the rest of the night—laughingly dictating everyone's actions. (Come Litha, however, the Holly King will turn the tables on the Oak King. . . .)* [135]

---

135. Since the Holly King/Oak King battles can also represent the rivalry between Winter and Summer, many Wiccans who follow the Celtic and Old Germanic custom of beginning Winter at Samhain and Summer at Beltane enact their duel on those Sabbats instead of the Solstices. In that case it would make sense for Winter's ruler, the Holly King, to win at Samhain, and Summer's ruler, the Oak King, to win at Beltane.

The seasonal battle of the Oak and Holly King probably derives from Celtic mythology, but such ritual contests between champions or teams garbed to represent the opposing seasons are well documented all over the world, with the victory of one or the other sometimes foretelling whether

* Stay up all night playing Witchy games and whatnot; spell and witness to ensure that the Sun does rise after the longest night of the year.

If Celebrating as a Solitary Witch

* Leap a strega cauldron fire to ensure goodly health through winter.[136]

* Or, walk as a Witch troupe singing traditional Pagan carols in your local Christmas parade. Carols can include "Deck the Halls," "The Cutty Wren" (also known as "Please to See the King"), "The Boar's Head Carol," and numerous other olde Wassail songs.[137]

* Or, feed the birds: slather pinecones with peanut butter, roll them over seeds, fruit bits, or berries, and suspend them from tree limbs. If you lack pinecones, do the same by substituting a ball of thick, coarse rope tied in on itself to prevent easy fraying.

If Planning to Lead a Public Yule Ritual

* Choose a theme such as ringing in the rebirth of the Sun God. At ritual climax, have participants shake loud and long a hand-bell, a sistrum, jingle bells, or other tingly musical instrument brought from home.

Or, conduct a candlelight processional downtown singing a popular Pagan God-based chant, such as:

"Neptune, Osiris,

Merlin, Manannan, Helios,

Shiva, Horn'd One."

---

the coming season would be harsh or mild. For example, Roman chariot racers were originally divided between a White faction to represent Winter and a Red to represent Summer. Sir James Frazer described a ritual contest at the onset of autumn among the "Central Esquimaux of North America" in which the "ptarmigans" (all persons born in winter) hold a tug-of-war with the "ducks" (all those born in summer); if the ptarmigans lose, "fine weather may be expected to prevail through the winter." (*The Golden Bough*, Ch. 28 sect. 5, "Battle of Summer and Winter".)

136. A fire made in a small or medium-size cauldron with an Epsom salt base and doused with isopropyl (rubbing) alcohol, as described in *The Goodly Spellbook* spell "To Induce a Trance for Scrying."

137 .Sources: *Make Merry in Step and Song: A Seasonal Treasury of Music, Mummer's Plays & Celebrations in the English Folk Tradition*, Bronwen Forbes, Llewellyn Publications, 2009; and http://piereligion.org/yulesongs.html.

Eat ham, pork, or (to be very traditional) a boar's head—all sacred to the Norse God Freyr, Who rides astride a boar promoting plenty (such as adequate food stores during the long winter months). Drink hot wassail (fruit cider such as apple), spice-mulled wine, or wheat ale. Pour a libation offering of it atop the roots of any tree that fruits.

TRADITIONAL MAGIC WITH FOOD AND DRINK

* *Promote generosity by fashioning a Yule Goat ornament sacred to the God Thor, from grain stalks festooned with red ribbons.*

* *Or, make a traditional spell focus or feast centerpiece to attract abundance: plant a fruit-tree sapling inside a soil-filled clay garden pot and decorate it by attaching to its spindly limbs pieces of toast soaked in your chosen libation. Plant the wee tree after a snow or during a frigid day; let outdoor critters eat the toast and naturally fertilize the plant with their droppings.*

* *Leave feast morsels adoors to feed birds such as ravens (from Old Norse "Huginn's Yule," meaning "raven's feast").*

Imbolc

Winter's peak: A time for new beginnings, purification and cleansing, weather divination. The lambing of the ewes. The coldest time of the year, it is also the time when the light is noticeably beginning to overtake winter's darkness.

Alternative names: Candlemas (Feb. 2, when some celebrate this Sabbat), Brigid, Imbolg (pronounced "i-MOLG"), Oimelc, La Chandeleur, Feast of Torches.

Propitiate: Weather.

Color palette: Snow white, candle-flame yellow, or icicle silver.

Related holidays: St. Brigid's Day (Irish Catholic, originally Pagan); Candlemas; Carnival, Mardi Gras, Fastnacht (Christian); Maslenitsa (Slavic); Groundhog Day (American, originally European); New Year (Chinese); Lupercalia (Roman).

If Celebrating as a Coven

* *Improve the Covenstead in ways both practical and symbolically fitting, such as by upgrading light fixtures. It's traditional to replace the "Maiden candle" with a new one at this time. Once during a weekend-long Imbolc Sabbat we took the opportunity to build a roomful of bookshelves to hold our huge occult library, books being sacred to Air (communication), white (paper), and Winter (introspection), and thus appropriate to Imbolc's sign Aquarius.*

* *Or, girls, single women, and those who identify as female can make and wear lit candle crowns during the Sabbat circle. For each crown, acquire eight slender white taper candles, preferably dripless. Run the blade of a butter knife under hot water and then use it to carve a notch on opposite sides of each candle, ½ to 1 inch up from their bases—high enough to ensure the candles' stability, but low enough that their tops will rise well above the wearer's head. Harvest long strips of grapevine or honeysuckle (bindweed), etc., and then weave the vine into garland-style crowns to fit each wearer's head circumference. Insert candles in the spaces between weaves, vertically equidistant around except for near the eyes. Secure each to the wreath using sinew, craft wire, green florist's tape, or twist-ties. Add colored ribbon if you like, and help cushion the crown atop the head by weaving soft evergreen boughs and red winter berry sprigs across the opening if desired. Help each other don and then light the candles at the appropriate ritual moment.[138]*

* *Or, divine your future by performing ambulomancy, walking sunwise around your neighborhood block and interpreting the meanings of the omens you see—in the starry sky, as animals loudly note your passing, or in the shape of flotsam and jetsam that you see on the ground. (For information on how to interpret them, see* The Goodly Spellbook, *"Omens & Portents.")*

* *During the Cakes and Wine Ceremony, substitute sheep's milk instead of the typical wine, ale, or Spirits.*

If Celebrating as a Solitary Witch

* *During the day, soak cornhusks in warm water and make them into strips (or use other pliable plant material such as reeds) to fashion and decorate adoors a corn dolly to represent the Goddess Bhride (pronounced "Breed," also known as Brigit).*

---

138. To make or buy larger, more permanent candle crowns (including battery-operated versions), research the Scandinavian tradition of "Lucia crowns."

* Make a separate comfy bed of evergreen boughs or leaves for your "Biddy," as this statuette is often called in Ireland. (You can use a shoebox, or carve a more elaborate bed out of white balsa wood from an arts-and-crafts store.)

* As you bring the Biddy into your house, thrice invite the Goddess to make Her bed in your home. Leave beside Her bed all night an offering of food and drink and a (safely) burning white candle. The next day or soon thereafter, cradle the Biddy in the boughs of a fruit-bearing tree, and leave Her there to attract garden fertility and spring/summer prosperity.

* Or, make a protective four-legged Bhride's Cross of reeds or rushes harvested adoors (or buy some from an arts-and-crafts store), and fold sixteen of them per fetish.[139] Hang it on your entryway door to promote health and prevent fires.

* Or, divine the weather: two widespread beliefs are that the weather on Imbolc proper is the opposite of how it will be during the remaining six weeks of winter (that is, till Ostara), and that hibernating animals such as bears, badgers, and hedgehogs exit their dens at this time to check on the status of the weather—hence the paradoxical American custom that if it is sunny enough for a groundhog to see its shadow on that day, there will be six more weeks of cold weather, but if the day is cloudy, spring will come early.

* At midnight, purify your home of winter stagnation by by lighting candles, a traditional French ritual that lends this holiday the name La Chandeleur. Then, light a fire to divine the specific kind of weather to expect in spring. Listen to it burn: if it's crackly, anticipate spring lightning; if hissy, prepare for spring flooding; and so on. At rite's end, help usher in spring by turning on every light in your home for a while.

If Planning to Lead a Public Imbolc Ritual
* Choose a theme that features light, such as outlining a ritual labyrinth path with luminaries (thin paper bags—some plain, some with magical cutouts such as five-pointed stars or crescents, etc.— with a light source inside them, such as a glow-stick or a wax or battery-operated tea-light candle set atop stabilizing sand or dirt.) Play introspective Pagani music to foster maze-treaders' thoughts.

---

139. For how-to instructions, view the easiest, color-illustrated instructions online at: http://www. fisheaters.com/stbrigidscross.html. (Fair warning, though: this is a very orthodox Catholic website.) Historically, three-legged triskelion versions were also made, and are probably older than the cross versions given that Bhride was originally a triple Goddess.

TRADITIONAL FOOD AND DRINK

Many believe this Sabbat's name comes from Old Irish *i mbolc,* which means "in the belly," possibly because this is when female sheep deliver their offspring. (Many other animals also give birth at this time: for example, squirrels usually deliver in February in Coven Oldenwilde's natural wildlife habitat.)

* *Eat lamb, fish, or dumplings.*

* *Drink water (folk used to imbibe from sacred wells after walking around them sunwise) or clear spirits. If we have an Imbolc Cakes and Wine ceremony, Coven Oldenwilde often imbibes Greek ouzo, which starts clear and turns blue when diluted with water.*

TRADITIONAL MAGIC WITH FOOD AND DRINK

* *Appeal to the Goddess Bhride to bless yourself, your sanctuary home, and your valuables by offering Her adoors portions of feast foods prior to human consumption, milk, and a rag or a piece of your clothing overnight. The rag or clothing acquires Her properties of healing, for you to use thereafter. A quick spring and no drought is predicted if foul weather follows the milk offering; however, should a bird make off with a beak-full of your cloth to feather its nest, winter weather will persist.*

Make crêpes, as the French do on this day. If you can flip a crêpe in the pan with one hand while holding a gold coin in the other, your household will be blessed with prosperity for the coming year. Eat the crêpes after eight in the evening.

Ostara

The vernal equinox: The end of winter and beginning of spring, when night and day are of equal length, new growth begins to appear, and life triumphs over death.

Alternative names: Spring Equinox, Spring Festival, Eostre.

Propitiate: Fire, light, victory.

Color palette: Pastels like a dawn sky, off-white like an eggshell, bright green like new sprouts.

Related holidays: Passover (Jewish); Easter (Christian); Hajj (Islamic), originally tied to the vernal equinox; St. Patrick's Day (Irish-American); Nowruz (Iranian); Holi and Maha Shivaratri (Hindu). Many cultures begin their new year at this time.

If Celebrating as a Coven

* Make an egg tree by poking a small hole in both ends of many fresh eggs and carefully blowing out their liquid contents. Air-dry the eggshells, then dye them using herbs, diluted coffee grounds, food coloring, laundry bluing, etc. Coat them in melted wax and carve away parts of it before dyeing the shells; when they dry, remove the wax to reveal your design. You can repeat or vary these techniques to achieve depth of color saturation.

* Glue a string into one of the egg holes—or, if you're especially deft, feed a loop of thread, floss, or string through both holes and tie the loose ends to a bead—and dangle your decorated eggs from the branches of a limb or a freshly cut sapling set upward inside a weighted vase.

* Or, do a ritual egg dance by ecstatically dancing around decorated eggs laid on a ritual room floor, trying not to break any: anyone who does so receives a magical penalty, such as bowing before the person in front and floridly extolling their virtues.

If Celebrating as a Solitary Witch

DO A TRANCE DANCE BY STEPPING BETWEEN THE LINES MADE BY PUTTING A COLORFUL MAZE OF MARDI GRAS BEAD NECKLACES ON THE FLOOR IN AN INTRICATE LABYRINTH PATTERN.

If Planning to Lead a Public Ostara Ritual

* Pick a theme based on tradition, such as an old-time egg race: have participants run one at a time across the circle while balancing in a wooden spoon a heavy, decorative stone egg, or a toy egg filled with a magical prize. For prizes, make, find, or buy ahead of time small items such as charms, teensy spell scrolls, little fetishes, chunks of resin incense, etc., that have magical correspondences or talismanic virtues—a wee compass that can find Quarter directions, a blue glass bead that can protect against the Evil Eye . . .

* Shout out a silly demand for each participant to fulfill mid-stride, such as continuing by hopping on one foot, by tiptoeing, or while running backward, or have two participants make the assay in the style of a three-legged race, with their left and right legs tied together. Encourage racers on with claps and whoops of delight. When all have raced, have everyone open their egg, and explain to each the magical meaning of their prize.

TRADITIONAL FOOD AND DRINK

Serve spiked eggnog during the Cakes and Wine ceremony. For the feast, serve egg-based dishes such as deviled eggs, pickled eggs, egg salad, or egg noodle casseroles; rabbit stew; chocolates or sweets.

TRADITIONAL MAGIC WITH FOOD AND DRINK

* *Make an egg-topped Priapic wand to conjure fertility and attract abundance, or make a spring door wreath with eggshell décor interspersed amongst spring shoots. Wrap each eggshell that you want to decorate in a separate piece of fabric whose design dye is non-colorfast (that is, will weep in liquid); secure each inside using a rubber band. Soak them in white vinegar until the fabric's pattern transfers onto the shell. Remove the fabric-wrapped egg from the liquid, unwrap, and air-dry. Tie dangling pliant baby vines or ribbon onto one end of a fennel stalk, and then glue a shell vertically atop it for a Priapic wand, or glue several in a round and hang on your front door as a seasonal wreath.*

* *Or, work "egg jarping," a Northeast England continuation of an ancient Greek tradition wherein two opposing people try to crack the others' hard-boiled eggshell without their own egg suffering a crack.*

* *Feet planted firmly on Mother Earth, one player slaps the pointy end of their egg atop the pointy end of their opponent's to try to induce a crack in the shell. If unsuccessful, their opponent gets a turn to try to do the same. Any crack means you're out of the game. No glue, varnish or other tampering to strengthen the shell is permitted. The winner consumes the loser's egg—doubtless a goodly food-boon for those who displayed deft restraint during winter dearth.*[140]

* *The morning after the main rite, send all off after they've ingested a big breakfast of a traditional recipe for "coddled eggs." In a pot over low heat, slowly whip together cracked raw eggs with milk, melted butter, and strained, water-soaked oatmeal. Add pepper or spices to suit (no salt or sugar), and cook until it reaches a silky consistency of pottage or porridge. (Leftovers can be ladled onto a tad of olive oil in an iron skillet to be fried into "pancakes".)*

---

140. For official rules, see WEJA, the World Egg Jarping Association at: https://www.theguardian.com/lifeandstyle/shortcuts/2012/apr/08/egg-jarping-hardboiled-eggs-blows.

Beltane

Spring's peak, when flowers and blossoms vie with one other to flaunt their new growth. A time of fertility and sexuality—but it's inauspicious to wed during "lusty May," for spring flings are usually temporary liaisons ("Marry in May and rue the day").

Alternative names: May Day, May Eve, Walpurgisnacht ("Walpurga's Night").

Propitiate: Human activity.

Color palette: All bright colors.

Related holidays: Pentecost/Whitsunday (Christian), *Shavuot* (Jewish), International Workers' Day/Labour Day (socialist), Earth Day (environmentalist), *Wesak* (Buddhist), Floralia (Roman).

IF CELEBRATING AS A COVEN

* Make May Day baskets: *using one sheet of colored construction paper for each basket, draw on, paint, or decorate it with magical symbols or spring designs such as hippie daisies, shamrocks, and so forth. Add ribbons or other embellishments as desired. Tape the straight paper into a cone shape. Cut a rectangular strip from one short side, to serve later as a handle. Tape the flat paper into a cone shape and then tape the handle onto opposite sides of the mouth of the cone.*

* *Fill with hand-picked blooms, grasses, candies, baubles, etc. Secretly hang the basket on a friend's, enemies', or stranger's entrance doorknob.*

* *Or, go "a-Maying" or "green-wooding"—make love with a mate or liaison at night in a forest.*

IF CELEBRATING AS A SOLITARY WITCH

* *Preserve your beauty by bathing your face in May Day morning dew.*

* *Or, "gather the May" by bringing into your home or workplace leafy budding boughs, blossoms, or flowers.*

* *Or, plant "companion plants"—herbs, vegetables, or flowers known to grow well when in proximity to each other, such as sunflowers and marigolds.*

IF PLANNING TO LEAD A PUBLIC BELTANE RITUAL

* *Opt for a ritual theme featuring a wildly dressed, exuberant "Lord of Misrule" ritual*

character who cuts capers and encourages participants to laugh and cavort. (Some Witches conduct a "Giggliana" or purposefully irreverent rite—the only time a year when we'd dare do so—by, say, casting circle with a chainsaw, blowing bubbles to call Quarters, etc.)

* Or, erect a Maypole and lead a spirited ribbon-weaving dance around it. Nearby, make leafy "bowers"—small shelters of woven branches where couples can sneak kisses.

TRADITIONAL FOOD AND DRINK

* During the Cakes and Wine Ceremony and feast, serve Shining Punch, an Appalachian Tennessee Pagan gathering favorite: moonshine or vodka mixed with pulpy iridescent lime juice. Or, serve "May Wine": white wine in which sprigs of sweet woodruff have been soaked for about fifteen minutes, then removed. (Use sprigs without open blossoms.)

* For the feast, eat fire-roasted meat[141] topped with a spring-greens salad featuring colorful edible blossoms.

TRADITIONAL MAGIC WITH FOOD AND DRINK

* Secretly mark a piece of ritual Cake with something such as—traditionally—a piece of cooled balefire charcoal. Mix the marked portion in with similar, unmarked slices onto the Cakes plate. After the Cakes are consecrated, the person who randomly selects the marked Cake gets up to three tries to leap the ritual fire: if they succeed, they get health, wealth, and strength, and become "Fool for a Day," encouraged to issue humorous demands.

* Or, pour a protective line of milk in front of your entrance doorway, and leave a goodly offering indoors to propitiate helpful house brownies, and adoors to lure charming fairies.

Litha

Summer solstice. End of spring, beginning of summer; the longest day of the year. The Sun God at His zenith, in His prime.

Alternative names: Summer Solstice, Midsummer.

---

141. If you can't barbecue, then hibachi; if you don't have a hibachi, broil in an oven, and so forth. If you can't cook meat, eat jerky (strips of dehydrated, preserved meat).

Propitiate: Sun, vigor, health.

Color palette: Sunny yellow, orange, gold. (Avoid red to prevent tempers from flaring.)

Related holidays: St. John's Day (Christian), Kupala Night (Slavic), World Humanist Day (Humanist).

IF CELEBRATING AS A COVEN

* *Reprise the solstice battle between the Oak King and the Holly King (this time, the Holly King wins).*

* *Or, camp adoors and harvest blooms, leaves, bark, and roots with which to make magical potions or herbal medicines. Chant and sing around an outdoor balefire, or do fire-leaping (make a wish if you fly o'er it unscathed). Throw wish-granting red soil into the balefire as Witches do in Wyoming. If near a lake or river, divine future events by floating flower garlands on its waves: lively movement presages health and love, while listlessness or sinking bodes ill.*

IF CELEBRATING AS A SOLITARY WITCH

* *Attract Will o' the Wisp fairies: after sunset, lie quietly in a forest fern brake. Don't touch the round neon-white, blue, or green orbs that come to investigate you. The largest are parents, the smallest, their offspring, and they often float single-file along man-made trails. Though they have no body, they move with intelligence. Don't follow these Fey when they retreat back into the forest, or you'll end up being "fairy-led" and never seen again. Instead, be a goodly ambassador of humanity toward them.*

* *Or, harvest St. John's Wort (hypericum perforatum): Air-dry the herb and make a tincture of it. Add drops or dropper-full squirts of it to any liquid, or sublingually (under your tongue), or make into a tea to drink to elevate your mood. (For the recipe for making simple herbal tinctures, see* The Goodly Spellbook.)

* *Or, press picked wildflowers:[142] Put as many buds, petals, or whole blooms with leaves and stems or stalks as will fit between two sheets of wax paper. Then, use an iron on a low to medium heat setting to gently melt the wax paper and seal in/preserve your plant matter; cool; then cut out the shapes to make pretty labels, decorative gift bag tags, mobiles, etc. Using this method you can also make gorgeous semi-sheer lanterns out of your ironed sheets. Attach two together using*

---

142. For myriad beautiful ways to use dried flowers and plants, read Lady Passion's favorite fully illustrated book on the subject, *Creative Design: Dried & Pressed Flowers*, Mary Lawrence and Sarah Waterkeyn, Gallery Books, New York, NY (from Salamander Books, London, UK), 1999.

strong clear tape; pierce a hole on opposite top ends, and poke some type of hanger through it, such as craft wire. Tightly secure the hanger to the sheets, and suspend a glow-stick from the hanger's bottom center, to dangle inside the lantern. The effect is like illuminated stained glass.

* Alternatively, press the flora between two sheets of wax paper inserted into the pages of a heavy book; then, when dried, use tweezers to delicately extract the blossoms from between the wax-paper sheets. Mat and frame the beauty, and hang it on your porch, under an eave near a garden, or in a solarium or greenhouse, or give as gifts.

* If you want to conceive, go to the beach and let nine sea-waves wash over you (one for each month you'll be pregnant).

IF PLANNING TO LEAD A PUBLIC LITHA RITUAL

* Have some circle participants hold taut aloft the outer edges of a white bed sheet while others walk or dance around them, tossing summer blooms atop the fabric. When the flower-tossers have expended the contents of their baskets, have all delight the Gods by helping to hold the linen's edges and spin the whole sunwise while chanting or singing Pagan songs.

* Or, make a different kind of Sun-wheel using natural cordage, or yellow or orange, Sun-colored yarn or paracord. Have participants circle, each using both hands to hold onto the circular-tied string as you weave from inside it a spoked Wheel pattern, a spider web, a dreamcatcher, or one of the traditional Cord Dance designs that we illustrated in The Goodly Spellbook chapter "Mystical Dance." Once it's complete, have everyone skip dance to help turn the Wheel sunwise in praise of the orb that gives Earth life.

TRADITIONAL FOOD AND DRINK

* In the morning after dew has evaporated, harvest edible and medicinal herbs such as fennel, rosemary, kudzu, lemon verbena, mallows, wild onion, and elder flowers. Add some to your feast dishes and store the rest as herb stock to use as a medicinal component with which to cure folk of ailments or to make magical potions.

* Eat cheddar cheese and solar-colored vegetables such as buttered corn, scalloped potatoes, sliced radish, or carrots. Enjoy cornbread; or olive-oil both sides of slices of baguette bread, top with tomatoes, and then sprinkle the top with spices, and grill or bake them in an oven: the flecks resemble the sparks of fireworks that culminate many countries' celebrations around the summer solstice (such as the U.S.A.'s Fourth of July).

* *For dessert, eat diced mangos topped with chilled lemon custard, or shave ice-cubes and top with tart lemon juice.*

* *Imbibe spiked mint lemonade (lemon juice, spring water, moonshine, muddled fresh-harvested mint leaves, and floating lemon slices), or screwdrivers (orange juice, well water, vodka, and floating orange slices).*

TRADITIONAL MAGIC WITH FOOD AND DRINK

* *Ingest calming St. John's Wort tincture to forefend flaring tempers common when the weather is hot and Sol is at His zenith.*

* *Foster reciprocal love as Lisbon citizens do, by giving someone you're attracted to a manjerico—a potted sweet basil plant with a bright flower and a romantic poem on a ribbon-tied scroll wrapped around the container.*

* *Or, do as the Swedes—erect a phallic spire adoors sacred to the fertility God Freyr. Pinch a swath of chicken-coop wire into a shape of desired height. Affix it in place by inserting its base wires into the ground, and then weave vines such as honeysuckle trumpet vine, morning glory, ivy, Virginia creeper, peas, beans, or tomatoes through the cone's honeycomb-like openings.*

* *Or, make a maize maze as a ritual focus: on circle ground, pour cornmeal in a labyrinthine pattern of the symbol of Sun with outward rays. Dance lively between the rows, chant, spell, play music around and about.*

Lammas

Summer's peak: The hottest time of the year. The "first harvest," start of the grain and fruit harvest. While some say that this Sabbat's name derives from "Loaf-Mass," others contend that it's from Lughnasadh, the feast of Lugh, a Celtic God of light and inspiration. Celebrated with games, entertainments, and crafts, honoring the God/desses and Spirits of Nature.

Alternative names: August Eve, *Lughnasadh* (Irish, Scottish, Manx), *Lúnasa* (Gaelic), Lambess, Feast of First Fruits (Anglo-Saxon).

Propitiate: Nature deities, such as Flidais (Flih-DAY), Goddess of the Wild Things.

Color palette: Riotous colors.

Related holidays: GƉyl Awst (Welsh), the Great Feast of the Transfiguration (Eastern Orthodox).

IF CELEBRATING AS A COVEN

* *Play an olde harvest game: Stack two opposite piles of straw or grass. Have two opposing groups defend the integrity of their own pile with the aid of willing others who may toot horns (or make noise) to distract. The person whose stack first falls pays a humorous penalty, such as eating a handful of oats.*[143]

* *Or hold an outdoor Pagan Olympics and give magical prizes to winners of the creative events you devise. The games can be bawdy, olde-timey, or traditional: Because the weather will be hot, folk will be scantily clad, so make the most of this.*

* *Or, if you're experiencing drought conditions, conjure rain by a spell from* The Goodly Spellbook, *"To Break a Drought." Get skyclad and rub all over your nude bodies snow that you saved from first snowfall in your freezer. (If you live in a region where snow never falls, substitute rain collected during a Full Moon.) Afterward, dance frenetically while shaking a rattle or sistrum, or turning a rain-stick up and down.*

IF CELEBRATING AS A SOLITARY WITCH

* *Visit your favorite grove, mountain, lake, stream, or other natural spot and cultivate the largess of its Elemental Spirits by making a "reverse offering" —removing man-made litter and trash, or working to repair human-caused destruction such as erosion or sedimentation due to irresponsible agriculture, clear-cutting of tree cover, or over-development.*

* *Or, make an indoor water fountain to hydrate yourself and your environment during the "dog days of summer" when animals and humans are prone to pant. Repurpose an old wok or shallow pot or ceramic dish as its water reservoir base. Install in this base an electric pump from an arts-and-crafts store, and cover it with river-smoothed stones, shells, gems, etc. Fill fount with distilled water to discourage scum from forming, and add drops of "anti-ick" upon occasion.*

---

143. William Hone, *The Every-Day Book* (1838).

Have participants make and wear a costume, headdress, or mask from fresh fronds, fruits, berries, wheat, molted bird feathers, vegetable matter, etc. Let creativity reign with flotsam hair extensions, flower garland crowns, body jewelry, yucca skirts, and so forth.

Traditional Food and Drink

* Serve bread, preferably homemade, artisan, "dosed" with butter, herbs, and spices, or drizzled with honey, maple syrup, or molasses. Also, eat seafood, berries, and pickles.[144]

* Drink red wine and juices such as pomegranate, red grapefruit, tomato juice.

Traditional Magic with Food and Drink

* Cast an olde British Lammas spell. Bake or buy a round loaf of bread. Consecrate it in a Cakes and Wine Ceremony, and then break off four pieces and ward (protect) your home or property by burying a piece in each of the four corners of your property boundaries.

* Or, show gratitude to someone who has helped you by gifting them fruit on their doorstep, or wrap a flower-chain around their entrance doorknob.

Mabon

Autumnal equinox: the end of summer and beginning of fall, when the night has grown equal to the day. The "second harvest," featuring grain, gourd and root vegetables, and wild game. School bells toll the end of summer freedom. The start of a time of darkness, when the Sun departs the upper world to rule in the nether realm. Associated with judgment, justice, and reaping what you've sown.

"Mabon" is a modern name for this Sabbat, drawn from the Welsh Arthurian myth of the kidnapping and concealment of the divine youth Mabon ap Modred. His name means Great Son of the Great Mother and is the same as *Maponus*, an ancient British Sun God.

---

144. Because hero-God Lugh established the original feast in honor of His mother-in-law Tailtiu, a Goddess Who represents the death of the plants that feed humanity (akin to the Greek Goddess Demeter), it makes sense to eat pickled, preserved foods during this Sabbat in order to prompt fellow Pagans to start stockpiling foodstuffs for the inevitable winter.

Alternative names: Fall Equinox, Harvest Home.

Propitiate: Fate, punishment ("karma").

Color palette: Hunter green, olive drab, flax, or beige. (Brown or even sepia if the weather's droughty.)

Related holidays: High Holy Days & Sukkot (Jewish), Michaelmas (Christian), International Day of Peace (worldwide).

If Celebrating as a Coven

* *Show appreciation for grain mill-ground for bread, pasta, and similar by dancing the traditional Mill Dance (reference the Witch steps illustrated in* The Goodly Spellbook, *Skills section, "Magical Dance").*

* *Or, make an aromatic meditative spellwork sand painting. Acquire 1 pound of table salt or rugged rock salt. Drop 5 teaspoons each into several clean, recycled jars. Add desired amount of food-coloring drops designed to stain the sand into the magical color correspondence you want, and add aromatic resins, oils, and scents. Stir with a wooden chopstick. Air dry the desiccated material, and then carry your specific salts, separated by color, on a tray into your ritual area— preferably onto an olde cement or earthen basement floor that won't be harmed by the salts' nitrites. Using your fingers, sprinkle pinches of salt where you will to make magical glyphs or to spell out a goal in a magical alphabet, etc.*

* *Or, work a spell to banish bad habits, ill luck, obstacles to success, old debts, etc., so you can start with a clean slate on the next Sabbat, Samhain (Witches' New Year).*

If Celebrating as a Solitary Witch

* *Make a magical shortbread-baking pan.* Use self-hardening clay from an arts and crafts store. Finger-form a flat, round, plate-size dish with an outer upturned rim. Use warm water to make the surfaces smooth. Let air-dry a bit, but before it's fully dry, use a sharp implement to score six equal pizza-style slices in the center circle reservoir, and then carve or impress whatever magical or natural designs you wish between the lines (vine leaves and grape clusters are traditional). Air-dry. Coat upper surfaces with olive oil prior to pouring shortbread batter into your mold. Flip baked bread over atop an empty plate, then lift and flip again to behold the beauty of the bread design that you created.

* Or, work a spell using fresh-dried herbs, spices, vines, straw, etc. For instance, you could make a ritual acorn headband crown: drill a tiny hole vertically through each acorn's middle; string together to fit your head circumference using thin copper jewelry wire; and secure at back by twisting both ends in a small, flat, spiral pattern.

* Or, sew or have sewn your cold-weather cape or Samhain costume in preparation for the upcoming Samhain Sabbat.

If Planning to Lead a Public Mabon Ritual

* Fashion a Goddess statue of fruits and veggies in season. Construct a tall, upright chicken-wire female hour-glass-like statue frame with arms raised high in a victory stance, and a stable, bell-shaped lower half that balances flat atop the ground or floor surface. (Or, substitute an upright pentagram scaffold of five equally long and slim limbs roughly lashed together and propped securely from behind.)

* Dress the Deity head-to-toe using whole and parts of seasonal fruits, vegetables, and end-of-summer verdure. For instance, think melon head; cascading corn-silk hair ringlets; sunflower eyes; squash blossom earrings; breasts of halved avocado; blackberry nipples; grape-cluster pubis, foliage skirt, etc. Bedeck Her with jewels such as colorful Mardi Gras bead or seashell necklaces. Animate Her by extolling Her virtues, then approach Her and offer Her fruits of the season, honey wine, and similar. Appeal for Her plentitude by dancing and chanting around Her. This is a highly creative, interactive, moving ritual.

* Or, research and reenact one of the myths representing the abduction of summer's spirit of growth and fertility by the spirit of winter, which holds it captive in the earth till the spring. The most famous of these is Greek myth of the abduction of Persephone, daughter of the Great Mother Demeter, by the God of the Underworld, Pluto. Less well known is the Arthurian myth of Mabon ap Modron—whose name means "Great Son of the Great Mother"—from the tale of Culhwch ac Olwen in the Mabinogion. Mabon was mysteriously kidnapped from Modron when he was only three days old, then hidden deep in a castle till found as a young man and freed by a questing band of seven knights and wizards from King Arthur's court. Beneath the surface of this medieval legend, Mabon is actually Maponus, the Celtic God of youth and light Who in Romano-British times was equated to the Sun God Apollo, and Modron is Dea Matrona, the Celtic Divine Mother Goddess.

Traditional Food and Drink

Eat grains such as wild rice, honeyed oatmeal, or bread made with equal parts barley, oats, and rye. Eat birds such as goose, duck, turkey, or squab; ham or beef; and blackberry or apple pie. Drink wheat ale or rye whiskey.

Traditional Magic with Food and Drink

* *Decorate your feast table with a potted plant of perennial Michaelmas daisies. Their Latin name aster (star) aptly describes their colorful blooms when most other plants have succumbed to withering summer heat or a freak snap-frost. Conjure ongoing prosperity by planting the perennial in a twelve-inch-diameter container.*

* *Thank a benefactor by tossing a handful of granola grains on their land or in the direction where they live.*

* *Mabon is when accounts are settled. Attract payment from those in your debt by spicing the feast with Greek oregano. When due payment is magically acquired, pay off your own debts so that you may enter Winter with a clean slate.*

CRAFTING RITUALS

"It's still magic even if you know how it's done."

TERRY PRATCHETT, *A HAT FULL OF SKY*

WITCH RITES GRANT FOLK LEAVE TO CUT LOOSE AND EXPERIENCE
REVERENT PLAY, CATHARSIS, AND EPIPHANIES THAT SPIRITUAL BLISS
REVEALS. USING MAGICAL GESTURES, PROJECTING A THEATRICAL
VOICE, AND ASSUMING A DIVERGENT PERSONA IMMERSE YOU FROM
THE INSIDE OUT IN THE FULLNESS OF THE MYSTICAL HAPPENING—
AND YOUR MASTERY OF THIS GRACE, GLIDE, RESONANCE, AND
OTHERWORLDLINESS WILL IMPRESS PEOPLE WHO PARTICIPATE IN
PUBLIC RITUALS THAT YOU CONDUCT.

A goodly rite's natural design should evoke supernatural effects, its primal or formal elements prove magic's relevance in a techno-alienated era. At some point during the doing, all should feel time bend, twist, warp—seem to speed up, slow down, or stop altogether. Participants may weep happy tears, feel awestruck or mutely introspective, or abandon boundaries and relish bonding with strangers. In a world where we're taught to keep to ourselves, stay in our own lane, and defend our personal space, this is a rare, heady freedom indeed.

Rituals can be quaintly plain or extravagantly elaborate: sometimes less is more; at other times, the more décor and props, the merrier. Whatever mystical theme you use as an anchor to wrap a ritual around, it should perpetuate one or more key Pagan principles, traditions, or myths.

Rites can only come across as paltry or haphazard if their conductors fail to take many pivotal factors into consideration during the planning and implementation phases. Generally, the tougher a rite is to pull off, the more courageous and persistent you must be to see it through to fruition—and the more rewarding the results will be when you try an olde way or dare an unprecedented feat.

As instances of what to *avoid*, as with all in magic, spurn the temptation to shoehorn in themes that don't fit well together, such as "a Freudian Fey Fantasy" or "Daylight Diana Delight": Freud and the Fey have naught in common, and Diana is a Moon Goddess.

MAGICAL GESTURE, VOICE & PERSONA

"Pamphile divested herself of all her garments, and having opened a certain small chest, took from thence many boxes, from one of which the covering being removed, she rubbed herself, for a long time, with an ointment contained in it, from the extremities of her feet to the crown of her head. When, also, with the lamp in her hand, she had said much in a low voice, she shook her limbs with a tremulous agitation; and from these, lightly fluctuating, soft feathers extend themselves, and strong wings burst forth, the nose is hardened and incurvated, the nails are compressed and made crooked, and Pamphile becomes an owl. Being thus changed, and emitting a querulous sound, she made a trial of herself, and gradually leapt from the earth; and soon after, being raised on high, she flew out of doors, with all the force of her wings. Thus she, indeed, was voluntarily changed, by her own magic arts."

—APULEIUS, TR. THOMAS TAYLOR, *THE METAMORPHOSIS, OR GOLDEN ASS*

Having memorized a script and been creative in how you planned a ritual does not mean that you are living up to your full potential as a Witch, nor is it enough to deeply affect, impress, and empower participants, or even ensure a spell's success. For a ritualist to achieve these goals, they must embody polish, poise—truly "own" their every gesture in circle, finesse their vocal inflections, and be able to adopt a mystical persona that others like and believe, that participants and onlookers feel is sincere versus contrived.

There are many times when working magic seems inconvenient: obligations and requirements of mundane life have a way of trying to distract people from spiritual pursuits. And there are times when a Witch just feels as normally sad, depressed, or out-of-sorts as anyone else—hence, doesn't think that they're up to the task of circling or casting spells.

These unavoidable eventualities are why you should *hone* self-discipline—make it second nature to be able to rise above any penchant for making excuses for magical inaction and, instead, go into ritual mode at a moment's notice. Magical gesture, voice, and persona are powerful Witch tools that enable this.

MAGICAL GESTURE

Facial expression can set a tone for others. Depending on its features, your countenance can give people permission to feel a certain way—or put them on high alert. Rather than affecting a mask of inscrutability, Witches allow their faces to show their feelings of serenity, bliss, mystical ecstasy, otherworldliness, or righteous indignation, concern borne of wisdom and experience, and so forth.

Similarly, like well-trained geisha or dancers, Witches' every flick o' wrist, our floating gait, graceful twirls, and sure-footed flourishes put the Art in "the Art Magical." As with your thoughts and spell intentions, be conscious of every move you make, every step you take. You'll know you're making progress in this area when you overhear admiring whispers from cowans (non-Witches, but Pagan friendly) to the effect of "She's so graceful," or "He's quietly commanding, don't you think?"

Witches prefer many non-verbal magical cues such as scented oil and incense, bell-ringing, etc., to hearing ear-splitting, barking commands during ritual. Substituting gestures for jarring orders amidst eloquent liturgy makes rites feel gentle to participants and appear confident and intriguing to onlookers.

Your hands go wherever you do. Unlike other potent magical tools, they cost naught. You can use them to wreak major magic in subtle fashion most anywhere, and can easily deny doing so if accused. Using hand-signs is a secure way to communicate with fellow Witches when you're all in mixed company or there's a chance that your rite may be espied by strangers.

Rites that feature mystical gestures feel more physically emboldening than meditating or doing mental magic. We and our Covenmates have done several completely elaborate, traditional, silent rituals only using American Sign Language for the deaf.

We illustrate many olde hand gestures that you can employ during rites, in *The Goodly Spellbook,* "Magical Gesture." You can call the Quarters with them and much more. And consider that it's not just *what* you do, but *how* you do it: try embellishing the look of your finger flourishes by wearing bracelets, lacy cuffs, or form-fitting gloves.

MAGICAL VOICE

By the same token, take pains to hone a stirring ritual voice. Having taught untold numbers of students, we know that "mousy" doesn't work any more than nervous trembling or muttering. As you learn to persuade with your words in a magic circle, so you master how to sway folks in the mundane world with your vocal manner.

A goodly ritual voice has thespian characteristics. It emanates from the soul, deriving deep from the belly, the diaphragm, or the bottom of the throat.

A "High Priestess voice" is dulcet, mellifluous, soothing, strong, and *audible* to all no matter how far away from her they may be. It is not forcibly loud or screechy; rather, it is so controlled that it seems to naturally resonate with conviction. A "High Priest voice" is neither pompous, robotic, nor monotonous; rather, it is sonorous and reverberant—similar to that of late actor Christopher Lee in the role of Lord Summerisle in the original *The Wicker Man* movie.

Record your voice and critique its quality, accent, tone, audibility, conviction, and intensity. If it grates on your own ears, it also will on others'.

Does your voice sound hoarse, nasal, cracked, shrill, or thin, "reedy?" Do you have a vocal scratch? Are you inaudible, unintelligible? Do you sound tentative? Do people often misunderstand what you're trying to say, so that you often find yourself replying "No, you don't understand . . ."?

Are you an "uptalker," someone with a high-toned or infantile voice inflection that makes your every statement sound like a question? Perhaps you, um, like, um, pepper your sentences with hesitation words such as "like," "you know," or "Do you feel me?" Don't let your *"So mote it be!"* come off as "So mote it, like, um, be?"

The most common off-putting error that inexperienced or insecure ritualists make is a sing-songy delivery—exaggerating their pronunciation of alternating syllables, as in *"i SUMmon STIR and CALL you UP, to GUARD our CIRcle and WITness THESE our RITES."* This comes from focusing too much on rotely reciting lines of script like a mediocre actor in a school play rather than expressing the words' feeling and intention. Regardless of your vocal type, practice eliminating its imperfections and clearly articulating your ideas, ire, or desires to others, be they Covenmates, Deities, or the public.

Also perfect the Power to Be Silent. Listen more than you talk. Make your words *count* by only speaking when you have something important to contribute to a conversation. You can easily dissipate your power when all you do is expend your breath on matters of no consequence. You'll know you're making goodly progress when you start getting compliments on your economy of speech and your speedy deftness in cutting to the chase during matters of contention.

Don't let a plodding gait detract from a superb ritual voice that you develop. Pay attention to your posture and footfall during circle. Become certain about where you are supposed to stand, when, and how. You don't have to adopt the artificially rigid erectness you'd have if balancing a book atop your head; instead, concentrate on preventing being prone to tripping on others' cape hems or flowing robes. Reserve stomping for special effect during a spell or dance: instead, glide, tiptoe, or sail through the air. Ditch machismo, homophobia, supposed societal stricture against dancing from the heart even if it makes you look the fool: This be ecstasy, so revel in it.

MAGICAL PERSONA

Witches often either enter circle embodying a unique magical persona, or spontaneously manifest Elemental airy, fiery, or flowing movements or Deity mannerisms during a rite when they feel ecstatic.

A magical persona is similar to an alter ego or alternate personality that comes to the fore when you're "all in" a rite's energy and purpose. It's also closely akin to being briefly inhabited by a Deity as described in *The Goodly Spellbook*, "From a

God's Mouth to Your Ear—Oracles." The more deeply true you know yourself, appreciate yourself, free yourself from conventions of how you assume you're supposed to act or dress, the more easily the Divine can speak to you and, through your ways, touch and inspire others.

The word *persona* is Latin for "mask," and it originally described the voice-amplifying masks that ancient actors wore when personifying mythic characters in public plays, and Deities during religious Mystery rites. These larger-than-life dramatic props included the iconic comedy and tragedy masks that became the familiar symbol of theater arts. In many cultures, donning a ritual mask is an important part of the process of assuming or channeling the Deity or Spirit that the mask portrays—it serves as a cue to the wearer, the attendees, and the Being evoked. Beyond masks, a persona can be augmented by powdered red ochre clay, mud, body paint, bindis, and so forth applied directly to the skin.

Color is another magical cue that is a potent part of a persona. For example, a Korean *mansin* (shaman) may embody a dozen different Deities and spirits in the course of a ritual. To summon each one, she dons a particular costume in a specific color or color combination.[145] Similarly, in a Moroccan Gnawa trance-music ritual, attendees who become possessed by one of the seven different *mluk* Spirits that the ritual evokes take up and dance with a scarf or veil in Its corresponding color.

Wiccan ritual color cues include the Triple Goddess's white, red, and black—signifying Her Maiden, Mother, and Crone aspect, respectively—and the color palettes that we give in the "Guide to Sabbat Rites."

You can devote as much time as you wish to perfecting the authenticity of your persona's look in detail. For instance, if your Sun sign belongs to the Element Air, you could sew or acquire impressive accessories and accoutrements associated with an Elemental Air Sylph, such as iridescent wings or a gossamer cotton or thin linen robe.

We've seen spectacularly creative examples, such as a Craft Elder covered head to toe in patches covering his hat, shirt, over-vest, pants, and shoes—each sport-

---

145. *Shamans, Housewives, and Other Restless Spirits: Women in Korean Ritual Life*, Laurel Kendall, Honolulu: University of Hawaii Press, 1985.

ing thought-provoking Pagan symbols and words of wisdom that he'd collected over decades' time; women who attach so many feathers, flowers, leaves, or feathers to their bodies with invisible, removable adhesive that they seem more fairy than human; kids who revel in running through woods in camouflage body paint and deerskin bikinis or leather loincloths; and much more. We've also been frequently pleased to know a Covenmate well, only to see them mutate into another Being at a gathering or rite, transforming themselves into something supernatural before our eyes.

A persona may captivate you by surprise, can even seem utterly opposed to your normal nature in every respect; or can radically change as you grow spiritually over time. Regardless of how, when, or what, the more you become the magical self you want to be, the more you feel you are deep down essentially, the more you can dress and act in ways that affect others and give them ideas of their own.

Some things Witches do to begin taking on their magical persona include painting their body; getting tattooed, whether temporary or permanent; glittering their brow; sporting a wild hat, mask, gloves, cane, or spike-heeled boots; or braiding or dyeing their hair and such. By layering effects, we change our appearance into the essence of what we want others to perceive us as, be it a dragonfly, fairy, Deity, animal, mythic character, etc.

Occasionally someone's insecurity or subconscious may come to the fore, and someone who thinks they're properly manifesting a persona is unaware that they're actually acting incongruously. For example, we once had a student who tended to go lupine during ecstatic rites—but then he'd blow the effect on participants by beating bones on flagstones or engaging in other antics that wolves cannot do.

Keep your persona believable: if you create a costume to support your persona, adjust its detail as experience proves that you should, such as for safety. For instance, don't put yourself in peril of burning by wearing a feather headdress while leaping a balefire.

Magical persona is about being what you are, or trying to be what you want. Either way, your voice or silence, movements, mannerisms, look, and purpose must be readily identifiable, consistent, and Pagani. Demonic clowns and such don't qualify.

PERFORMING PUBLIC RITUALS

"Many handis make light warke."
(Many hands make light work.)

—JOHN HEYWOOD, *THE PROVERBS AND EPIGRAMS*, 1562

In days of yore, public Sabbats, market fairs, carnival festivities, and inter-tribal gatherings were routine. Yet since the Burning Times, many Witches feel that they are expected to practice alone: they fear the discovery of their beliefs and practices and attendant persecution. They feel that they should continue being "the Hidden Children" of the Gods. Others treasure working in secret, and delight in the knowledge that no one else knows their capabilities or what they're up to magically. Still others remain "in the broom closet" simply because it's easier and less challenging than being an open, proud, and active Witch who represents the Olde Religion by the good they accomplish in their communities and the world at large.

They don't call it "the Work" for nothing. But what glorious, satisfying work it is! Coven Oldenwilde encourages every Heathen, Pagan, Wiccan, or Witch to be publicly proud, because we've seen firsthand the ongoing progress being made even in the culturally conservative Southern American states called the "Bible Belt."

We've witnessed firsthand how creating and conducting public rituals imparts important life skills and Craft ways to all who lead and participate in them. Ritual organizers and attendees collaborate toward a common vision, creating instant moveable art and evoking a mass transcendent experience. Public ritual teaches us how to stand up boldly for who we are in the face of antagonistic officials, police, or protestors—and how to do so peacefully and responsibly, since it trains us to sense, manage, and plan for the movement of people and props on a large scale.

The flow of coordinated, focused mass energy is empowering on a scale impossible to imagine until you dare do it. Can't imagine speaking articulately, magically, lucidly in front of hundreds? Try. Can't imagine leading a hand-in-hand circle that stretches across an entire football stadium? Try. Plan well and practice ahead of time—in your mind's eye as well as in person—so that you'll be worthy of the trust attendees place in you, and your experience will be as blissful as theirs.

Nowadays in much of the world, too many of the olde festivals have been replaced with pallid, nationalistic observances celebrating dead male leaders or living despots. The ones that remain attract tourists far and wide, because they constitute some of the last vestiges of wild color and arcane traditions that people can still participate in.

This need not be, for devising and conducting a public Sabbat is well worth the effort it takes to remind folks in your area that they have a right to free, sacred fun— that there's *more* to life than saccharine or violent socially acceptable diversions.

Among modern Pagans, however, certain clichés have arisen about "typical" Pagan rites, because too many groups who conduct them do too little or too much: for example, unimaginatively passing out strips of paper with pre-written goals such as "banish fear" or "visualize prosperity" to be burned in a balefire, or endlessly "processing" their feelings before attempting ritual and doing nothing unless everyone agrees on every minute aspect of the ritual plans. Still others pontificate inaudibly, performing lengthy ritual actions better suited to a living room than a large public space, apparently unconcerned that the expectantly circled participants might be less than happy to have traveled hundreds of miles just to stand stiffly mute and resentful of these ritual leaders' vainglory.

Frankly, the first example is simplistic and a bit insulting to Pagans' intelligence and capabilities; the second is a maddeningly tedious and timid approach to magic; and the third is insulting not just to the other participants, but especially to the Gods, because of the lack of energy those rites raise. Witches can and should do better.

As such, it's better not even to plan a public rite than to perform one so badly that attendees feel the need afterward to enact their own private rites just to purify themselves and rectify their spiritual disappointment. Witches must never be lackadaisical in public, and never promise something that they don't deliver, for this is dispiriting to those who admire our courage and creativity.

BIBLIOGRAPHY

Aradia: A New Translation. Charles G. Leland, ed. Mario and Dina Pazzaglini, Phoenix Publishing, 1998.

Christianity: The Origins of a Pagan Religion. Philippe Walter, tr. Jon E. Graham, Inner Traditions, 2006.

Crossdressing in Context, Vol. 4: Transgender & Religion. G.G. Bolich, Psyche's Press, 2008.

Dancing the Fire: A Guide to Neo-Pagan Festivals and Gatherings. Marian Singer, Citadel, 2005.

De officiis ("On Moral Duties"). Marcus Tullius Cicero, numerous editions and translations.

A Dictionary of Archaic & Provincial Words, Obsolete Phrases, Proverbs, and Ancient Customs from the Fourteenth Century. James Orchard Halliwell, various editions, 1847 et seq.

Drawing Down the Moon, 3rd Edition. Margot Adler, Penguin Books, 2006.

Dr. William Price: Wales's First Radical. Dean Powell, Amberley Publishing, 2012.

Etruscan Roman Remains. Charles Godfrey Leland, repr. Cosimo Classics, 1892/2007.

The Folklore of Plants. Thomas F. Thistleton-Dyer, Merchant Books, 1889.

The Golden Bough: A Study of Magic and Religion, Sir James George Frazer, various editions, 1890 et seq.

The Golden Verses of Pythagoras and Other Pythagorean Fragments. Florence M. Firth, various editions, 1919.

The Goodly Spellbook: Olde Spells for Modern Problems. Lady Passion & *Diuvei, Sterling Publications, 2005, 2014.

History and Astrology: Clio and Urania Confer. Ed. Annabella Kitson, Unwyn Hyman Ltd., London, 1989.

The Key of Solomon the King (Clavicula Solomonis). Ed. S. Liddell MacGregor Mathers, Samuel Weiser, Inc., 1972.

Living Religion. Janet Morrissey et al., South Melbourne, Vic. Cengage Learning Australia, 2016.

Make Merry in Step and Song: A Seasonal Treasury of Music, Mummer's Plays & Celebrations in the English Folk Tradition. Bronwen Forbes, Llewellyn Publications, 2009.

The Meaning of Witchcraft. Gerald B. Gardner, Magickal Childe, Inc., 1959.

The Metamorphosis, Or Golden Ass. Apuleius, tr. Thomas Taylor, W.J. Cosby, Universal Press, 1822.

Northern Mythology: From Pagan Faith to Local Legends. Benjamin Thorpe, Wordsworth Editions, 1851/2001.

Plant Lore, Legends, and Lyrics Embracing the Myths, Traditions, Superstitions, and Folk-Lore of the Plant Kingdom. Richard Folkard, S. Low, Marston, Searle, and Rivington, 1884.

Season of the Witch: How the Occult Saved Rock and Roll. Peter Bebergal, Peter Tarcher/Penguin, 2014.

Shamans, Housewives, and Other Restless Spirits: Women in Korean Ritual Life. Laurel Kendall, University of Hawaii Press, 1985.

Teutonic Mythology (Deutsche Mythologie). Jacob Grimm, tr. James Steven Stallybrass. London: G. Bell and Sons, 1835/1882, chapter 3, page 1052.

The White Goddess: A Historical Grammar of Poetic Myth. Robert Graves, Macmillan, 1948/2013.

Witch Blood!: The Diary of a Witch High Priestess. Patricia Crowther, House of Collectibles, Inc., 1974.

Witchcraft for Tomorrow. Doreen Valiente, Phoenix Publishing, 1978.

Witchcraft Today. Gerald B. Gardner, Citadel Press, 1954/2004.

INDEX

ABOUT THE AUTHORS

LADY PASSION (DIXIE DEERMAN) IS AN EXPERIENCED BLIND
SEER, REGISTERED NURSE SINCE 1988, HIGH PRIESTESS OF COVEN
OLDENWILDE SINCE 1994, AND INTERNATIONALLY BESTSELLING
AUTHORESS SINCE 2005. HER MAGICAL SPECIALTIES ARE DIVINATION,
MAKING MAGICAL MEDICINES, AND CONDUCTING ELABORATE
PUBLIC RITUALS.

Lady Passion's successful spiritual, environmental, and social-justice activism is documented online, such as her elimination of North Carolina's anti-divination law; protection of R.N.'s from being fired for advocating for a patient's rights (*Deerman v. Beverly Corporation of America*); her saving of century-old trees on a public park and an old haunted stone jail beneath; and much more.

The Lady counsels folk worldwide, and frequently works magic for the media such as *Extra!*, CNN, and BBC London.

She and *Diuvei live snug in their 3-story Covenstead in the bowl of Asheville surrounded by the breathtaking Appalachian Blue Ridge Mountains.

Diuvei (Steven Rasmussen) grew up in the San Francisco Bay Area's Silicon Valley in a diverse family that embraced science, spirituality, and service. After being kicked out of Princeton University for disobeying an assistant dean, he studied metaphysics with Kythera Ann, served as president of the South Bay Astrological Society, and worked in computer musicology at Walter B. Hewlett's Center for Computer-Assisted Research in the Humanities. In 1988 he began studying Witchcraft with Don Frew and Lady Bhride of Coven Tobar Bhride in Berkeley, California, and became an Initiate in the California Line of Gardnerian Wicca, obtaining his Elevation to the Third Degree in Coven Triskell in 1992.

He and East Texas native Lady Passion met and fell in love the following year at a national Witch convention in Black Mountain, North Carolina, where they bonded over their mutual devotion to Hecate and to magic olde and wild. They handfasted in 1994, and together have followed their true calling ever since.

Today, as High Priest of Coven Oldenwilde, he strives to practice Pagan Virtues as a civic activist in Asheville, North Carolina, and as a spiritual activist wherever he finds himself.

Readers are welcome to contact Lady Passion and *Diuvei through Coven Oldenwilde's popular Wiccan websites: wiccans.org; oldenwilde.org; and oldenworks.org.

OTHER BOOKS BY THE AUTHORS

Ask-A-Priestess: Magic Answers & Spells From a Real Witch, Lady Passion, Smashwords.com, 2009

Simply Savory: Magical & Medieval Recipes, Lady Passion, smashworks.org, 2010

The Goodly Spellbook: Olde Spells for Modern Problems, Lady Passion & *Diuvei, Sterling Publications, 2005, 2014

Italian translation: *Il Libro Degli Incantesemi: Antique Formule Magiche Per Risolvere Problemi Attuali,* Lady Passion & *Diuvei, Gruppo Editoriale Armenia, Milan, 2006, 2015